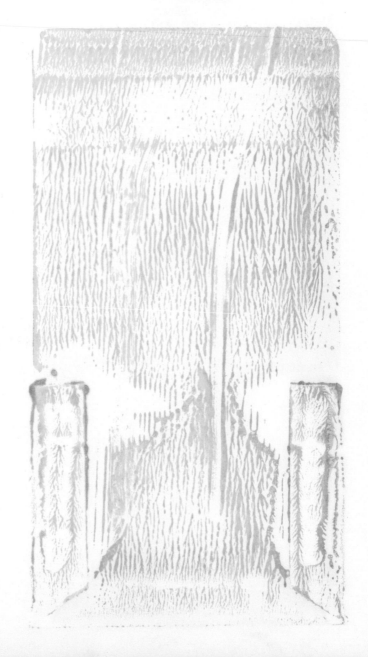

STRINDBERG'S
DRAMATIC EXPRESSIONISM

STRINDBERG'S
DRAMATIC EXPRESSIONISM

By

Carl Enoch William Leonard Dahlström
University of Michigan

Second Edition,
with the author's essay
"Origins of Strindberg's Expressionism."

Published by Benjamin Blom, Inc.
New York 1968

Printed in U.S.A. by
NOBLE OFFSET PRINTERS, INC.
NEW YORK 3, N. Y.

FOREWORD

THIS study was originally undertaken in partial fulfilment of the requirements for the degree of Doctor of Philosophy at the University of Michigan. The investigation was continued during a period of fourteen months spent in Europe, mostly in Germany, Sweden and France.

The introductory chapters to each part of the book indicate clearly the limits of the study. In the first part I have established something tangible in the rather chaotic mass of critical literature that professes to deal with the expressionistic movement in Germany. I have systematized this critical material and established norms for the study of expressionism in drama. In the second part I apply the norms to the study of Strindberg's dramas to determine the nature and extent of his dramatic expressionism.

Chapters II, III and IV of Part I set forth the ideas of several critics of expressionism. The accounts given in these chapters follow the critics so closely that at times I approach a paraphrase of the original material. On the other hand, I am wholly responsible for the material given in the synthetic studies of Chapters V and VI in which selection has been imperative. Part II shows itself obviously to be entirely an original study.

Responsibility for all statements and conclusions rests wholly on the author. The subject of the thesis was directly inspired by the lectures on contemporary drama offered at the University of Michigan by Professor Oscar J. Campbell, who is the godfather to this study. I wish to express my appreciation to Professor Campbell not only for inspiration but more especially for the wise and genial direction that has attended my studies and the writing of this book. To Professor Louis Bredvold also I wish

V

to express appreciation for his continued interest in this work and for suggestions in the final revision of the manuscript; to Dr. C. N. Wenger, colleague and friend, for several pertinent and helpful references; and to Professor Eugene S. McCartney for his help in preparing the manuscript for publication.

ORIGINS OF STRINDBERG'S EXPRESSIONISM

CARL E. W. L. DAHLSTRÖM

Portland State College

STRINDBERG'S dramatic expressionism has been defined technically by means of a critical apparatus and analyses of certain
plays. There is little question but that, in view of the materials published during the last thirty years, better results could now be obtained.
Yet it is doubtful if the gain would be sufficient to warrant a repetition of the analyses already made. For the most part we are satisfied
that in *To Damascus, A Dream Play,* and *The Ghost Sonata* Strindberg created dramas quite different from those that had previously appeared but basically related to many that were written after his death.
What we now need is a study that will complement the technical examination of the plays, if possible a study that will offer or suggest a
raison d'être for the new development in literary art. It is the object
of this essay to define Strindberg's expressionism through its origins in
the cultural atmosphere of the nineteenth century. Since much is necessarily subjective, the definition will not be developed wholly in accordance with the demands of formal logic, and thus it may prove
acceptable solely to those who have experienced in relatively the same
way the cultural changes of the nineteenth and twentieth centuries.

We shall employ the following procedure. First, we shall consider
the facets of the nineteenth century that were of peculiar significance
to artists. Second, we shall observe what Strindberg did as man and
artist in this milieu. Third, we shall close with an attempt to define in
brief compass the nature of Strindberg's expressionism.

The scientific perspective of the nineteenth-century European was
clearly forecast by the Renaissance when men began to devote more
attention to this world while relaxing attention to the supernatural.
The Reformation gave added stress to man as an individual, and the
wide split in the western branch of the Christian Church weakened the
influence of the religious institution. Science then began to free itself
from outside controls and to forge its instruments of observation, ex-
perimentation, and systematization. While for hundreds of years a
religious orientation continued to be paramount in the European milieu,

° Author's article reprinted from vol. 34, No. 1 of "Scandinavian Studies,"
by permission of "Scandinavian Studies."

it lost this position when the Christian Church was no longer supreme in the affairs of men. Political organization took precedence over the religious and even dictated to the latter, whether Protestant or Roman Catholic. Officially, to be sure, God was in his heaven and all was well on earth. Unofficially, however, as Edward FitzGerald made clear in 1859 and Nietzsche proclaimed in 1872, God was dead. Indeed, the situation was far worse. Science had no place for God and no way of accounting for him in the total objectivity of thisworldliness. It was not simply that God was now dead; to all intents and purposes he was nonexistent, had never been, and could not be. In the second half of the nineteenth century God was already disappearing from the minds of many educated Europeans, although habit frequently kept them going through the motions of worship. Men might still declare that religion was of prime importance, but their practices belied their declarations. The form was thus empty because faith had lost its essence.

According to public pronouncements the religious order of the universe was still treated as though it was paramount; yet it became increasingly clear that the scientific order was becoming intellectually dominant in men's terrestrial affairs. Throughout the nineteenth century, and even earlier, statements were made to the effect that the two orders were actually one, God being the God of science, technology, and commerce as well as the God of the Scriptures. Scientists and nonscientists referred to God as the Great Artificer or Lawgiver of the Universe, the Principle of Order, and Ether, and tried to convince themselves that this abstract God was somehow the same as the personal God of the earlier persuasion. When contradictions appeared they could be denied or explained away without difficulty, for the deity's movements in mysterious ways provided a rationale for all inconvenient data. This does not mean that large numbers of people were awaredly dishonest, deliberately engaging themselves in crooked thinking; it means that they were culturally so conditioned that they could scarcely think otherwise.

One source of difficulty lay in the compelling urge for absolutes, a characteristic of the Graeco-Judeo-Christian cultural development. Because of this urge the European was so reared that his thinking was automatically based on absolutes. Thus when science fashioned a new world, it brought to the mind of a Newton the concept of absolute space. At this time a seemingly unresolvable contradiction was introduced. Whatever is absolute must be unique; hence unless they were merely different names for the same idea, God and space could not both be absolute. The people who clung to their religious faith either ignored science or else made it subordinate to religion, and those who maintained the scientific perspective had to abandon religion or treat it as subordinate to science. In no other way could they preserve the character of the absolute, something they seemed determined to do regardless of evidence and regardless of consequences.

The persistence of the absolute is especially revealed in the European's failure to recognize the actualities, let alone the potentialities, of his languages. He was employing language in science to set up the abstractions which develop a plane of fact, he was using language in belles lettres for planes of nonfact, that is, for meanings and values, and he was also using language in mixed planes of fused fact and nonfact.[2] Yet he spoke as though the last class of planes alone existed, and the failure to understand his own tongue caused him decades of confusion and anguish. He could not see that the scientific enterprise complements that of the humanities although ironically enough he had been required to make distinctions in language usage when he worked logically as scientist and when he created rhythmically as literary artist. The failure can be understood once we realize that man's cultural conditioning blinded him to his own use of language in the very enterprises which he himself had established.

Because he could not understand his own language usage, the European confused the truths of logic with those of rhythm. According to his practices, logic dealt with the true and the false. It was formal, analytic, and abstract, and it could successfully be applied to objective matters. Further, the logical procedures could be tested by anyone with adequate training, and thus it was a means of bringing men into impersonal, equational agreement. On the other hand, the European artist for centuries had been employing rhythm subjectively to present experiences of meanings and values, and to present them as wholes. The experiential truth was profoundly personal and could not be tested by formal means, its validity being established solely by a community

[2] For a number of years I have been working on language and the planes of reference. A brief treatment of the planes of reference may be found in my article "An Approach to Tragedy" *Modern Drama*, 1 (May, 1958), 36–41.

of sympathy and interest based on similar experience. The one kind of truth neither supported nor opposed the other, each being set up according to the perspective of its own enterprise. Yet men persisted in seeking an absolute truth as though logical determination and rhythmic presentation could somehow be one; or, we may say, in their general use of language men unawaredly fused fact and nonfact. The failure to distinguish between the findings of logic and the expressions of rhythm was responsible for much of the distress as well as the folly of nineteenth- and twentieth-century men.

Unable to resolve the contradictions in his cultural perspective, the European found himself in a most unhappy situation. Since it had to be either religion as paramount or science, the artist eventually found himself with neither. The socio-religious orientation of his culture had long given him artistic substance, with meanings and values which had been experienced individually and commonly by generations of people until they were inherent in European languages. When the artist abandoned these, he did so because in his pride of intellectual emancipation he was convinced that religion had presented an unreal world, one marked by untruth and superstition. He was equally certain at the time that science alone could give him a world of genuine reality; hence science must have the basic stuff out of which he could create works of art. Realism and naturalism then became the way of life for a goodly number of writers. But the satisfaction with the new materials was shortlived. Long before the scientists of the twentieth century frankly announced that their enterprise had nothing to do with human meanings and values, that they were concerned with abstractions and ideal mathematical systems, the artist had discovered that science lacked rhythmically deployable substance. If he tried to use the findings of science, the writer still had to relate them to the cultural basis of his age, that is, he had to give them human significance. Having mistakenly discarded the cultural substance with the formal religious institution, the artist could not use the ideas of science except in utterances of nostalgia and despair for what had been lost. He quite logically drifted into nihilism.

For a time the writer sought artistically to contain the chaos of the two incommensurable orders, that of religion and that of science. To do this required a response quite different from the kind that had been made by his predecessors, for the latter molded into artistic form the order of meanings and values which was inherent in a unified cultural milieu. But containment of the chaos was not enough; it simply concentrated the confusion and the distress in the mind of the artist. Moreover, to people in other professions the new literature appeared to be a sign of madness. A solution then seemed to be afforded by artistic isolation. The artist could withdraw from the cultural confusion of his age and devote himself to rhythm for its own sake. The result was virtuosity in technique accompanied by abstractionism. The artist had nothing of substance to communicate to his fellow men because his environment had provided him with no artistically valid meanings and values. Yet since he was artist with a compulsion to employ rhythm, he turned his art into a kind of intellectual play, often so abstruse and esoteric that it could be enjoyed only by the artist himself and his fellow professionals. To the nonartist he appeared to be depicting distortions of reality or else to be trying to escape from it, but the nonartist usually failed to understand the presentation of rhythm for rhythm's sake.

If we keep in mind some current movements we can observe four possible classes of development in Western art since the Renaissance. First, for a number of centuries, the cultural atmosphere offered a world order of meanings and values, the basic substance readymade for the creative artist who was conditioned by his rearing to respond positively to the milieu. Second, when the cultural environment became a chaos of two different orders, each presumably absolute, the artist used rhythm in an endeavor at containment. But this could not long endure, because the artist could create only a specious order out of a cultural disorder. Third, the artist accepted cultural nihilism and turned to himself, reflecting as best he could his own character and personality in abstract works of technical virtuosity, though communicating little or nothing to the great majority of his fellow men. Fourth, the artist, driven by the necessity to employ his technique on something other than itself, seized out of the past and present whatever meanings and values appeared to be universal and transmuted them into the substance of a possible new cultural world. In these four steps the artist moved from prime agent in reflecting a cultural milieu to the position of prime agent in fashioning a cultural atmosphere. It is far too early for us to say whether this fourth step, already initiated by European writers, can be completed. It is a fair guess that it will not be successfully pursued unless the artist is joined by the philosopher, the religious, and a significant body of appreciative lay people. That is, it is doubtful if the artist alone can provide modern materialistic man with a human orientation.

As we turn to Strindberg we note that he came upon the European scene during the disintegration of a society which had been unified through its religious orientation. The Swede struggled courageously to fulfil himself in a world of contradictions. That his work was largely spun out of his own mind was a consequence of the circumstances under which he labored. Nothing was left him externally of genuine substance, and the compulsion of the artist led him to use what was available. He also looked longingly toward a cultural world fashioned by the creative imagination, but he could not extricate himself from the chaos of his age.

In his youth Strindberg responded to the socio-religious culture of Sweden, at that time a provincial country. He was early indoctrinated with concepts that equipped him with what seemed to be unshakable and hence eternal truths about God, man, and the universe. The world was controlled by divine will, by an absolute God capable of rolling back the waters of the sea, stopping the sun in the heavens, or hurling down the stars from the firmament. There was no contradiction between divine and natural order, because everything was created by God, his word was law, and he therefore could add, take away, or alter at pleasure. Man was the special creation of God, formed in his image, and given jurisdiction over the earth. He was, however, to rule according to God's command, not his own will, and his life on earth was a pilgrimage, a period of testing to determine if he merited paradise. To the young Strindberg we may be sure that the deity was a personal God, all-loving and all-merciful, yet also the implacable judge whose divine justice required him to sentence the great majority of human beings to an eternity of unspeakable tortures. It was a very disturbing world qualified by extravagant hope and extreme fear, but it was an ordered world, and Strindberg was at home in it.

At the same time the cultural atmosphere had disquieting elements in it, for scientific method and the Industrial Revolution were making their impact on the Swedes. As a result thisworldliness was in competition with otherworldliness, although both were socially in good standing. For Strindberg this meant that at the very time that he was responding to pietism, his environment was leading him into scientific perspectives which would challenge the whole structure of his religion. His brief stay at Uppsala turned him toward science sufficiently that he flirted with the idea of a medical career and thus spent some months in the home of a physician. Although he did not pursue the medical profession, the intellectual curiosity regarding scientific matters was a powerful force throughout Strindberg's life. When, however, as a consequence of his studies of science he announced that he was an atheist, he was never actually more than a verbal and logical unbeliever, his early conditioning having thoroughly indoctrinated him with concepts of supernatural powers.

In part because of his hypersensitive nature and in part because of the confusion of the milieu Strindberg found himself on a path of disillusionment that was ever lengthening out and ever widening. His personal failures at Uppsala, in pre-medical training, in teaching, and in the theater cannot be ascribed to a lack of ability; rather they must be ascribed to his sensitivity and to the confusing cultural environment in which he lived. The two never fitted each other, and since they could not be reconciled, the weaker—Strindberg—was constantly being whipped by the stronger, the environment.

Although Strindberg rather early developed himself as a writer, he did not readily find an outlet for his talents. He was too poor in material wealth and too proud easily to succeed or to be satisfied with slow advancement. Furthermore his struggles with art in the milieu in which he was reared were not of the kind that he or others could then understand. The traditionalists desired all artists to continue repeating what had been done earlier, not recognizing that the changing culture was making meaningless a repetition of earlier works; so they rebuffed Strindberg. Like others in the same milieu Strindberg could not see that he was caught in a fearful battle of two absolutes, religion and science, and that the struggle for artistic survival, let alone integrity, would be long and intense. He did not understand that he was using language in one way in his art, in another way in science, and in a fusion of fact and nonfact in common utterance. It was natural that he should flounder, particularly since somehow or other he had to earn a living as well as solve his problems of art. He employed a kind of realism and a kind of naturalism, and as late as the nineties he was feverishly busy in laboratory work which he called scientific experiments. Whatever may have been Strindberg's inner convictions, he formulated a literary naturalism that was by no means scientific, though there was a response to scientific findings and pronouncements.[3] Too much of the subjective, too much of Strindberg himself with too little of objective control prevented his naturalism from being scientific in any major way. But even this creative work was not satisfying, for he could not fulfil himself as artist.

Along the path of disillusionment science was another false hope. It had seemed to promise so much, and yet something was lacking that not even the artist himself could consciously define. Strindberg did not understand that in religion and science as two competing absolutes he was faced with a contradiction that could not be resolved. Though he turned his back on the religious institution he was still dominated by religious persuasions. Moreover as an artist he was in need of meanings and values. He felt that he had to reject religion because it did not offer truth; so he turned to science as the new and infallible source of truth. He failed to note that science was not functional in art, that it could give him only mechanical analyses and synthetically contrived systems both of which were of necessity thoroughly dehumanized. There were a number of clearcut ways out of the situation,[4] but Strindberg was so close to the cultural problem that he could only blunder his way in and among the contradictions of his milieu. He did his best to contain the cultural chaos in his rhythmic creations, and in so doing he created a kind of literature different from that of his predecessors. Indeed we may say that he was subjective in a new way.

Art is always subjective, but there is a profound difference between the creative ego that expands and seizes upon the given order of its

[3] See my article "Strindberg and Naturalistic Tragedy," *Scandinavian Studies*, 30 (February, 1958), 1–18.

[4] There are at least six possible ways: (1) The individual may cling to the socio-religious culture of his fathers and either repudiate or ignore science; (2) he may accept science as a subordinate part of the socio-religious culture, reconciling by rationalization any differences that appear; (3) he may ignore the socio-religious order or repudiate it and devote himself wholly to scientific enterprise; (4) while devoting himself to science he may publicly proclaim his religious faith and accept God as the prime scientist; (5) he may subscribe to both religion and science as equally valid and thus provide two compartments for his life and thought; (6) he may turn away from both religion and science, in which event he will have to provide some tertium quid or else accept nihilism.

cultural world and the ego through which the debris of a cultural chaos is funneled. A hundred years before Strindberg's time the cultural world was still sufficiently intact that an artist felt himself a part of it and could give it rhythmic form. During the nineteenth century, however, the cultural world became progressively so disorganized that at the dawn of the twentieth century the artist found himself estranged from the milieu and without adequate substance to put into form. He then had to create his own universe, and he had to do this out of his own mind.

The task was too much for anyone, but Strindberg did the best that a writer could do under the prevailing conditions. He began to create a world in his own image. He was, however, so torn by the clashes in his environment that he could not mold the discordant elements into a harmonious whole. He could only circumscribe them and thus he created an extended oxymoron, the literature of rhythmized contradictions that we find in *To Damascus*, *A Dream Play*, and *The Ghost Sonata*. Each work is carefully designed. At the same time, not one is a rhythmic expression of a unified culture; each is a containment of a cultural clash. As a consequence settings, dramatis personae, and plots are all distorted as regards the picture that we would expect to have either from the traditional socio-religious order or from that of science and technology. Of the forces from which the actions spring—the situational complex—we find that the egoïc dominates. Since the order created by this force is peculiar to a given individual, reflecting his experience without necessarily communicating it clearly, it stands to reason that a work of art created egoïcally will not be widely understood. The other traditional forces are more or less useless because they are associated with enterprises that have been found wanting. The physical, biological, and some of the social belong to science and technology; the divine is the heart of religion. The only possibility of force other than the egoïc is that of the unknown, the mystical, that which is beyond all rational considerations. It is no wonder then that the literature created by Strindberg, arising as it does from the egoïc and the unknown powers, should be marked by dream content and dream form ranging from the delightful to the nightmare, from that which seems rational to that which is patently fantastic. That we also have something reminiscent of musical form is simply the natural result of the employment of art's indispensable referential device: rhythm.

XV

At the very time that Strindberg was artistically trying to contain the chaos of his milieu, he seemed to be pushed in one direction while he was vainly striving to move in another. I refer to the gravitation toward nihilism and the aspiration for human significance. The artist desperately wanted to be something that was humanly functional; he wanted a world of human beings. But he had no means of bringing his struggles to a successful conclusion. As science and technology became dominant in the nineteenth century, they reduced everything to objective data and thereby eliminated the qualitative aspects of human existence. With the absence of meanings and values, life was dehumanized, nothing remaining but agglomerations of molecules, animate and inanimate. Because of these circumstances Strindberg's expressionistic dramas are neither tragedies nor comedies. They are not marked by defeats because there is nothing to give them substance for either victory or doom. They are not comedies because the works are too serious and at times too painful. The action is much like the ceaseless bobbing up and down of flotsam on an infinite sea. One can select any place and any time for a beginning and do the same for the closing because the experience has been one of action without progress. Even the Unknown in *To Damascus*, despite all the wanderings, makes no genuine progress. He enters the monastery not because at long last he has been led there by his deep convictions but because there are no answers to his questions. It is almost a matter of indifference whether he does one thing or another, but the monastery offers an escape from human associations and responsibilities.

Throughout all, the cloud of futilitarianism notwithstanding, Strindberg does not give up hope that something eventually will emerge or that somehow meanings and values will restore humanity to men. He himself cannot find a solution to the problems that beset him. He cries out that mankind is to be pitied, for he sees in men and women the conflict of ideals and practices. It is such a disturbing contradiction to discover that men can dream such splendid dreams, nourish profound sentiments of human decency, and yet in their actions betray natures that are brutal, deceitful, and unbelievably petty. The positive element in Strindberg's expressionistic dramas can be found, we must admit, but it never attains the force found in a Nikos Kazantzakis.[5] In

[5] See, for example, Kazantzakis' *The Odyssey: A Modern Sequel* and *The Saviors of God: Spiritual Exercises.*

other words, while the Swede stoutly resisted the centripetal pull of nihilism, he was too much alone to muster up the requisite power to rise above the chaotic situation in which he was forced to live.

What we have presented is very brief, but I think that we should have little difficulty defining Strindberg's expressionism as an artistic consequence of an unusually disturbing milieu. The new kind of literature was a product of an age of cultural disintegration, of the unresolved and often unadmitted clash of two absolute orders. It was the result of a chaos produced by the incommensurability of traditional religion and nineteenth-century science. The European's insistence on some kind of absolute spelled his failure to understand what he was doing with his own language in science as well as in the fine arts, to say nothing of general communication. The chaos in culture meant that the creative artist no longer was able to mold the traditionally developed order of meanings and values into significant form. He was in effect culturally demoralized. Having nothing outward to feed him, he was forced to turn inward, to feed upon himself. The consequence was an egoïc literature which the Germans have rightly qualified as *Ausstrahlungen des Ichs*. The distortion that appeared in Strindberg's works was the inevitable result of the disqualification of the only two orders that men had, that of logic and that of holoistic experience. The drift into nihilism was strong and led to the outbursts which have been variously labelled *cry*, *Schrei*, and *howl*. Yet those outbursts were also cries for help, demands for a human world for human beings. In short, Strindberg's expressionism was a response to a situation that was almost impossible for an artist. He felt the urge to create, or, as he himself put it, he felt rhythms coming. Yet there was nothing to rhythmize except chaos, disappointment, and a hope so faint that it could be mistaken for despair. Since rhythm is itself order, he employed it to give artistic limits to the clashing and therefore essentially undeployable materials. Finally, Strindberg's expressionism stands as a transition between traditional art and the later developments. It looks toward abstractionism and virtuosity in technique. Perhaps we can say that it also looks forward to the artist triumphantly creating a cultural atmosphere.

XVII

CONTENTS

PART I. CONTROL FACTORS IN EXPRESSIONISM

Contents

PART II. EXPRESSIONISM IN
STRINDBERG'S DRAMAS

PART I

CONTROL FACTORS IN EXPRESSIONISM

Ich sage euch: man muss noch Chaos in sich haben, um einen tanzenden Stern gebären zu können.

— Nietzsche, *Also sprach Zarathustra*

CHAPTER I

INTRODUCTION

THE term " expressionism " has generally been used as loosely as the term " romanticism," and the same confusion has beset both. Paintings, works of sculpture, music and literature of all sorts have been described as expressionistic. Yet, with one or two exceptions, critics have been reluctant to make a broad scientific study of either the theory or the practice of expressionism. Too often the studies of the subject have become imaginative vagary, or incidental comment totally lacking in generalizations which could be accepted as safe guides in such a study as I propose to make.

The aesthetic doctrines professed by the proponents of expressionism are most noble. Nevertheless one encounters at the outset of his studies the noisy confusion made by both the prophets and the dilettantes who " glauben in das Nothorn des Geistes zu stossen und blasen nur eine Kinder-Trompete."[1] There are times when one not only agrees with Dessoir but takes a step farther with Alfred Kerr: " Liebe Leute, der sogenannte Expressionismus, das versteht sich von selber, hat nicht ausschliessendes Recht: aber (unpathetisch) ein Recht. Wie meine Teuren, auch der . . . ich will mal sagen: Sublimismus ein Recht hat, oder: der Klassizismus, oder: der Kirchhofismus, oder: der Ichpfeifdraufismus. Raum für (fast) alles hat die Erde."[2]

Yet it is easy to laugh at any movement, to be indignant or to be disgusted, without first being fair. When great confusion

[1] Dessoir, Max, *Vom Jenseits der Seele*, p. 329.
[2] Kerr, Alfred, " Dramen-Expressionismus," *Die neue Rundschau,* August, 1919.

attends the birth of a movement, be it in art, politics, religion or science, the world usually divides itself into two camps which fight under the principle that " all is fair in war." The birth of expressionism offered no exception to this general rule, with the result that the student of the movement finds himself torn almost to pieces by the centripetal attraction of the proponents and the centrifugal force of the opponents. In addition, there is within the movement itself the polaric differences indicated by Dessoir: to wit, the great gulf between that which expressionism desires to do and that which is actually accomplished. We are thus given a warning: any attempt to define expressionism by practice alone, or by theory alone, will not tell the whole story, for in neither case will the evidence be complete.

The method in this work will be synthetic in the endeavor to discover norms for the study of dramas. It will be expedient first to give a little information regarding the history of the term and the movement, and to sketch in very lightly the intellectual and social background. Then we shall be prepared to discuss expressionism in painting and literature before proceeding to the synthetic study itself.

HISTORY OF THE TERM

THE term " expressionism " was first applied to works of art, primarily to painting. Kühn, in declaring that the year 1910 marks the birth of the movement, implies that we need search no farther for the origin of expressionism and the use of the term. In 1910, he says, Picasso was painting, futurists were appearing in Italy and the two magazines *Aktion* and *Sturm* were born. Kühn puts especial emphasis on Picasso and Kandinsky, two expressionistic painters: " 1910 als Picasso es wagte, den Geist selbst, das Gesetz, das Ewige, kristallinisches Wachsen aus innerem Zentrum zu malen, damals begann die Revolution. Als Kandinsky die Seele malte, die Landschaft des Ewigen, das

Sein des Wertes, da begannen Sehende zu ahnen, dass eine neue
Zeit begänne, eine Zeit in der der Mensch erwacht.
" Das unendliche Ich erstand!
" Das unendliche Ich lohte empor, rasend, berstend, die Himmel erfassend, leuchtende Fackel." [3]
Yet Kühn focusses our attention on what he chooses to call
the beginnings of the movement, and leaves us rather ignorant
of the term itself. He is also too patently a protagonist to bother
with dates and sound evidence. Fritz Knapp offers us more
usable information when he declares that the word " expressionism " was coined at an exhibition of Matisse's works in France
in the year 1901.[4] It is, however, from that literary encyclope-
dist, Soergel, that we obtain the most pertinent material:

Man hat sich gewöhnt, unter Expressionismus einen Sammelbegriff für
alle die jungen Kräfte zu verstehen, die zwischen 1910 und 1920 sich
durchzusetzen suchten. In Wirklichkeit ist das Wort zunächst nur Ausdruck eines künstlerischen Stilwillens. Schon 1901 gebraucht es der fran-
zösische Maler Julien-August Hervé für eine Zyklus seiner Bilder. Matisse
wendet es oft an; der Kritiker des *Gil Blas*, de Vauxcelles, macht die
Öffentlichkeit in Frankreich mit dem Worte bekannt. Es ist nicht un-
möglich, dass das neue Schlagwort zugleich auch in andern Ländern auf-
tauchte; forderte doch das Losungswort der jüngsten Vergangenheit, Impressionismus, zu der Gegenlosung Expressionismus geradezu heraus. Wie
denn auch Däubler erzählt, Paul Cassirer habe es ' einmal im Wortgefecht
hingeworfen. Es heisst, man habe bei einer Jurysitzung der Berliner Se-
cession, wahrscheinlich vor einem Bild von Pechstein, gefragt: Ist das noch
Impressionismus? Worauf die Antwort: Nein,, aber Expressionismus!'
Wie dem auch sei, die wir heute kurz als Expressionisten bezeichnen,
nannten sich einst nicht so oder wollten nur sich so genannt wissen, nicht
aber die Nebengruppe im eigenen Lager, nannten sich Neopathetiker —
lange schon, ehe Hans Ehrenbaum-Degele, Robert R. Schmidt und Paul
Zech seit 1913 die lyrische Zeitschrift *Das neue Pathos* herausgaben —,
nannten sich Abstrakten, Aeternisten, Futuristen, Aktivisten, Sturm-
künstler. Aber alle diese Richtungen lassen sich in zwei Hauptrichtungen
einordnen: in die Expressionisten im engeren Sinne und die Aktivisten,
in denen das Kunstwerk bei aller Einfügung der Kunst in die Aufgaben

---

[3] Kühn, Herbert, " Das Wesen der neuen Lyrik," *Die neue Schaubühne*,
December 1, 1919, p. 368.
[4] Knapp, Fritz, " Impressionismus und Expressionismus," *Neue Jahrbücher für Wissenschaft und Jugendbildung*, Vol. I, 1925, p. 522.

des Lebens einen Sonderwert behält, und die, denen das Werk nur ein
Mittel des Wirkens ist, das zu jeder Zeit mit einem wirksameren zu vertau-
schen wäre.   Hier Politikgläubige, dort Kunstgläubige, hier mehr Tätige,
dort mehr Beschauliche, hier Dichter, dort solche, denen das Wort 'Literat'
das schönste Ehrenwort ist.[5]

In painting, at least, the word " expressionism " was already
in use by 1901, and the critic de Vauxcelles gave further currency
to the term in France.   The use of the term in Germany, however, is decidedly recent; in fact, it came more like an after-
thought to qualify a movement in full swing.   Soergel points out
that there are expressionistic tendencies in the works of German
writers during at least a score of years previous to 1910, and in
some works just preceding the decade 1910–20 there is almost
full-fledged expressionism.   The majority of critics also agree
that Sorge's *Der Bettler* [6] and Hasenclever's *Der Sohn* [7] are two
wholly expressionistic works that gave dynamic impetus to the
movement in drama.   Yet Binding assures us that the word
" expressionism " was not applied to literature before 1915.[8]   A
bibliographical study also gives further evidence that in Germany, at least, the term was rarely if ever used in titles of
articles on painting before 1913, and of articles on literature
before 1916.

The history of the term " expressionism " is enlightening only
as it limits our field of inquiry.   It is clear that the term has
generally been loosely applied to the literature produced by the
young German writers of the decade 1910–20, irrespective of
the nature of their works, and to the paintings of various European artists active from 1901 to date.   It is also evident that
limitations on the use of the term could scarely occur until close
to the end of the stormy decade.   Consequently, we ought not

---

[5] Soergel, Alfred, *Dichtung und Dichter der Zeit*, p. 357.
[6] Written 1910, produced 1912.
[7] Written 1914, published 1916.
[8] Binding, R. G., " Allgemeiner und dichterischer Expressionismus,"
Faust, November, 1921, p. 5.

to put too much trust in the critical literature that appeared when the term first became current, that is, in 1916 and 1917. It is not that we can ignore this early literature with all its glow of praise, or its bellowing of anger and disgust, but rather that we must work through this material to the calm of later criticism that has some distance between itself and the movement. Obviously enough, this distance cannot be very great when the dates of the movement are put at 1910–20; but the criticism written since 1920 ought to reveal more balance, certainly, than the earlier documents.

GENERAL BACKGROUND

WHILE it is not possible within the limits of this study to give definitive treatment to the background of expressionism, it seems nevertheless desirable that we take at least a fleeting glance at the so-called foundations of the movement. It is not at all rare, for instance, for a critic of the movement to include within the range of expressionism all the works of genius not only from our own Western World but even from the Classical World. The Greek dramatists, Shakespeare, Goethe and many other notables have been gathered in the forum of expressionism. This is rather loose talk, especially when Classical and Western are mingled in the same breath. It is, however, significant in that it indicates a broad cultural sweep and not a tiny aesthetic program.

In this background Gothicism is also stressed as one of the most noble forebears of this modern movement. The masterful Gothic spire of a Chartres points everlastingly the way toward the infinite with a loftiness that sets it apart from all other styles of architecture. Such a spire is a "metaphysics crystallized in stone," according to one figure of speech, and "frozen music," according to another. Gothicism represents the soul of mankind striving toward the absolute, struggling to realize its oneness with the all, conscious of its high destiny. Even the grotesques in Gothic art bring one close to expressionism; the artists have turned away from observed reality and have employed a principle of distortion.[9]

In literature the period of *Sturm und Drang* is given as the finest example of a movement very much like the modern one; and the subsequent rise of romanticism offers opportunities for drawing parallels to expressionism and its possibilities. In both ideals and practice these early movements are said to have much in common with the modern school.

In philosophy Nietzsche's individualism caught the entire youth of Germany. Furthermore, Bergson's intuitive philosophy, Husserl's phenomenology, the *Einfühlung* theory of Lipps and its expansion by Worringer, the *Als-Ob* philosophy of Vaihinger, the philosophy of the unconscious by Hartmann, and the scientific studies of the unconscious by Freud, all these have pointed the way toward a new concept and a new expression of reality in art.[10]

Added to all this we have the steady trend of mechanization in our civilization that gave increased impetus to the search for spiritual values. Science, political life and art bade one think materialistically, and left little room for considerations of the soul's world. Scholarly criticism of the Bible destroyed the authority of the church, and also relegated to categories of superstition and ignorance much that had been previously linked with values of mysticism and with spirituality in religion. Likewise, a comparative study of religions led many to discard religion without looking for new values in religious experience. The theory of evolution was also part of the combination that planted

[9] See below, pp. 15–18.

[10] For a detailed study of background material see Soergel, *Dichtung und Dichter der Zeit,* pp. 383–400 *et alibi;* Bachmann, Frieda, " Die Theorie, die historische Beziehungen und die Eigenart des Expressionismus," *The Germanic Review,* July, 1927, pp. 229–244.

man in earth-stuff and convinced him that he was *almost* entirely, if not completely, dust.[11] Psychology threaded its way along the highways and byways of the nerves and placed all spiritual values on the level of traffic problems in the nerve-system. Chemistry counted, weighed and differentiated atoms; and it continually preached the finality of matter as evidenced by the atom. Then physics built a world within the atom with renewed emphasis on energy and matter, but with no concept whatsoever of spirituality. Political life sought expression in a low order of socialism and stressed material welfare. Literature and painting desired only to reproduce observed reality as exactly as possible. Indeed, it would seem that in nearly all realms of thought and endeavor naturalism held sway, and its consequent mechanization of all values allowed no play of the spirit.[12]

Thus far it seems that no critic has pointed to Spengler's *Der Untergang des Abendlandes* as a source book for the background of expressionism. Irrespective of the validity of Spengler's historical thesis, the book is of the utmost importance for the correlation of expressionism with its artistic antecedents, especially Gothicism and Romanticism. Moreover, though Spengler seems to be unconscious of expressionism as a *literary* movement, or else thoroughly disgusted with it,[13] he offers more opportunity for the interpretation of expressionism than any other work: to wit, the recurrence of the " Faustian concept " as a necessity and not as a program; the advent of the " second religiousness "; the paradox of the esoteric " Faustian Ego " commingled with the " Magian We " in the socialistic tendencies of expressionism. In our present study of systematization we shall have to put

---

[11] Note G. B. Shaw's treatment of the subject in the preface to *Back to Methuselah*.

[12] See Soergel, note 10 of this chapter; Lemke, Ernst, *Die Hauptrichtungen in deutschen Geistesleben*.

[13] See I, 376; II, 122 (English translation I, 294; II, 103).

aside the interpretation of expressionism. Spengler's book, however, must be recommended both as an aid and as a challenge to the understanding of this modern movement.

A study of the background material of expressionism, as presented by the critics of the movement, leads one to the very commonplace observation that every movement is well rooted in the past, that every new movement is a reiterated emphasis, with increased facility in terminology, on something that has occupied the minds of men again and again throughout the ages.[14] The past always yields its influence: that which favors a new movement directly by its similarities is accepted wholeheartedly and offered as evidence that the past has not been wholly lacking in wisdom; whatsoever stands in opposition lends its service by placing greater emphasis through contrast on the ideals of the new movement. The result is that one becomes wary and cautious enough to indicate that at most a new movement cannot be more than a new permutation of old forces, with a different placement of emphasis.

One should not be surprised, therefore, when some critics declare that there is nothing new about the " new movement," except the name! This book, however, has no great concern for the *validity* of expressionism, even though that validity be no more than a new patch on an old garment. The movement in literature and in the arts in Germany between 1910 and 1920 is called " expressionistic." I propose to systematize the critical literature concerned with this period in order that I may establish norms and determine the character of Strindberg's dramatic expressionism.

[14] According to Spengler, if a new movement is an historical phenomenon it must come as a necessity in cultural growth, even as the romantic idealism of a youth may often be coupled with his adolescence.

CHAPTER II

EXPRESSIONISM IN PAINTING

C RITICS of expressionism often discuss the movement without reference to any particular field of art. Yet it is a generally accepted fact that expressionism in painting exerted an immediate influence on the later movement in literature. At least, the theory in painting was consumed and digested by the protagonists of the literary movement, for the theory in literature is too similar to that of painting to be the result of accident. A synthetic study of the critics of the literary movement, therefore, depends somewhat on an understanding of the concepts of the movement in painting.

Of the works examined, Marzynski[1] and Pfister[2] seem the most valuable for our study. The former, while very sympathetic to the movement, presents his material critically, without fervent pleas for faith in that which is beyond comprehension. Marzynski offers the further advantage of carefully outlined material regarding both the theory of expressionism and its method. Pfister, on the other hand, is primarily interested in psychoanalysis, but he has a rare degree of intellectual honesty that forbids him consciously to warp evidence to his favor. He steps aside as psychoanalyst long enough to investigate the validity of expressionistic aesthetics. It is our firm conviction that the studies of both Marzynski and Pfister are inclusive enough to present a fairly complete picture of expressionism in painting.

[1] Marzynski, Georg, *Die Methode des Expressionismus.*
[2] Pfister, Oskar, *Expressionism in Art, Its Psychological and Biological Basis.*

11

MARZYNSKI ON EXPRESSIONISM

MARZYNSKI's book on expressionism is concerned with two phases of the study, theory and method. By way of introduction, the author tells us that expressionistic art is the first that has ever turned its back definitely on observed reality. Art ceases to imitate either observed or imagined reality and discards entirely that type of reality that comes through the physical observation of the eye. Obviously, it is this factor that forms the basis for all the difficulties of comprehending expressionistic painting; what is on the canvas cannot be compared with anything that can be observed in nature. The new art imposes on the critics the necessity of establishing new criteria which consider new aesthetic values. Therefore it is essential that we first turn to the philosophical concept of this new art if we are to comprehend the method.[3]

The first step in philosophy is to turn from the view of universe and self as two separate entities associated more or less by chance. In such a view the ego is merely one among many objects all of which make up the concept *universe*. The subject is given a false valuation, an ego-centrism in which all inner qualifications are lacking. It is the conquest of this point of view that marks the beginning of philosophizing and the end of philosophical naïveté.

For the expressionist, the ego is the essential part of our world, is indeed the heart of its reality. The two are inseparable and an ego without the universe is nothing. Conversely, the universe exists only as a world of projected ego. Subject and object are handy tools for the differentiation of ego and universe, but the two are actually one thing. *It is my ego and my world which flow together in the unity of the supersubjective individual.*

[3] We are *following* Marzynski throughout and not attempting either to refute or defend his statements. See the third paragraph in the *Foreword* to this book.

Preëxpressionistic art was concerned with the reproduction of the object, and emphasis was placed on the sublimation of the object. In expressionism, however, with its concept of the supersubjective individual in whom ego and universe are united in flux, the artist turns from the object as completely as possible. Observed reality·is a *condition* for experience, but the objective material that the artist presents on the canvas is only a bridge over which aesthetic excitement passes. Complete emphasis is shifted from the object to the subject, and the sublimation of the subject becomes the aim of the expressionist. The subject must always occupy the central position, irrespective of what happens to the object.

Before expressionism, emphasis on the object was so decided and complete that the subject was left weak and inconsequential. It is the subject that now must be reclaimed and given primary position, for world and ego flow together in the supersubjective individual.

It is evident that expressionistic art can by no means be compared with a field of knowledge like science, since the latter is concerned primarily with the object. Rather, this art must be viewed in a plane parallel to the planes of religion and mysticism, if one is fully to comprehend its subjective nature. It is more comparable to a specific sort of knowledge, a cognition whose method is the enlargement of the subjective.

This cognition is *Einfühlung*. The common concept of *Einfühlung* offers for definition simply a projection of the ego in a foreign form. This definition of the term, however, sets too narrow limits on the concept. *Einfühlung*, in the broader sense, is really a cumulative process: ". . . sich einfühlen in einen Menschen, in ein Kunstwerk, bedeutet eine Umschichtung der Elemente, eine Lockerung der individuell erstarrten Komplikation, eine Verflüssigung und Verbreiterung des Lebens, die Restitution von Möglichkeiten, die im Verlauf der individuellen

Entwicklung aufgegeben werden mussten. Einfühlung bringt im gewissen Sinne Ausweitung und Bereicherung, weil die individuelle Persönlichkeit ihre Individualität und ihre Festigkeit nur erlangen kann durch einen Prozess fortschreitender Verarmung und Erstarrung." [4] *Einfühlung* thus becomes the experiencing of the flow of ego and world into the unity of the supersubjective individual. It is not bound to the narrow limits of feeling oneself into a foreign form, but is rather the integration of ego and the foreign form into a cosmic unity of both.

In concluding his discussion of the metaphysics of expressionism, Marzynski repeats the outstanding points of his analysis. Subject and object, a duality, remain fast in an inseparable union, though each as a separate concept is necessary for the existence of the other. Formerly, art aligned itself on the side of the object; expressionism, however, belongs to the subject, and its work is the objectification of the subject. It is a form of art that is comparable to that kind of cognition that is termed *Einfühlung.*

Marzynski treats of the method of expressionism more completely than the metaphysics. In this study he presents two phases that deserve emphasis beyond all others: art as optical counterpoint, and the principle of distortion.

One cannot read far into critical works on expressionism, whether in painting or in literature, without encountering again and again the statement that expressionism is trying to realize in other arts what is so fully accomplished in music, the sublimation of the subject. Marzynski tells us that expressionistic art, at least in its radical form, is a kind of optical counterpoint. The artist attempts to build up a work of art abstractly out of colors and patterns. This naturally entails the complete separation of the art-form from observed reality in nature. The majority of expressionistic painters recognize that music is the

---

[4] Marzynski, *Expressionismus,* p. 34.

purest of autonomous arts, the only completely expressionistic art; but they realize that optical music has a limited outlook. The result is that the separation of the art-form from the object in nature is not expected to be complete, nor do many painters attempt it in practice. A glance at pictures of the abstract type, characterized as optical music, verifies the statement that the limits are exceedingly narrow. Marzynski offers Fernand Léger's *Formenvariation* [5] as an example of this type of painting. Such works illustrate clearly that variation in line and form, with complete absence of forms comparable to observed or imagined reality in nature, is decidedly limited.

The element of distortion accounts for much that occurs in expressionistic art. It is not that the artist arbitrarily decides on distortion; it is not simply mutilation of the object. His very concept of art, his insistence on the sublimation of the subject, compels the artist to distort the object. It is inescapable that the artist should become oblivious to a faithful representation of the object.

In the first place, distortion is the result of the attempt to paint the whole psychic experience, to paint all the associations that the ego may acquire in its relation to an object. The object is only a means to an end, and is so lacking in importance that an accurate reproduction of it becomes positively an impediment to the expression of the subject. The object is essentially nothing more than a medium for the expression of the psychic complex. Form and color are therefore inconsequential and may be distorted, really *must be distorted*, according to the dictates of the psychic complex. Distortion is thus a psychological trick; the objective side of experience is cast away entirely, as in optical music, or is warped, in order that the subjective side may gain.

[5] *Ibid.,* Plate 5. For pictures of this type see also Pablo Picasso's *Violinspielerin* and *Der Dichter* in Küppers' book *Der Kubismus,* Plates 16 and 17; also Rudolf Bauer's *Zeichnung* and Oswald Herzog's *Revolution* in Brandt's book *Sehen und Erkennen,* pp. 420–421.

Again, distortion occupies such a predominant position because reality after all is such an indeterminable factor that accurate reproduction or faithful representation is not simply rare, but is actually not possible. Observation gives various results according to factors operating on the object observed and the observer. Conditions of light, distance and atmosphere will occasion in the observer a process of distortion, and this distortion is carried even farther by the quality of attentiveness, interest, consciousness and all other physical and physiological elements that enter into the perceptive process. Distortion inevitably conditions observed reality, and emphasis on the sublimation of the object is quite futile since one cannot so much as reproduce what actually qualifies the object. This futility points directly toward the subject, that which experiences the object, as the essential plane for artistic activity. The consequential distortion of the object is not important in itself, however, for *all* reproductions of objects are distortions.

It is through the concept of distortion that we discover the unique phase of expressionism, the selection of elements. In previous schools of art the selection of elements was quite mechanical, the distortion being determined immediately by the conditioning elements of the perceptive process. In expressionism, however, selection becomes individual, and once the selection is determined the process of reproducing the elements becomes mechanical. Expressionism refuses to accept the ensemble effect of distortion on the object, a process that centers attention on the objective side; but, on the other hand, insists on determining which of the experience-effects from the object are to be given place. Only by a process of selectivity from the psychic complex can the artist hope to give more complete attention to the subject. This selectivity, moreover, is not made from distortion-effects of the object, in which the attention is focussed on the fact of distortion; rather, it is made from the experience-effects for which distortion of the object is an immediate condition.

The selection of elements leads further to a consideration of arrangement in space. Since the image of nature in the psychic complex is not particularly concerned with space, nor with order in space, it follows that the mechanical reproduction of the image in the psychic complex will give no heed to the law of space that conditions observed reality. Consciousness orders, gives arrangement to, the disjunctive parts of the image-complex; and, as a result, the emphasis on any single element or small group of elements may disappear. Consequently, a whole series of elements may be given place in the art-form in the same distorted spatial arrangement that exists in the psychic complex. This gives rise to the so-called telegram-style where the unity in variety is objectively broken, but is subjectively maintained by the control of consciousness.[6] It is obvious that this form, pushed to such an extreme that it would more and more remove emphasis from individual elements, would lead eventually to the interfusion of the objective elements. This interfusion would again tend toward the abstract form in which no objects of observed or imagined reality could play a part.

In his conclusion Marzynski indicates that expressionism has a certain kinship to romanticism in its turning away from observed reality. Actually, however, the modern movement is wholly non-romantic.[7] The romanticists flee to a better world because this one is too *life-impoverished*, and the emphasis is placed on a dream life built up on the embellishment of the objective world. Expressionists, on the contrary, forsake observed

[6] See Marc Chagall's *Ich und das Dorf* in Marzynski, *Expressionismus*, Plate 23; and in Brandt, *Sehen und Erkennen*, p. 424.

[7] See, however, p. 9 above, apropos of Spengler's *Der Untergang des Abendlandes*. If Romanticism and Expressionism are both manifestations of the resurgent "Faustian idea" of Gothicism, the kinship of the two movements is fundamental and the differences are only superficial.

reality not because it is too impoverished, too monotonous, but rather because it is simply naturally objective, instead of artistically subjective. Again, for the romanticist art is a more intense natural life; the expressionist, on the other hand, *desires to reshape reality until the art-form emerges from the nature-form.*

Marzynski's book tells us that in theory expressionism is pointing wholly to the subjective side of life. The expressionist understands that object and subject are after all essentially inseparable, but he wishes to remove the old emphasis on the object in order to give the subject more play. As the musician transmutes experience into tone combinations and qualities, without pointing to the objective experience itself, so the expressionist would put on canvas his experiences transmuted into color and form without betraying the stimulating object. The artist points to the sublimation of the subjective as the key to whatsoever reality exists in this subject-object world of ours.

With regard to method, the concept of distortion plays by far the most important part; at any rate, it is the most significant element in contributing to one's comprehension of what the artist is trying to do, whether or not one actually appreciates the art-product. It would be more enlightening for us if Marzynski had made comparisons between expressionism and other forms of art that have been governed by distortion: for instance, Egyptian standardization of primitive forms; Gothic grotesques; the various forms of caricature, including everything from paintings of renown to modern newspaper and magazine products; and also the method of perspective which is distortion to gain three-dimensionality on the canvas. Yet it is quite clear from Marzynski's treatment of the subject that the stress on distortion is a conditioning factor of the sublimation of the subject in expressionism. It is equally important for its emphasis on the part played by the psychic complex. The principle of distortion illustrates very well that the artist is not painting the observed object, but actually his own psychic complex!

THE judgment of the psychologist, and more especially the psychoanalyst, is clearly in demand when one faces an art so involved with the psychic complex. Dr. Pfister has already filled the rôles of both psychologist and psychoanalyst in his study of expressionism.

Pfister's book is divided into two parts. The first part, fully two thirds of the book, is devoted almost exclusively to the results of psychoanalysis applied to a John Doe character, called José in the book, and his expressionistic pictures. This part of the book is obviously of more interest to the student of psychology than to the student of art. The last third of the book, however, is concerned with " The Psychological and Biological Background of Expressionism " and forms an excellent complement to the material already covered in Marzynski's book.

The final judgment of the psychoanalyst is early found in several sentences. " It is the old story; the neurotically-bound must put his own hating and loving, his own disruption or weakness into other people, even into the universe itself. This finds expression in the fact that he links on to any other persons he chooses, uncritically, the historical features of images which haunt him. Thus the subjective artist, and to a certain degree every artist must be subjective, creates the world according to his own image." [8] While he has respect for certain lofty characteristics of expressionism, Pfister is nevertheless convinced that expressionistic practice in painting has " floundered into introversion." This conviction seems to be so strongly rooted in Pfister that the reader at first suspects the psychoanalyst of having begun his thesis with preëstablished conclusions and of

[8] Pfister, *op. cit.,* p. 50.

picking his evidence to favor his thesis. Further reading, however, convinces one of the fairness with which Pfister offers and
uses evidence.[9]

In discussing the aims of expressionism, Pfister shows himself
essentially in accord with the views of other critics. The expressionist, he says, " objects to the low level of the photog-
rapher's camera, reproducing natural colours. The expressionist
wants to reproduce the intrinsic meaning of things, their soul-
substance. But this grasping of the intrinsic, i.e. the only genuine
reality, is not done through an intellectual study of the external
world . . . no! the creating mind feels itself as the measure of
things, because the world is nothing but self-development of
Mind. The subjective idealism of a Berkeley, of a Fichte, of a
Schuppe reappears in Expressionism, not as the result of a
keen critique of knowledge, but as an immediate artistic
experience. . . . The expressionist creates out of the depths of
things, because he knows himself to be in those depths. To
paint out of himself and to paint himself means to reproduce
the intrinsic nature of things, the Absolute. The artist creates as
God creates, out of his own inner Self, and in his own likeness." [10]

Here, as Pfister tells us, not only the subjective side of expressionism is emphasized, but, most strikingly, the desire of the
artist to depict his own psychical states. More than this, the
artist so limits himself to the limning of his psychical complexes,
and so insists on the limitation, that his world becomes an individual cosmos of uncritical reactions to experience. Marzynski,
speaking from the platform of theory, would probably insist that
the expressionist does not become so completely engulfed within
himself since he admits the subject-object inseparable duality
of the world and ego; and he would explain that the artist goes

---

[9] Naturally, Pfister is not entirely without bias, but he is pleasingly free
from that kind of partiality that permits the indiscriminate use of evidence.
[10] Pfister, *op. cit.,* pp. 189–190.

to extremes in practice because he is making a special plea for emphasis on the subject in order to counteract the former exclusive catering to the object. Pfister would indicate that theory and practice should not be so completely divorced; and he could well point to expressionistic practice in which the subject is not widened, nor is it enriched, for the expressionist apparently abandons his theory in practice and admits no critical understanding of the subject-object relation. In practice there is every proof that the subjective becomes autistic through introversion. Pfister, moreover, is.not ignorant of the *highest* form of expressionism, for he quotes Fritz Burger's statement of the aims of the movement. Expressionism " does not want to be any longer the object of an aesthetically educated caste, but the embodiment of that incommensurable world which comprises our Inner Self. It will not deliver from the World but bring about for us the possession of the World's Inner Greatness, the wonderful wealth of variety in form of the Creative Power itself, which is the salvation and the ruin of us all. As a moulding world-view it desires to be a religion freed from the past of history. At the moment that the optical and chemical sciences are able to reproduce the coloured empirical Reality perfectly, a dream of millenia comes true — Art will retire into her holy realm, her very own, and will curse the enjoying eye and the limping wisdom of the aesthete as well as the vulgar joys of the mob, and will conclude an unheard-of alliance with Philosophy already meeting her half-way. Both turn away from the Empirical World mapped out according to the dictates of Natural Sciences, in order to grasp formatively the meaning of life within a world-view often permeated with mystical ideas. With that Art is brought back to its oldest original purpose." [11]

Nevertheless, in spite of this recognition of the aims of the *highest* form of expressionism, Pfister is quite dissatisfied with

[11] *Ibid.,* pp. 190–191.

expressionistic practice. He is able to find defence for the qualification of autism not simply in expressionistic practice but even
in articles on the theory. " The characteristic which most impressed all the theoreticians of Expressionism is that which the
psychoanalysts call Autism . . . the active turning away from
the external world and the living within the Inner World of
Fancy or Phantasy." [12] This claim is supported by quotations
from articles by several critics (Raphael, Jollos, Stockmeyer)
who put emphasis on the negation of the object and the turning
of the artist to his soul as the source of all things. Expressionism
for Pfister, with evidence both from theory and practice, is
" thorough-going Introversion-painting." [13]

Further characteristics that may be garnered from Pfister's
book will be enlightening for our later study on literary expressionism, but will need no extensive discussion. Expressionism
regresses toward pre-cultural forms.[14] It is also marked by a
great number of characteristics of the infantile.[15] All the pictures
of the expressionist contain the fulfilment of secret desires, which
are wholly hidden even from himself.[16] Expressionistic painting
springs from the suffering of the soul.[17] This form of art has a
definite parallel with automatic cryptolaly and religious glossolaly.[18] Things in reality are caricatured to the point of being
unrecognizable.[19] Expressionism caricatures to the point of
almost obliterating the object, or in the representation of psychic
states may abandon all attempts at giving a likeness.[20] Expressionistic art borders on the pathological realm of dream and hallu-
cination.[21] Many expressionistic pictures are the wild shriek of
tortured minds, but just as inartistic as a yell.[22] This art, if
pushed to its logical extremes, means an absolute rejection of the
empirical world.[23] The non-psychopathic expressionists possess

---

[12] Pfister, *op. cit.*, 196.
[13] *Ibid.*, p. 198.
[14] *Ibid.*, p. 194.
[15] *Ibid.*, p. 196.

[16] *Ibid.*, p. 201.
[17] *Ibid.*, p. 210.
[18] *Ibid.*, p. 217.
[19] *Ibid.*, p. 224.

[20] *Ibid.*, p. 242.
[21] *Ibid.*, p. 227.
[22] *Ibid.*, p. 245.
[23] *Ibid.*, p. 266.

besides their art a sufficient number of bridges to span the abyss between the Ego and the external world.[24]

The foregoing paragraph is presented in what the expressionists themselves would call *telegram-style*. Yet, for the limits of our study, it would not pay to make an exhaustive study of Pfister's book, most especially since the psychoanalyst is clearly interested in the psychopathic cases. This meat-loaf paragraph contains the gist of Pfister's material on the nature of expressionistic painting.

We must, nevertheless, bear in mind that Pfister has tested his conclusions by aesthetic as well as scientific investigations; he has considered both the theory and practice of expressionism. He sees no possibility of the expressionist realizing aesthetic form, or even of delivering himself through his painting, as long as the artist locks himself within the ego and dynamites all the bridges between subject and object. Total abandonment of the empirical world is not simply dangerous; actually, the destruction of the subject-object inseparable duality can only deliver the individual to the madhouse. It is consciousness that is supported by the linked subject-object, and consciousness unsupported at one end will sink into unconsciousness.

Most important for our study is the presentation of characteristics of expressionistic art, for it is control factors that this study seeks. We make note of the primitive and infantile forms which appear in expressionistic practice; in painting, a regression toward the savage state of man. Furthermore, expressionism, springing from the suffering of the soul, also results in automatic cryptolaly and religious glossolaly, and is comparable to yell. The element of distortion appears once more for our consideration, another vital agreement between Pfister and Marzynski; this form of art so caricatures the object that the latter is at times obliterated. It is the rejection of the empirical world.

[24] *Ibid.*, p. 259.

From Marzynski's point of view, distortion is a necessity and results from aesthetic doctrine. According to Pfister, distortion is not necessary, but inevitable, and comes from pathological disturbance.

In the presentation of expressionistic characteristics there is much in harmony between Pfister and Marzynski, as we have already noted. The former, however, in examining the practice of painting, especially with reference to its autonomous character, insists that not only aesthetics but also psychoanalysis has a definite rôle in the analysis of this modern art-form. He also emphasizes for us the confusion that exists in theory and practice, especially if one tries to discover in expressionistic paintings the subject-object inseparable duality so strongly affirmed in the theory. Expressionism, to Pfister, is subjectivism of much the same order that one finds among religious ecstatics, or among the patients in our institutions for the feeble-minded and the insane.

CHAPTER III

GENERALITIES ON EXPRESSIONISM IN THE ARTS
AND IN LITERATURE

PFISTER has pushed expressionism to its logical conclusions, and given us the results of the extremists. In the arts and literature one may find a specific movement, Dadaism, which has gone to the extreme point of expressionistic practice. Yet this no longer remains expressionism, but rather a narrow portion of the entire movement. Dadaism broke the bridges between subject and object in a rather wholesome manner by pointing to the results of expressionism if pushed to the extreme. The result in literature is well illustrated by the following example, a stanza from Hans Arp's so-called poem *Das bezungte Brett*.[1]

> hochnehmst millionemill um bitt
> fallammelmahl fallobst toast
> bum bum barin rucktwitelsack
> und tabledhoten ihn von ast. . . .

This " poem " brings us to an appreciation of Pfister's statement that expressionism at times comes very close to automatic cryptolaly and religious glossolaly. Yet, in literature, the appearance is almost exclusively in the Dadaistic movement and not in expressionism proper. We, of course, cannot be concerned here with infantile babbling, *ur*-yell, and other balderdash, even when valid as a satire on expressionism. Consequently Dadaism with its theories and results may well be left undiscussed without injuring the validity of this study. It is enough to know that Dadaism was a conscious breaking of the bridges to reality and

[1] von Allesch, G. J., " Expressionismus," *Zeits. f. Ästhetik* . . . , Bd. 19, 1925, p. 119.

was directed at first as a satire against the wildness in expressionism and the whole coterie of -isms then bobbing up in art.[2] In literary expressionism we find practically all the characteristics given both by Marzynski and by Pfister. There is, however, one exception that is perfectly obvious. In literature the art-product has enough contact with reality to be comprehensible without too elaborate explanations either on the part of a psychologist or his neighbor, the psychoanalyst. The objective side in literature cannot be eliminated without reducing the content to senseless, even if tuneful, jargon.[3] Dadaism is the natural consequence when the objective side is completely ignored, and literary expressionists were too desirous of creating a new world, a world with mankind in the center, to annihilate the means of attainment which they possessed.

BAHR AND EDSCHMID

IN SPITE of ecstatic ranting, Hermann Bahr and, more especially, Kasimir Edschmid occasionally pronounce a sentence that

---

[2] For further studies in Dadaism see the following works:
  (a) De Torre, Guillermo, *Literaturas Europeas de Vanguardia*, Caro Raggio, Madrid, 1925. See pp. 178–227, "El movimiento 'Dada.'"
  (b) Erenyi, G., "Aesthetischer Nihilismus," *Gegenwart*, October, 1920, pp. 362–365.
  (c) Flake, Otto, "Prognose des Dadaismus," *Der neue Merkur*, September, 1920, pp. 404–408.
  (d) G., J., "Heil dem dadaistischen Zentralblatt," *Gegenwart*, March 1, 1920, p. 89.
  (e) Hülsenbeck, Richard, *En avant Dada*, Steegemann, Hannover, 1920. (Hülsenbeck was at one time "Oberdada" among the Dadaists.)
  (f) Hunck, J., "Dada und Expressionismus," *Allgem. Künstlerzeitung*, IX, 84, 1920.
  (g) Matthias, Leo, "Über Dadaismus," *Der neue Merkur*, September, 1920, pp. 397–403.
  (h) Soergel, *Dichtung und Dichter der Zeit*, pp. 623–634.
  (i) "Der Dadaismus," *Auslandspost*, May 1, 1920, pp. 2–3.
  [3] See "absolute poetry" written by Rudolf Blümner; an example is given by Soergel, *Dichtung u. Dichter*, p. 618.

is cool enough to be handled in a critical study. Bahr, as usual, was first in the field, putting a book on the market as early as 1916.[4] His work is concerned for the most part with expressionistic painting, and is not of sufficient importance to our study to warrant considerable treatment. It is more of interest than of importance, for Bahr, himself a literary man, is one of the first writers to use the cant that especially qualifies literary expressionism. He gives decided impetus to the cry for *Seele*, a cry that becomes *Schrei* in a rather short length of time. " Da schreit die Not jetzt auf: der Mensch schreit nach seiner Seele, die ganze Zeit wird ein einziger Notschrei. Auch die Kunst schreit mit, in die tiefe Finsternis hinein, sie schreit um Hilfe, sie schreit nach dem Geist: das ist der Expressionismus." [5] Bahr, an excellent barometer of art, has sensed in painting the *Schrei*-element that was to become so strong in literature; but it is as yet a poetic cry that Bahr hears in 1916 and not the savage yell that Pfister hears after 1920.

A little later in his book, Bahr tells us more beautifully than the average critic that the primitive instinct also manifests itself in expressionism. " Wie der Urmensch sich aus Furcht vor der Natur in sich verkriecht, so flüchten wir in uns vor einer ' Zivilisation ' zurück, die die Seele des Menschen verschlingt." [6] Here, Bahr does not point to regression toward the primitive but rather indicates the character of literary primitivity. The artist is not simply a reproducer of primitive art, not simply a modern individual who reverts to primitive man; rather, the artist is *Le Penseur* who dwells in an *ur*-atmosphere of *ur*-feeling, of *ur*-emotions and of *ur*-activity. He is quite nude, without the clothes of modern civilization, but he is a thinker and not a shrieking or yowling savage. There is a philosophical quality to this *ur*-ishness that is not given in words like primitivity,

---

[4] Bahr, Hermann, *Expressionismus,* Delphin, München, 1916.
[5] *Ibid.,* p. 123.   [6] *Ibid.,* p. 127.

original state, source and the like. *Ur*-ishness is an emphasis on
the spiritual quality of man, not simply as free from the artifice
of convention, the tags of civilization, but as something enduring
before and beyond the quirks of written codes and public opin-
ions. *Ur*-ishness points to the unattached cosmic spirit that gives
man his essential and enduring worth.

Though discoursing on expressionism in painting, Bahr has
bridged the way to criticism of literary expressionism. The
literary man cries out for the *subject,* turns to his own soul, and
may even shout wildly for pure unadulterated feeling; but this
remains in part only gesture, for literary expressionism never
entirely forsakes the object. The cry of distress is for intellect,
for *Geist,* as well as for feeling, for *Seele.* The literary expressionist does not regress toward the primitive, where unqualified
subjectivism would deliver him, but rather he struggles for the
expression of what is eternal from the *ur*-man throughout all
succeeding mankind. Furthermore, he seeks for deliverance from
the insufferable bonds of an all too materialistic civilization.

Kasimir Edschmid [7] declares that no one doubts that apparent
reality is after all not essentially real, that observed reality is not
the essence of an object. The classified facts are not enough
for us, not enough to give us a true picture of the universe and
a concept of its essential core. It is in the vision of the artist
that we obtain this genuine view, not from the mere form or
representation of stuff that the artist gives us, but from the
essential reality that the artist wrests from matter. The artist's
intuition is the functional element that makes possible the
wresting of reality from matter.

The artist fastens upon reality not by seeing, but by observing;
not by depicting, but by experiencing; not by reproducing, but
by fashioning; not by taking, but by seeking — a selective act.[8]

[7] Edschmid, Kasimir, *Über den Expressionismus in der Literatur und die neue Dichtung,* 3. Aufl., Reiss, Berlin, 1919.   [8] *Ibid.,* p. 52.

He sees the human element in the harlot, the divine in the factory; all individual elements are fashioned by him into that whole which constitutes the world. Moreover, all is related to the eternal. It is the artist's business to fashion his view of the world according to the vision of reality that he gets by peering behind the individually manifested facts.

The human being is no longer just an individual bound by all the traditions of duty, morality, society and family. In expressionism, the human being is the most exalted and the most miserable.[9] He becomes *human*. This, then, is the new phase of the art, that man no longer is represented as an individual, classified according to his rôle in an artificial society. The hand of the artist goes behind all classifications, goes behind the mere individual, and shows us mankind: " keine blonde Bestie, kein ruchloser Primitiver, sondern der einfache, schlichte Mensch." [10]

When one has delivered man from his individuality, from his social pigeonhole, there are new possibilities for him. " Nun ist der Mensch wieder grosser, unmittelbarer Gefühle mächtig. Er steht da, so deutlich in seinem Herzen zu erfassen, so absolut ursprünglich von den Wellen seines Bluts durchlaufen, dass es verscheint, er trüge sein Herz auf der Brust gemalt. Er bleibt nicht mehr Figur. Er ist wirklich Mensch. Er ist verstrickt in den Kosmos, aber mit kosmischem Empfinden." [11]

Soon, however, Edschmid alarms us by bringing expressionism to introversion, and expressionists to the vestibule, at least, of the madhouse. There is a danger that Edschmid is proposing to uncouple the subject-object relation and drop consciousness into oblivion.

Er kügelt sich nicht durch das Leben. Er geht hindurch. Er denkt nicht über sich, er erlebt sich. Er schleicht nicht um die Dinge, er fasst sie im

---

[9] Note a kindred statement by Havelock Ellis: " No creature on earth has so tortured himself as Man, and none has raised a more exultant Alleluia." *Dance of Life* (Houghton Mifflin Co., New York, 1923), p. 358.

[10] Edschmid, *Expressionismus*, p. 58.   [11] *Ibid.*, p. 59.

Mittelpunkt an. Er ist nicht un-, nicht übermenschlich, er ist nur Mensch, feig und stark, gut und gemein und herrlich, wie ihn Gott aus der Schöpfung entliess.

So sind ihm alle Dinge, deren Kern, deren richtiges Wesen er zu schauen gewohnt ist, nahe.

Er wird nicht unterdrückt, er liebt und kämpft unmittelbar. Sein grosses Gefühl allein, kein verfälschtes Denken, führt ihn und leitet ihn.

So kann er sich steigern und zu Begeisterungen kommen, grosse Ekstasen aus seiner Seele aufschwingen lassen.

Er kommt bis an Gott als die grosse nur mit unerhörter Ekstase des Geistes zu erreichende Spitze des Gefühls.

Doch sind diese Menschen keineswegs töricht. Ihr Denkprozess verläuft nur in anderer Natur. Sie sind unverbildet. Sie reflektieren nicht.

Sie erleben nicht in Kreisen, nicht durch Echos.

Sie erleben direkt.

Das ist das grösste Geheimnis dieser Kunst: Sie ist ohne gewohnte Psychologie.[12]

This art is positive, says Edschmid, because it is intuitive. Men in this realm of art abandon themselves to the divine; they are immediate, primitive, simple, because that which is most simple is also most complicated and intricate. They have a cosmic art which enables them to reach greater heights and penetrate farther into the depths than any other art.

We note, however, that *Gefühl*, *Geist* and *Seele* whirl aloft in the nebula of ecstasy toward God, with so complete a disregard for critical understanding and intellect that we cannot accept at face value Edschmid's declaration: " doch sind diese Menschen keineswegs töricht." At the same time, however, we remember with growing forbearance that Edschmid was also in the vanguard of critics of expressionism; and, like Bahr, he often has too much of the " soap-box prophet " and too little of the critic in his utterances.

There are still other great secrets of this art which Edschmid reveals to us. He stresses again the fact that the *typical* plays an important rôle in expressionism; furthermore, that the typical carries in it the idea of motion, of becoming, of the dynamic state. What is presented, for instance, is not a thought, but

[12] Edschmid, *op. cit.*, pp. 59–60.

thinking; not an embrace, but embracing. As the individual is a representation of something isolated and static, so is the typical a manifestation of movement.[13]

Language naturally undergoes some change when an art is pregnant with great secrets and delivers itself of new and unheard of concepts:

Die Sätze liegen im Rhythmus anders gefaltet als gewohnt. Sie unterstehen der gleichen Absicht, demselben Strom des Geistes, der nur das Eigentliche gibt. Melodik und Biegung beherrscht sie. Doch nicht zum Selbstzweck. Die Sätze dienen in grosser Kette hängend dem Geist, der sie formt.

Sie kennen nur seinen Weg, sein Ziel, seinen Sinn. Sie binden Spitze an Spitze, sie schnellen ineinander, nicht mehr verbunden durch Puffer logischer Überleitung, nicht mehr durch den federnden äusserlichen Kitt der Psychologie. Ihre Elastizität liegt in ihnen selbst.

Auch das Wort erhält andere Gewalt. Das beschreibende, das umschürfende hört auf. Dafür ist kein Platz mehr. Es wird Pfeil. Trifft in das Innere des Gegenstandes und wird von ihm beseelt. Es wird kristallisch das eigentliche Bild des Dinges.

Dann fallen die Füllwörter.

Das Verbum dehnt sich und verschärft sich, angespannt so deutlich und eigentlich den Ausdruck zu fassen.

Das Adjektiv bekommt Verschmelzung mit dem Träger des Wortgedankens. Auch es darf nicht umschreiben. Es allein muss das Wesen am knappsten geben und nur das Wesen. Sonst nichts.[14]

Just when we are convinced that expressionism is decidedly new, that it offers new aesthetic doctrine and is in a fair way to re-create language as a medium of expression, Edschmid declares that after all the art is extremely old. Moreover, expressionism is not simply a vogue in art, and has never been just that. It is actually a *Weltanschauung.*

Es ist eine Lüge, dass das, was mit verbrauchten Abwort das Expressionistische genannt wird, neu sei. Schändung, es umfasse eine Mode. Verleumdung, es sei eine nur künstlerische Bewegung. . . .

Diese Art des Ausdrucks ist nicht deutsch, nicht französisch.

Es ist übernational.

---

[13] *Ibid.,* p. 65.

[14] *Ibid.,* pp. 65–66 (Soergel also quotes the same passage in *Dichtung und Dichter der Zeit,* p. 353).

Sie ist nicht nur Angelegenheit der Kunst. Sie ist Forderung des Geistes.
Sie ist kein Programm des Stils. Sie ist eine Frage der Seele.
Ein Ding der Menschheit.
Es gab Expressionismus in jeder Zeit. Keine Zone, die ihn nicht hatte, keine Religion, die ihn nicht feurig schuf. Kein Stamm, der nicht das dumpfe Göttliche damit besang und formte.[15]

Although Edschmid, like Bahr, is more concerned with expressionism in general than with the literary movement, he does nevertheless give consideration to the latter. Once more the familiar words appear: *Seele, Geist, Wirklichkeit, Mensch, Kosmos, Gott, Erleben, intuitiv, Gefühl* and their like. In addition we also find stress laid on the typical and on movement, *Bewegung*. The typical alone can qualify the essential reality that lies behind the objects we observe; and the typical alone is in a constant state of becoming, of dynamic activity. Furthermore, in literature, we have another change, that of language. In fact, it is only too obvious that Edschmid's book is a constant example and reminder of the new style of German.

Apropos of the language changes which Edschmid discusses, we may very opportunely add a little more material from the pen of Oswald Pander: " . . . jedes radikal expressionistische Gedicht, das in der bunten Ecke der Zeitungen auf den Scheiterhaufen öffentlicher Lächerlichkeit gezerrt wird: seht! kein Subjekt, kein Objekt, kein Prädikat, keine Deklination, keine Konjugation, keine Grammatik, und, ach! keine Logik; wir verstehen das nicht, es hat keinen Verstand! "[16] While Pander is in sympathy with developing the language into a better medium for expression, he nevertheless would maintain some limits.

Pander also points to the philosophical nature of this new movement in art. " Expressionismus will dem Erleben abgestorben Sprache aus Erleben neu gebären. Expressionismus ist nicht

---

[15] Edschmid, *op. cit.,* p. 70.
[16] Soergel, *Dichtung und Dichter der Zeit,* pp. 354–355 (taken from Pander's article in *Jungen Deutschland,* 1918).

wilder Ausbruch des Ich. Expressionismus drückt der Welt das Gesicht des Menschen auf."

MAX PICARD ON EXPRESSIONISM

A FIRST reading of Picard's article [17] seems only to add confusion to an already unwieldy mass of data. After a second reading one is positive that even Picard cannot order the material in his own essay. Yet, by repeated attacks on the article, it is possible to reach behind the superficial confusion of words and wrest some order that can be employed later. One learns, furthermore, that Picard has something of value to present.

Like many of the writers on expressionism, Picard begins with a discussion of impressionism:

> Durch den Impressionismus hat sich der Mensch der Verantwortung enthoben.
> Die Dinge im Impressionismus sind in so enger Beziehung untereinander, dass man ein Ding gar nicht isolieren kann, man kann gar nicht sagen, was eines ist, es ist immer schon von dem anderen dabei.
> Man braucht also nicht ein einzelnes Ding verantworten, man braucht nur ein Ding mit irgend einer Beziehung zu einem anderen beantworten.
> Statt des Gewissens für ein Ding braucht man nur das Wissen um seine Beziehungen.[18]

Impressionism thus posits a world of relativity in which one is concerned not with things in themselves, not with essential reality, but with the relations that bind each thing with everything. Responsibility for getting at the heart of things is so evaded that no *thing* is ever tangible. " Denn jedes Ding soll rasch aus irgend einer Beziehung herauswachsen und ebenso rasch wieder in irgend eine andere Beziehung verschwinden." [19] It is a world of *relativitization* and *reactivity,* a world in which relativity is multi-

---

[17] Picard, Max, " Expressionismus," *Die Erhebung,* herausgegeben von Alfred Wolfenstein, Fischer, Berlin, 1919, pp. 329–338.

[18] *Ibid.,* p. 329.

[19] *Ibid.,* p. 331 (see the discussion of evolution and evasion of responsibility in the preface to G. B. Shaw's *Back to Methuselah*).

plied by relativity and reaction by reaction. Nothing essential happens in it, and no essential thing is found in it.

The remedy for such a world is found naturally enough in expressionism. " In der expressionistischen Zeit soll ja alles anders sein. Aus dem Chaos, in dem die Dinge kaum einem Namen haben, damit sie von allem und zu allem gerufen werden können, aus diesem namenlosen Chaos ruft der neue, expressionistische Mensch das Ding heraus zu sich. Er ruft die Dinge bei ihrem Namen an: Du Wald, sagt er, und du Stadt, damit der Wald und die Stadt sich aus dem Chaos wieder auseinander ordnen." [20]

The impressionist would hear only the " du " which establishes relationships between objects; he is not so interested in the object itself. The expressionist, on the other hand, is not at all concerned with the " du." He hears the terms " Wald " and " Stadt," terms that isolate objects from one another.

At the present time relativitization has so increased and complicated matters that the expressionist must call out in a loud voice if he expects anything in chaos to hear him. " Der Expressionist ruft darum laut und ist pathetisch, nicht aus einem primären Lebensgefühl heraus, sondern aus Zwang." The employment of pathos is especially required if one is to grasp anything out of the confusion of chaos, but it is not sufficient in itself.

Das Pathos aber allein genügt nicht, ein Ding aus dem Chaos zu fixieren. Man muss ein Ding noch verwandeln, als ob es niemals mit den anderen Dingen des Chaos in Beziehung gewesen wäre, damit es von ihnen nicht mehr erkannt wird und nicht mehr auf sie reagieren kann. Man muss abstrakt sein, typisieren, damit das Erreichte nicht wieder in Chaos zurückgleitet. Man drückt also so viel Leidenschaftlichkeit in ein Ding hinein, bis es fast auseinanderbricht und das Ding sich nur damit abgeben kann, die Spannung des eigenen Bruches zu bewahren; es kann sich dann gar nicht mehr zu einem andern hinspannen.

Oder man statuiert Typen. Wie bei Mariotten spürt man, wenn die Bewegung beginnt, auf einmal, plötzlich gerade als ob die Bewegung nicht mehr im Ding selber wäre, sondern als Ding von aussen hinzukommen müsse, gerade als ob es hier zwei Dinge wären: Typus und Bewegung. Be-

---

[20] Picard, *op. cit.*, p. 332.

wegung und Ding sind getrennt. Man ist also im Expressionismus nicht leidenschaftlich um der Leidenschaft willen, nicht typisch um des Typus willen, man benützt die Verschwendung der Leidenschaft, die Abstraktion, die Typisierung nur, um aus dem Chaos das Bewegte in die Ruhe zu isolieren.

So sehr ist man jetzt bestrebt zu fixieren, dass man sogar die Herkunft der Abstraktion aus der Bewegtheit zu verbergen sucht. Man sucht zu verbergen, dass die Abstraktion aus der Anschauung des Chaos entstanden ist. Darum konstruiert man zum Begriff der Abstraktion den polaren Begriff der Einfühlung. Anstatt dass sich ein Gefälle von der Anschauung des Chaos hin zur Abstraktion bewegt, fixieren sich die polaren Begriffe Abstraktion und Einfühlung. Das bewegte Vorstellungsgebilde soll in ein fixiertes verwandelt werden.[21]

This process of transforming the active imaging factor into a fixed image has been systematized into a *Weltanschauung*, and Picard supports the statement by a quotation from Mynona.[22] According to the latter every positive thing experiences its negative, and the secret of reality lies exactly in the middle, at the point that both positive and negative are paralyzed. A thing, then, can only be grasped, that is, freed from chaos and isolated in typical form, when it is contemplated in polaric opposition. The impressionists conceived this opposition to be conditioned by centrifugal force, and the anti-poles were pictured as flying from each other into new relationships. The expressionists, however, find that the opposite relation is the true one. The anti-poles of abstraction and *Einfühlung* are attracted centripetally and struggle with terrific tension toward each other. This is the *Weltanschauung* of the expressionist with its explanation of the polaric nature of things and the essential reality that is born of the centripetal struggle of opposites.

As an example Picard cites the struggle of man and woman, polarized by sex, and attracted by this terrific and tense centripetal force that conditions sex. It is not just *a* woman in struggle with many men, nor a chance struggle of *a* man with

[21] *Ibid.*, pp. 333–334.
[22] Mynona is the pen-name for Salomo Friedländer (see Soergel, *Dichtung u. Dichter*, p. 860).

many women. It is *the* man and *the* woman, the only man and
the only woman that chaos can produce. Furthermore, this
type-man and type-woman must struggle as though all the hate
or all the love of chaos be present in them. Other examples of
polarization and centripetal struggle are found in the oppositions
of father and son, the old generation and the new; the intellectual
and the burgher, the liberal and the conservative.

This possibility of reducing chaos by snatching a thing out of
it, isolating and fixing it in antithesis, has now become almost
a formula for expressionists who first fashioned experience in
opposites. Thus, one experiences religion, for example, not as
an absolute, as God, but rather as an absolute antithesis between
metaphysical contemplation and ethical activity.[23]

That this tendency to isolate a thing from relationships, from
chaos, has reached philosophic status, is further substantiated
by a quotation from Husserl: " Wir wollen uns nicht mehr mit
einem symbolischen Wortverständnis zufrieden geben . . . Be-
deutungen, die nur von entfernten, verschwommenen, uneigent-
lichen Anschauungen — wenn überhaupt von irgend welchen —
belebt sind, können uns nicht genug tun." [24]

The expressionist wants to fix pure absolute being. In so
doing he turns away from psychology and makes his appeal to
logic. Psychology creates a fertile readiness for nuances, all of
which are relative. Expressionism, however, is desirous of pre-
venting further relativitization, because it wants to isolate and
fix one single typical thing.

Picard quotes from Kurt Hiller to illustrate the resentment
that expressionists have for psychology. Hiller claims that
psychology is really a swindle, for it solves no problem at all; it
prolongs the agony of a situation without giving solution and
leaves the individual simply the experiences of pain.

[23] Picard credits this to Hans Blüher.
[24] Picard, " Expressionismus," *Erhebung,* p. 335.

" Man will im Expressionismus nicht den Schmerz um ein
Ding, man will das Ding selber haben, der Schmerz mag dabei
sein oder nicht. Schmerz und Freude an einem Ding will man
nur darum kennen, damit man sie von dem Ding trennen kann,
damit hier das Ding sei, das ganz für sich allein sein kann, und
dort die Affekte, die überall sein können. Man will also den
Gegenstand von der Relativität der Affekte lösen, man will ihn
nicht sich verwandeln lassen durch Schmerz oder Freude. Man
kümmert sich nur darum, dass ein Ding sei, isoliert sei." Not
pain, not joy, not the *affects* from a thing, but the thing itself is
what the expressionist demands.

Thus the expressionist is not a psychologist. He is much more
a psychoanalyst, contradictory as that may seem. Yet psychology lets a thousand things come from one thing whereas psychoanalysis unites a thousand into one. It assembles thousands of
experiences out of chaos, unites them and fixes them into a single
experience.

The tendency to orientate in chaos, the fixing in chaos, is so
great that it exposes the following paradox: " das ungeheuer
Bewegte und ungeheuere Bewegende, wird nicht mehr wie im
Impressionismus als das ungeheuer Bewegte und ungeheuere Bewegende erlebt, sondern eben paradox: fixierend-orientierend."
This paradox is what is revolutionary in expressionism. It is not
experienced for the sake of Dionysian transport, but for the sake
of an Apollinian form in which the transport is ordered.[25]

Toward the end of his article Picard explains that expressionism
is unscientific. It refuses science because the latter will provide
too many things. The expressionist is concerned only with one
thing at a time, a thing apart from all relations that may exist
with other things.

Das Symbol dieser expressionistischen Zeit wäre etwa nicht Buddha,
der nach einem Blick in die Welt, die Welt aus seinen Händen entlassen

---

[25] *Ibid.,* p. 336.

hat, sondern ein Herakles, der nach einem Blick in die Welt unendlich viele Hände haben möchte, damit er mit jeder dieser unendlich vielen Hände eines der unendlich vielen Dinge des Chaos erfassen kann.[26]

Picard gives us Marzynski's metaphysics of expressionism in rather involved language, but the substance is there; and the two writers are not in such disagreement as they at first may seem to be. Picard's world of things in which every positive thing experiences its opposite is not vastly different from Marzynski's subject-object inseparable duality. In each case essential reality is found somewhere between the anti-poles. Picard's main thesis is that everything must be conceived in polaric division, if it is to give meaning to a concept of reality; and the opposites must struggle toward each other with terrific force. Furthermore, inasmuch as individuality is conditioned by relativity and becomes lost in the *affects* thereof, the expressionist searches for reality in the typical which is decidedly more free from entangling relations. Picard's article is of especial value for its emphasis on typification and on antithesis.

[26] Picard, *op. cit.,* p. 338.

CHAPTER IV

EXPRESSIONISM IN DRAMA

THE CRITIC JULIUS BAB

THE dramatic critic Julius Bab has contributed articles on expressionism for a decade and a study of a number of his essays is decidedly profitable for the establishment of control factors. In spite of the fact that he is not in sympathy with expressionism, that he discounts greatly the literary fruits of the movement, Bab is first of all an honest and balanced critic. Whatever opposition he registers is based on aesthetic judgment and not merely on personal prejudice or antagonism. Besides being better informed than the majority of his fellow critics, he is content to write his criticisms in essay style; there is no ecstatic rant, no expletory expansion, no polarization from which one must wrest whatsoever reality there is in expressionism. All in all, Bab offers the best material for individual treatment. The other critics must be left for the general discussion that follows.

As early as 1916 Bab was discussing expressionism. In an article written during that year [1] Bab says that the striving toward dramatic form for the expression of inner powers really began eleven years earlier, that the term " expressionistic " might well have been applied to works of the earlier date. Even then, he says, the dramatists were demanding that form be determined not by the nature of the materials, but rather by the " Leiden-schaft des Gestaltenden." At this time, however, Bab seems

---

[1] Bab, Julius, " Die Expressionisten und das Drama," *Die Schaubühne,* September 19, 1916, pp. 266–270.

rather dubious of this modern movement with its convenient name, expressionism. He does not think that the young writers know what they really want nor where they are going. With one breath these young writers seem to demand undaunted brutality coupled with the superlative in elegance, the most intimate closeness and the most monumental distance, the most brotherly resignation and the most aristocratic seclusion. Further, it is Bab's opinion that the young writers are not overcoming these contradictions and oppositions but rather are multiplying them as they gain in the practice of expressionistic art.

In an article that appeared in the same magazine [2] one week later, Bab discusses Hasenclever's *Der Sohn,*[3] one of the early expressionistic dramas. Apparently, this form of drama " soll es nun ausmachen, dass die Figuren, mit denen der Sohn ringt, alle ohne objektives Leben, nur Ausstrahlungen seiner Innerlichkeit sind." But this, declares Bab, is merely an indication that drama is dropping into lyrical form, that the actor becomes simply a reciting attribute instead of a creative factor in the drama. This lays the expressionistic writer open to all the dangers of dilettantism, for the materials of drama establish an imperative with which one cannot trifle.

Ignoring Bab's criticism, its validity notwithstanding, we seize upon the equational factors " Ausstrahlungen seiner Innerlichkeit " and lyricism. They again refer us to the subjectivism that has been so constantly stressed by all critics. More than that, this radiation from the inner man seems, on the surface at least, to sever all connections with the objective side of life. In Hasenclever's drama, the one character, the Son, is struggling with shadowy figures that are projected from his ego.

Two years later Bab is still showing discontent with this new type of drama.[4] He says that the product of the young German

---

[2] See note 1 of this chapter.   [3] Written 1914, published 1916.

[4] Bab, Julius, " Der dramatische Jugendstil," *Die Weltbühne,* August 22, 1918, p. 176.

dramatists is " eine Art horror vacui, ein Schwindel vor der Leere, vor diesem abstrakten Raum, worin nur die Gespenster pathetischer Ausrufungszeichen umgehen. Wenn die allerneuesten Aesthetiker, die hinter diesen neuesten Produzenten natürlich schon herlaufen, uns einreden wollen: diese Leere, dieses kaum lyrische, sondern mehr rhetorische Kreisen der Phantasie um die ekstatische Stimmung des vom grossen Totendrang geschwellten Ich, das sei eben das neue grosse Kunstprinzip — so ist das natürlich Unsinn. Die Theorie, dass ein Drama möglich und notwendig sei, worin die ganze Welt nur als Spiegelung der Seele des dramatischen Helden vorkommt, halte ich, soweit sichs um eine Normsetzung handelt, für objektiv falsch. Aber sie ist hier auch subjektiv unbegründet — denn wo ist in diesen gespenstisch armseligen Stücken die ' ganze Welt,' die Gleichnis der Dichter- oder Helden-Seele werden soll? Beim späten Strindberg ist dies Innendrama, dieser ungeheuer dramatische Lyrismus freilich auf eine Art Wirklichkeit geworden, weil sein Ich die ganze Welt mit all ihren ungeheueren Spannungen und Kämpfen in sich geschlungen hat." But, says Bab, the " knaben "-dramatists of young Germany have no such *Ich* and consequently have no possibility of portraying the world.

In this article, as in the earlier ones, we have repeated emphasis on the " Ausstrahlungen des Ichs," this time expressed as " Spiegelung der Seele "; and, again, the lyricism of expressionistic drama. Bab is obviously discouraged with the abstractness, the emptiness and the more rhetorical than lyrical qualities of this new drama. This literary product seems little more than ecstatic rant from puffy egos. Nevertheless, Bab does admit that a kind of reality is obtained by a writer of the caliber of Strindberg, a writer whose ego has so been filled with the strain and battle of a world of experience that the radiation from his ego does put an aspect of reality on the stage.

The latest available article on expressionism by Bab is included in a book on the German drama edited by R. F. Arnold.[5] In this work the critic stands at some distance from expressionism, especially from those phases which he discussed between 1916 and 1918. Bab is still skeptical of expressionism, still lacking in positive sympathy, for in his review of the products of the movement he finds scarcely a work that is of genuine literary worth though there are a number of value in literary history. Time, however, has enabled the critic to establish his values with cooler judgment than heretofore.

In this essay Bab's method is that of individual treatment of expressionistic dramatists. He includes in his study a rather large number of contributors to the new movement: Sorge, Strindberg, Sternheim, Kaiser, Hasenclever, Werfel, Kornfeld, von Unruh and others of equal or lower rank. The inclusion of Strindberg in this study is naturally based on his influence on the expressionists.

Sorge's *Der Bettler* [6] is acclaimed as one of the most remarkable dramas that ever appeared in German literature, though the qualification " remarkable " by no means guarantees the aesthetic worth of the play. In many respects, indeed, the drama is the product of childish dilettantism. The author himself, who has written a play and cannot dispose of it, is the theme of the drama. But, says Bab, there are also characteristics of genius in the work.

In this drama, *Der Bettler,* " die ganze wirkliche Welt ist undicht geworden. Geist, Vision, Gespenst entquillt ihr bei jeder Bewegung. Der Dichter steht selber als Hauptfigur auf der Szene, und wie er hinblickt und hinfühlt, so verändert sich die gedichtete Welt: äussere Vorgänge werden zu inneren, innere zu äusseren." [7] This drama was written and even published several

---

[5] Bab, Julius, " Expressionismus," *Das deutsche Drama,* Beck, München, 1925, pp. 783–811.   [6] Written 1910, produced 1912. .

[7] Bab, Julius, " Expressionismus," *Das deutsche Drama,* p. 784. (This quotation is a restatement of the objectification of the subject in which

years before expressionism actually became known as a literary
movement, and yet it contains essentially the characteristics that
make an expressionistic drama. It is immediately qualified as
drama which is bodied by the radiation of the ego, by *Ausstrahlungen des Ichs.*

With respect to the influences operating on Sorge, " war wohl
der weitaus stärkste der Strindbergs." And Bab points especially
to *Nach Damaskus* and *Ein Traumspiel* as the two most influen-
tial of all Strindberg's works. He also explains the characteristics
of these two dramas before he proceeds with his study of the
German dramatic expressionists:

"Im Damaskusspiel werden nahezu alle Gestalten zu blossen Spie-
gelungen des Dichters, des 'Unbekannten,' der, ewig dem eigenen Ich
nachjagend, seinen Kräften, Schwächen und Gefahren in immer neuen
Visionen begegnet. In Gestalten, wohl bemerkt, deren Realität der Dichter
nicht ausdrücklich aufhebt — dazu müsste er ja eine andere, echte Realität
daneben stellen; sie treten alle wie wirkliche Geschöpfe auf, aber sie
verraten immer wieder in gespenstischer Weise, dass sie Leben und Kraft
nur aus der Seele des Unbekannten empfangen. Und im 'Traumspiel'
wird unsere ganze soziale Welt als der Traum einer Göttertochter, die
Menschenlos erfahren will, vorbeigerollt; die Vorgänge werden nicht mehr
nach naturwissenschaftlichen Möglichkeiten, sondern in der unbegrenzten
Freiheit des Traums nur noch nach Gefühlsassoziationen verknüpft. . . .
Vor allem, Strindbergs Wirkung war eine viel reiner ästhetische als die
Ibsens. Es waren nicht dröhnende moralische Kampfrufe, sondern reine
Gefühlsbezauberungen, die aus Stücken wie 'Damaskus' und 'Traumspiel'
wirkten." [8]

There is no doubt in Bab's mind regarding the expressionistic
character of at least two of Strindberg's plays: *To Damascus*
and *A Dream Play.* The critic also considers them decidedly
pertinent to his study of German expressionism, and takes pains
to point out that Sorge's expressionism was strongly influenced
by Strindberg. Furthermore, the distinguishing expressionistic
element seems clearly to be *Ausstrahlungen des Ichs.*

---

earlier objective experience has been transmuted into psychic complexes.
The result is that the objective world becomes distorted when it emerges
as psychic complex from the subject. The *real* world is then "leaky.")

[8] *Ibid.,* pp. 785–786.

Sternheim, the next dramatist considered by Bab, shows strongly the influence of Wedekind. He develops the dispatch-style which Wedekind has already used. *Die Kassette* [9] shows that Sternheim has sloughed all dispensable words, prepositions, articles and pronouns. His sentences become louder and shorter, until the dialogue finally races forward " in blossen Ausrufen " — a forerunner of *Schrei*-drama. Yet Sternheim is not essentially a member of the expressionistic school for he is lacking in one of the primary requisites of drama radiating from the ego, *Seele*. The evidence of telegram-style, which also appears among expressionists, is not enough to qualify Sternheim as an expressionist in the face of a deficiency in far more important characteristics.

Georg Kaiser, " der Denkspieler," [10] is another dramatist of much the same order as Sternheim. Kaiser also develops the Wedekind-Sternheim telegram-style, and his two plays *Europa* [11] and *Gilles und Jeanne* [12] are more pantomime texts than they are dramas. Furthermore, the characters in some of his dramas are certainly not individuals but types, as in *Gas* [13] and *Noli me Tangere.* [14] Yet Kaiser, though a skilful artisan in the technique of the drama, is also lacking in *Seele* and is on the border-line of expressionism rather than well within the limits.

August Stramm carried on the Wedekind-Sternheim-Kaiser technique in the further development of the telegram-style. Indeed, he went to such an extreme that the dialogue is often carried on by single words. Stramm made attempts at pantomime texts, but, according to Bab, accomplished nothing. His work is negative and nihilistic. All in all, Wedekind, Sternheim, Kaiser and Stramm can only be considered frontier figures in expressionism.

[9] Produced in 1911.
[10] So called by Diebold.
[11] Published 1915.
[12] Produced 1923.
[13] Published 1918.
[14] Published 1922.

Hasenclever's *Der Sohn*[15] is the literary work that actually marks the official appearance of the young generation. " Dies Stück ist inhaltlich primitiv, formal ein Potpourri. Da gibt es Wedekindsche Wüstheiten und Hofmannsthalsche Lyrismen, Eulenbergsche Romantik und Strindbergschen Spuk, Sternheimsche Zynismen und plötzliche seherische Ausbrüche, die ganz ersichtlich von dem jungen Sorge stammen."[16] This drama, *Der Sohn*, makes a positive break from Naturalism, and announces the new type of dramatic art. Later, in *Die Menschen*,[17] Hasenclever uses the most severe style of Stramm; the telegramstyle appears as pantomime with " Ausrufeworten."

Through Hasenclever and his circle, the movement was officially baptized " Expressionism," and the product, " expressionistic drama." The theoretical nature of the new dramatic form was soon making its way to the press in numerous essays. The pronunciamento of this circle of theorizers has been summarized by Bab as follows: " Sie verkündeten den subjektiven Charakter aller Figuren auf der Bühne: alle Gestalten nur Spiegelung des einen Ich, das in der Mitte steht! und deshalb die Formen der Wirklichkeit für das szenische Geschehen belanglos! — Dergleichen war freilich in grossartiger Weise durch Strindberg in seinem Damaskusdrama gezeigt worden — ja die deutsche Literatur besass ein erhabenes Beispiel dieser Art Dramatik in den Szenen von Fausts Tod in zweiten Teil der Goetheschen Tragödie."[18]

Bab considers a rather large number of other dramatists and discovers certain elements of technique in this so-called expressionistic drama. Reinhard Goering employs typical characters in his drama *Seeschlacht;*[19] and this play had much influence

[15] Produced 1916.
[16] Bab, " Expressionismus," *Das deutsche Drama,* p. 793.
[17] Published 1918.
[18] Bab, " Expressionismus," *Das deutsche Drama,* p. 794.
[19] Produced 1918.

on other writers, though the dramatist and his drama are, in
Bab's opinion, essentially weak. Toller makes an important
variation in the type of drama by introducing the social-political
framework in his *Wandlung*,[20] in *Masse Mensch*,[21] and in *Die
Maschinenstürmer*.[22] In addition to the social-political framework Toller adds to these plays an atmosphere of dream. He
even goes so far as to describe some of the scenes as pictured in
a " dream distance."

The staging of drama, especially in Toller's *Wandlung,* gave
evidence of the influence of expressionism in art, most especially
in the cubistic effects of scene arrangement. In spite of these
so-called contributions, Bab remains rather unsympathetic to
Toller's dramas. Aesthetically, they are of little value, though
Bab concedes that the works may have some place in literary
history.

Among other dramatists discussed by Bab is Fritz von Unruh.
He also makes use of types instead of individuals, and his dramas
run rather often into a high ecstatic fever. Bab considers von
Unruh vastly overrated. Paul Kornfeld proclaims the pure soul-
drama, and declares that since psychology has done as little as
anatomy to portray what is essentially human, it must be discarded in dramatic efforts. Max Brod attempts to make the
stage portray soul-reactions, but he has no significant degree of
success. Franz Csokor, Will Peukert and Hans Kaltneker all
follow the Strindbergian way to Damascus.

Franz Werfel early wrote lyrical scenes in the style of the
first expressionists, though these scenes never reached the theater.
Werfel is essentially a poet, a lyricist, but was caught in the
whirl of the day and impelled to write dramas. *Spiegelmensch* [23]
is dressed in the robes of *A Thousand and One Nights,* Goethe's
Faust, Strindberg's *A Dream Play* and Ibsen's *Peer Gynt.* Yet,
in this drama, Werfel fails to employ the very lyrical powers

[20] Produced 1919.   [22] Produced 1922.
[21] Written in prison 1919.   [23] Produced 1921.

that he possesses. Both *Spiegelmensch* and *Bocksgesang* [24] appeal to Bab as rather puffy literature. It is very obvious that the critic thinks Werfel would have done far better to ply his art in poetry instead of attempting to attune his song to expressionistic dissonance and yell.

In his article Bab also gives us Georg Simmel's definition of expressionism:

> Simmel hat von Expressionismus die tiefe Definition gegeben, er sei ein Ausdruck des Willens, das Leben absolut, jenseits all seiner Inhalte zu erfassen.

And Bab adds his own comments:

> Diesem Bedürfnis nach dem Absolutem dient wohl gleichmässig jede Zerstörung des Organischen durch Verselbständigung der Lebenselemente — gleichviel, ob das in der Richtung auf die reine Seele oder auf den reinen Körper geschieht. Und so erklärt sich, dass in dieser Generation die Krämpfe der völlig entkörperten Seele sich unmittelbar und in bester Kameradschaft neben den Orgien des ganz entseelten Körpers finden. Das Antiorganische ist die tiefe Gemeinsamkeit.[25]

Without indulging too much in repetition it is possible to gather factors from Bab's articles into words and phrases: namely, confusion, *Ausstrahlungen des Ichs,* lyricism, abstractness, rhetorical ecstasy, *Seele,* childish dilettantism, spirit, vision, specter, objectification of subjective experience, dream-character, telegram-style, *Schrei,* pantomime, typification of characters, social-political framework and the abandoning of psychology in the search for what is essentially human. These factors could well be grouped under a few headings, but inasmuch as that labor must be performed in the following synthetic study of a large number of critics it is wiser to delay the grouping until the evidence is more complete. Bab has the essential elements of expressionism in hand; but, like the majority of expressionistic critics, he has discussed the elements in direct relation to specific works of art. The ordering of control factors remains to be done.

[24] Produced 1922.
[25] Bab. "Expressionismus," *Das deutsche Drama,* p. 804.

CHAPTER V

GENERAL CHARACTERISTICS EVIDENCED BY A SYNTHETIC STUDY: I, ELEMENTS OF THEORY

THE three preceding chapters are intended especially as a preparation for the synthetic study that is to follow. The critics were chosen because their articles are more inclusive than others, or are in other respects immediately pertinent to this study. We should be able to establish norms even now, but to make this work more valid a synthetic study will be made of a large number of critics.[1] Documentation becomes of no importance, for the ideas presented are common property and represent as nearly as possible an agreement among critics rather than an itemization of the special individual contributions. Due credit will be given, however, when reference is made directly to a critic whose material is more aptly and clearly presented than that of any other.

The study divides itself obviously into two parts: elements of the theory of expressionism, and elements of dramatic practice. The critics are not always clear, nor beyond contradictions, in the statement of theory; and emphasis, of course, too often varies according to the personality of the critic. Yet, by exercising care, one can gather enough positive material from this rather unwieldy mass to establish the validity of the control factors already indicated. As a matter of fact, these control factors are already largely established by the critics that have been discussed. It remains now to add a little more leaven to this critical dough.

[1] See bibliography.

48

In searching for material among the early critics, those who wrote while the movement itself was growing, one finds himself as a rule in a maze of rant, unqualified praise and of scoffing by the scorners. The rant cries out for expression of the soul, the spirit, the absolute, the infinite, the cosmic ego; and it calls on all the idealistic philosophers and all the great writers of every age to bear witness that expressionism rests on the topmost plane of thought and artistic endeavor. The unqualified praise points a finger to dramatic works of the expressionists as certain proof of the lofty character of the art, and there is almost as much lack of critical understanding and evaluation here as among the autistic painters. The scoffers either indulge themselves humorously or else declare themselves overwhelmed with a cosmic disgust at the pretensions of such dilettantism. It is really only in the period following 1919 that the rant actually shows signs of exhaustion and criticism becomes collected and calm enough to make judgments. The majority of articles selected for this study fall then, naturally, in the years 1919 to date.

The following elements should not be considered in absolute division, that is, these are not disparate factors in expressionism. All the elements are related and are conditioned by one another. The division, nevertheless, is not purely arbitrary; it has been precipitated from the omnium-gatherum of a large number of critical works.

AUSSTRAHLUNGEN DES ICHS

FOREMOST among the elements is the concept of the *Ausstrahlungen des Ichs* — the radiation, expansion and unfolding of the ego. This is partly explained by the phrase " stream of consciousness " which is current in our English terminology. Yet " stream of consciousness " offers too frequently the possibility of itemization of the elements of consciousness, lingers too close to the realm of psychology. For the expressionist, consciousness is no manifoldly died punch press turning out countless items of similar or dissimilar pattern. It is rather a unifying instrument that moulds oneness of the countless items poured into it. The ego is the predominant element in our universe; it is, indeed, the very heart of the world's reality. For the artist, the ego is a magic crystal in which the absolute is in constant play. It is the subject that registers the everlasting *state of becoming* that qualifies our world; and this subject has an anti-pole *object* which is functional only in giving meaning to the subject. Conversely, the subject must give meaning to the object. It is this ego, this subject, this magic crystal that actually gathers reality in its ultimate character.

The expressionist obviously cannot be satisfied with reality as reported to us by our senses and classified for us by the scientists. He is not content with mere earth-stuff, nor with those superficial meanings that obtain from the observation of outward play of object on object. Even in this field science has proved again and again that its long road to the heart of reality has not been very successful, that its findings along the way have often been colossal blunders, that with all its research it has given no more meaning to reality than the Greek philosophers offered. Science, of course, will not permit the play of subject on object; it merely wishes to report the play of object on object without interference on the part of the subject. This, to the expressionist, means that the scientist will never approach the ultimate character of reality, never will get at the meanings that lie behind objects and their play upon one another.

The expressionist thus turns everlastingly unto his " self," turns his gaze within the ego. It is not through science and for-mulae that man can comprehend reality and wrest meaning from chaos, but rather intuition. The quick of reality can only be gathered or apprehended intuitively by virtue of the integration of manifold experience; in the words of Marzynski, by the flow of ego and world in the supersubjective individual.

From this element it is clear that the theory of expressionism tends toward solipsism. And this is rightly so, for only if all is a manifestation of the ego, is inextricably bound up with it, can this same ego intuitively comprehend the all, and the essential reality that lies behind its material face. The ego is a magic crystal in which the absolute is in constant play; it is in fact the only existent thing.

The ego as the source of reality determines the supersubjective character of expressionism. *Ausstrahlungen des Ichs* gives added evidence of the very small part that the object plays. It is not at all independent. It becomes more and more like the tail-piece of an aëroplane, essential for balance; and, when it is lost — see expressionistic paintings! The expressionist may declare that he maintains the inseparable duality of subject and object, but, as even Marzynski concedes, the emphasis is placed exclusively on the subject. Through the function of *Ausstrahlungen des Ichs*, the expressionist aspires to the sublimation of the subject.

THE UNCONSCIOUS

THE unconscious plays a definite rôle in this scheme of things. Intuition cannot be credited alone to consciousness, for then the scientist could immediately fasten upon this faculty and explain it to us. Intuition must be viewed more or less as an experience-permutation, or experience-combination, projecting definitely, if not clearly and fully, into the conscious. We note that in dreams we do not always encounter manifestations of recent objective experience. In fact, it seems that the whole mind has to fasten on an objective experience and brood on it to occasion the appearance in a dream that closely follows the experience itself. Usually, there is a queer combination of past events, things that have slumbered away from consciousness and memory and dropped into the unconscious, secret desires or events lacking conscious vividness, that make up the character of our dreams. So it is with intuition; it does not gather immediately from consciously controlled objective experience; it arises more or less as an experience-permutation from the unconscious.

The expressionist, then, is anxious to examine the unconscious not from the analytical method of the psychologist, but from the synthetic method of the psychoanalyst. He does not wish to add to the *affects* [2] reported by science, but desires to synthesize all *affects* in order that they may be functional in that form of cognition that is called intuition. He desires, in fact, to get behind the *affects* and seize upon the essential reality of which they are merely manifestations. The expressionist seeks to give meaning to all that happens within the ego, to grasp into the chaos of the unconscious and bring to the light of consciousness whatsoever meaning there is to this existence of ours.

EXPERIENCE

For the expressionist, objective experience is merely the stimulus for inner experience; the latter is the important element. Here again the play of the objective world is significant only as it is gathered by consciousness, remoulded in the unconscious and presented once more by intuition for objectification. If experience means simply objective contact, it can lead only to habit and not to contemplation; it can do little more than stimulate activity toward what is pleasant and what is unpleasant and develop habitual responses. It will discover and classify an infinite number of things, but it will not give a synthetic concept of essential reality lying behind all things. It can develop the animal in its maintenance of existence, but will never reveal the secret of existence.

Thus, for the expressionist, objective experience must be trans-

[2] For meaning of *affects* see p. 37 above.

muted into inner experience before it is functional in the search for reality. This inner experience is the play of the absolute in the magic crystal of the ego. It is this that the expressionist would isolate in an art-form in order that the essence of being may become more tangible.

It should now be clear that the expressionist is, in a sense, an idealistic monist! All things are one thing. Soul and body, material and immaterial, subject and object, these are anti-poles for the concept of reality but are not endowed with separate existence; they are antitheses from which reality may be wrested. There is an inseparable dualism of " you " and " I " that is a function of the unity in reality. It is like Christian theology in its presentation of the godhead: Father, Son and Holy Ghost. These, though separate manifestations, are nevertheless considered in an hypostatic union which forbids three gods to rise out of the monotheistic concept of deity. Behind these manifestations and attributes, these *affects,* stands a unified God. Likewise behind all the *affects* of our universe there is a unity in reality.

Science, too, has worked toward the same end. The large number of elements, differentiated according to the nature of the respective atoms, at one time demanded a *polyistic* view of objective reality. Now, however, matter has been unified again by investigations within the atom. The elemental stuff of each atom is like that of every other atom, but the arrangement is different in each. Yet science has been too much concerned with the object alone, has reduced to nil the strength of the subject. The expressionist holds that the scientist is bound to be baffled in his attempt to get at the heart of reality that lies not simply behind the object but indeed within the subject-object inseparable duality.

The expressionist attempts to seize upon the world in its one-ness. He does this intuitively by emphasis of the subject, though not by total rejection of the object,[3] since the object after all has responsibility in stimulating inner experience. He believes that only through this concept of " Welt als Einheit " can reality ever be apprehended.

SEELE UND GEIST

SEELE accounts for the pure untrammeled feeling in man. It is an expression of his yearning for the absolute, his ecstasy in apprehending, if not fully comprehending, the essential reality of our universe. It is the uncontrolled expansive element in the unconscious that is impatient at the bonds of convention and intellect developed in consciousness. It is the content side of our being minus the form. It is expression without symbols that lend interpretation. In its single state, unformed, not conditioned by the critical understanding that consciousness brings, *Seele* can find expression only in yell, in babble, or in meaningless strokes of the brush.

A number of the critics breathe forth prayers for more *Seele* and more *Geist* in literature, as the proper road to expressionism. This would be very promising were it not for the fact that the two are so often confused that they become identical, to the annihilation of *Geist* which then becomes synonymous with *Seele*. Diebold, however, has sensed the confusion and has given us the distinctions that obtain among the more clear-headed critics.

Diebold [4] says that *Seele* feels the chaos, whereas *Geist* thinks the cosmos. As already indicated, *Seele* tends toward dynamic formless feeling; *Geist*, on the other hand, is an ordering element. " Kubismus, Architektur und Fuge; Klassik, ' Form ' und elea-tisches Sein; tätiger Glaube, Ethos, Wille — das ist wesentlich

---

[3] Except, of course, the extreme cases of autistic painting, and the dadaistic offspring of expressionistic literature.

[4] Diebold, *Anarchie im Drama,* p. 25.

vom Geiste. Expressionismus, lyrischer Schrei, Melodie und verschwimmende Farben; Romantik, 'Ausdruck' und heraklitisches Werden; Heiligenkultus, liebende Hingabe — das ist wesentlich von der Seele." The only criticism of Diebold's differentiation of the two is that *Seele* is obviously already conditioned by *Geist*, the ordering element, when it takes on comprehensible and tangible form.

The earliest critics of expressionism, naturally the protagonists, put such an emphasis on *Seele* that *Geist* was often relegated unto Sheol; or else these critics employed the term *Geist* as a means of avoiding the repetition of the word *Seele*. Later critics, however, recognize that *Geist* and *Seele* cannot be separated any more than subject and object. Again, the inseparable duality prevails.[5] One cannot put out one eye with the hope of obtaining better sight; neither can one exclude the ordering element of *Geist* and expect *Seele* to rise to a higher plane. The expression of pure feeling could only be an indication of chaos, a content without form, an unqualified something that could never be ordered in consciousness. It would also make the expressionist's search for the heart of reality as hopeless as that of the scientist, for reality lies neither at one anti-pole, object, nor at the other, subject. It lies somewhere between the two.[6]

Though expressionism may be content to emphasize in its theory that *Seele* is important almost to the point of excluding *Geist*, practice reveals the fact that form must be employed to some extent. The result otherwise is something like dadaistic literature. A survey of dramas reveals also that expressionistic form has had far more vogue than expressionistic theory, a clear

[5] If one played a bit with genders *die Seele* and *der Geist* would offer still more room for speculation. One might use three books as a basis for this study: Otto Weininger's *Geschlecht und Charakter;* Leopold von Wiese's *Strindberg — Ein Beitrag z. Soziologie d. Geschlechter;* and Spengler's *Der Untergang des Abendlandes,* II, 401–403 (English translation, II, 327–329).   [6] See above, pp. 35–36.

indication of the tangibility of *Geist* and the intangibility of *Seele*. It takes the genius artist so to mould *Geist* and *Seele* that the latter may radiate from an art-product unencumbered by an obtrusive form.

OTHER RELEVANT FACTORS

UNDER this head we shall discuss the parallel with music, the relation to religion and the " worth of man." These elements are very common to expressionistic criticism and cannot well be included under the factors already discussed.

The Parallel with Music

A large number of critics point to music as the purest of expressionistic arts. They say, in fact, that music alone can truly be expressionistic, can so mould *Seele* and *Geist* that the former may find expression without emphasis on the latter. Music is, indeed, pure *Seele*, is wholly feeling, when it reaches the ears of the listener. Music transmutes objective experience into subjective experience so thoroughly that in the objectification of the latter the original experience is wholly lost from consciousness. The scores give evidence of order, of form, of the regulating *Geist;* but when music comes to us as sound it comes as unbodied *Seele*. It formulates no scientific theories, it gives in orchestrations no social creeds, it pronounces no religious doctrines and indeed offers no philosophical concepts. The form is quite functional in presenting *Seele* without attracting attention to *Geist*.[7]

Painting and literature would also present inner experience without undue reference to the stimulating object, would give us *Seele* without the obtrusive *Geist*. Painting has tried its hand at optical counterpoint, and literature has become more lyrical

---

[7] Bach's compositions in counterpoint may be considered as exceptions, but certainly no music-lover would call the form *obtrusive*.

in this attempt to transmute objective experience into expressive *Seele*. But painting became autistic with the extremists, and expressionistic literature was responsible for the rise of dadaism. Perhaps the services of a psychoanalyst are again in demand to explain why music can build out of *Seele* so completely and still not deliver the composer to the madhouse.

The emulation of the effect of music is an additional cry for more subjectivism in painting and literature; indeed, for super-subjectivism. The musician has in his soul a magic harp on which the absolute constantly plays. The painter and the literary artist cry out for the magic crystal of the ego in which the absolute is in constant play. And, more than that, they pray for eyes that may see and interpret what is revealed in this magic crystal. Sounds float unbodied, in constant motion, in constant union with the absolute, and give us an intuition of essential reality. Why should not colors and lines function thus for the painter, and words for the writer? Irrespective of his lack of outstanding success, the expressionist has felt and declared that there must be means in the arts for expressing reality as music does.

The Relation to Religion

Expressionism is not comparable to science, but rather finds association with philosophy and religion. It does not, however, confess union with any particular creed or institution; it allies itself with the spirit of all religions. It cries out for God, for a spiritual concept of life, and it rejects the crass materialism of the institutionalized forms of religion.[8] The result is that expressionism develops something of a passion for the Orient, the mother of religions, and for mythologies, the foster-children of religions. Distance from institutions, whether time or spatial distance, makes possible an emphasis on spiritual values. This

[8] See Spengler, *Der Untergang des Abendlandes*, I, 544; II, 380 (English translation, I, 424; II, 310) regarding the "second religiousness."

concept of religion is necessarily closely qualified by mysticism, for a confessionless religion becomes more and more mute as it becomes less explicative.

Even here the cry for God is one with the cry for *Seele*. It is a cry for spiritual values unhampered by heavy theology and convention. It is not a desire to escape to God, to flee the world, but a yearning to realize God, to find oneself in God, and God in self.

Professor Hans Naumann has laid much stress on this God-seeking among the expressionistic lyricists.[9] Indeed, as time passes, this religious element of expressionism assumes greater importance.[10]

The Worth of Man

Stress on mankind, on human values, surges through expressionistic drama and is an important element. Werfel, as quoted by so many critics, shouts, " The World begins in Man! " Away, then, with all these things that tend to rob man of his opportunity to realize himself! Away with the materialistic notions that enslave man to machines and machine-made concepts! Socialism, which caters to a materialistic brotherhood, cannot serve here. Rather, one needs a spiritual brotherhood among men. Socialism is busy with the objective side of life and even blots out the spirit by its uniformity and its insistence on the will of the group. For expressionism, there is no problem of the individual and the group to be solved mechanically and captioned Anarchism, Republicanism, Democracy, Socialism, Communism, or any other -ism.[11] Again, expressionism would point out that the individual on the one hand and the group on the other are anti-poles; the heart of reality lies somewhere between the two.

---

[9] " Rainer Marie Rilke and the Transition to Expressionism," lecture at the University of Michigan, January 24, 1929.
[10] See Wilhelm Knevels, *Expressionismus und Religion*.
[11] Except expression*ism*.

This heart of reality lies in the spiritual brotherhood of man, and can only be attained by a reëvaluation of the meaning of *human*. Expressionism points to essential human values rather than to the product of man's hands or intellect.[12]

Rudolf Wolff reveals the fact that woman plays a new rôle in the expressionistic order of things. There is a definite hope among men that blessings may come to them through woman. She is no longer considered merely *wife*, the opposite sex; rather, she is a comrade, a friend, a fellow-creature whose social rank in the *struggle for being* is on the same plane as that of man. It is no longer a blind love that draws the two sexes together, but rather the understanding love that one fellow-being has for another.[13]

The yearning for the establishment of human values is an evidence of objectivity in expressionism. No matter how much one stresses *Seele,* how much one cries out for the spiritual brotherhood, human relationships of an objective nature must have some place.[14] It is even questionable that these objective relationships may be so transmuted by inner experience that the objective experience itself could not be found. Indeed, it would seem desirable in establishing the worth of man that his objective experience be held in the light of consciousness. Yet one thing is certain: though expressionism at times may savor of socialism and at times the opposite political extreme of anarchism, it assuredly fosters no political party even as it confesses to no religious creed. It is crying out for a restatement of values in all our relationships. Indeed, it wants to get behind all these relationships and fasten on something that is durable.

[12] This by no means invites a sickly sentimental humanitarianism.
[13] Wolff, Rudolf, *Die neue Lyrik,* pp. 7, 12.
[14] Unless we have here, through the influence of the Jewish expressionists, something that is comparable to Spengler's interpretation of the " Magian Soul."

RÉSUMÉ OF FACTORS IN THE THEORY

THIS theory of expressionism is admittedly no well-defined system of thought, and may well deserve the smile of superiority and condescension which some give it. It is not entirely coherent, is not without contradictions, and is not free from the charge of naïveté. It reminds one too often of the child's gesture of reaching for the sun's rays, an attempt to grasp the intangible. It is almost a " form that cannot be formulated " into a definite system. At best, this theory can only be ordered intuitively; it cannot be framed in orderly language.

This by no means invalidates the material for our use, for in this work critical understanding has been applied to *selecting* from the writers on expressionism, not to justifying or repudiating what they set forth. There are, moreover, elements on which we can fasten our study. The factor *Ausstrahlungen des Ichs* with stress on the subject, and the consequent concept of cosmos in constant play in the ego give us a clue for our study. The rôles of *Seele* and *Geist* give another; the unconscious and inner experience, with the parallel to dreams, establish more norms. Likewise, the relations to music and to religion, and the emphasis on the worth of man afford norms for our study, though they are norms that must be used in association with others.

It must be repeated that no one of these factors is sufficient in itself to warrant the qualification *expressionistic*. The factors must be considered *in sum* as an interpretation of the theory of expressionism. Furthermore, it should be obvious to the casual reader, as well as to the critic, that systematization gives an X-ray picture and not a charming flesh-and-blood portrait. Expressionism must not be damned just because the critical appraisal of it may be dull and lifeless.

CHAPTER VI

GENERAL CHARACTERISTICS EVIDENCED BY A SYNTHETIC STUDY: II, FACTORS IN DRAMATIC PRACTICE

IN THE following section we are attempting to group the elements as nearly as possible under headings that have already been employed in Chapter V. This is not entirely successful owing to the fact that some factors in practice may well be determined by several elements of the theory. Moreover, these factors in expressionistic practice are by no means free from confusion.

It must not be assumed that the practice was wholly an outgrowth of the theory, even when in accord with it. The theorizing, as already indicated, was done for the most part by the Hasenclever circle, immediately following the production of *Der Sohn* and several years after Sorge's *Der Bettler* had been produced.

Furthermore, it must also be remembered that Strindberg's dramas were appearing on the German stage with ever increasing frequency several years before the expressionistic movement really broke through as a distinctly new art-form. In the two seasons, 1913–14 and 1914–15, there were all together 1035 performances of 24 different Strindberg plays in 62 German cities.[1] The German critics generally recognize the influence of Strindberg and credit these performances with some responsibility for the shaping of expressionistic drama.

It is evident that expressionistic theory and practice are not

[1] *Strindberg und die deutschen Bühnen* (essays by various writers), p. 17 ff.

directly linked in the formative background of the movement. The school of Wedekind, Strindberg, and the preëxpressionists added to the shaping of both expressionistic theory and practice. The theory which is set forth in Chapter V comes largely from critical material appearing after 1919 and thus gathers something from all that has been offered.

AUSSTRAHLUNGEN DES ICHS

DRAMA of the kind that projects the inner experience, the ego-world, on the stage has immediate place for autobiography and confession. Sorge's *Der Bettler* [2] is a fine illustration of this element. In this drama the author himself is the main character, and his inability to get a play produced is the subject of the drama. Other characters on the stage are creatures of the dramatist's stage ego.

Again, Werfel's *Bocksgesang* [3] illustrates *Ausstrahlungen des Ichs* from another angle. This play is not directly autobiographical nor confessional; Werfel does not project himself definitely into the play as the main character. Yet he does let his inner experiences radiate into the play. The drama is actually a symbolic representation of Werfel's experiences in the revolution which followed the World War. [4]

This objective experience with revolution is indeed not lost in *Bocksgesang*, for it plays an important part in the drama. Nevertheless, to put this play on a naturalistic basis, to call it merely an uprising of landless against landowners is to place it in the category of Hauptmann's *The Weavers*, in which it obviously does not belong. It is also misunderstanding the drama to classify it as naturalistic. Here is essentially no report of revolution for its own sake, no slice from a particular kind of life,

---

[2] Written 1910, produced 1912.
[3] Produced 1922.
[4] Specht, *Franz Werfel*, p. 236.

nor is it a revolution seen "through a temperament." The
struggle of the landless versus landowners is a symbol of the
ever present struggle in humanity, that between the *ur*-man and
the convention-bound man of a Culture World. In Picard's
statement of expressionism we learned of antitheses, of polarization of abstraction and *Einfühlung*, of the struggle of opposites.
This concept can be applied to Werfel's drama. What he wishes
to wrest from chaos is the worth of man, and he first puts forth
the antithesis of *ur*-man and cultural man. But this is too
abstract and needs further typification; consequently, we have
the more concrete symbols of landless and landowners, something
that is tangible. The one represents all the results of the active
spirit of man; the other, all the results of the intellect of man:
the dynamic and the static elements of the whole concept, man.
Werfel does not point to the landowners for the worth of man,
nor to the landless, nor indeed to the relation of the student and
Stanja, daughter of the rich. There is always a center between
two anti-poles and from this center emanate human values.
Neither anti-pole is functional without its opposite; consequently,
function itself is a derivative of the struggle between the opposites. Neither landless nor landowner can dominate to the exclusion of the other, neither *ur*-man nor cultural man. The
revolution was put down, in this drama, but Stanja bore the seed
of the *ur*-man within her and would in time give birth to another
creature, a monstrosity in the eyes of convention-tied man.

This drama so points to the objective experience that many
critics seem to lose sight of the symbol, and the drama as
Ausstrahlungen des Ichs seems to them patently false. Yet it
forms an excellent example of objective experience transmuted
into inner subjective experience which in turn radiates from the
ego and takes on dramatic form. Only from this point of view
does Werfel's *Bocksgesang* take on meaning. It must be admitted, however, that the art-product itself does not clearly offer

this interpretation, except that the monstrosity is quite without meaning unless one applies the expressionistic interpretation. It should be obvious even to the critic unacquainted with expressionistic theory and practice that the play *Bocksgesang* presents symbols that must be given more concrete values. The idea is rather clearly presented in the drama that the *ur*-man surges forth again and again, and cannot be rooted out by the Culture World.[5] A revaluation of the worth of man, likewise, can only come from the polarization of *ur*-man and cultural man, *Seele* and *Geist*, with the essential reality between the two.

Another element in the factor *Ausstrahlungen des Ichs* is the necessity for type characters, as well as typical situations. At first glance one is tempted to say that subjective drama cannot deal with types, but must employ individuals.[6] Ernest Boyd in his article " Expressionism without Tears "[7] commits this error. " Since the universe, by definition, is subjective, a projection of the ego," he says, " there are no types in the literature of Expressionism, only individuals." [8] Yet, even if one were led into this error by a superficial knowledge of the theory plus an inordinate desire to express oneself about something new, one should have been enlightened by a little contact with dramatic practice. Typical characters surge throughout dramatic expressionism, and usually leave their telltale marks indelibly written

[5] Note that the title of the play *The Goat Song* takes us back to the original meaning of τραγῳδία. Does Werfel thereby indicate for us in still another way the *ur*-character of his drama, and the consequent symbolic interpretation?

[6] It is easy to go astray either through superficial knowledge or else through considerable knowledge of expressionism. Through superficiality one may easily jump to the conclusion that this drama employs only individuals. Through constant study one meets a three-angled paradox that readily muddles the brain: the " I " of ultra-subjectivism, the " We " in the stress on the worth of man, and the " It " in the demand for and the use of types. See also above, pp. 9–10, 33–38, 49–51.

[7] Boyd, Ernest, " Expressionism without Tears," *Studies from Ten Literatures*, pp. 231–251.

[8] *Ibid.*, p. 239.

into the dramatis personae. Moreover, even the theorizers themselves mention with a great degree of frequency that typification is the rule in expressionistic drama. At most, only one character in an expressionistic drama has anything more than a shadow of individuality; when the author portrays himself and projects all other characters out of his ego as reflections of this dramatic representation of self, then there is opportunity for individuality.

Yet even this one character, the author, is generally a type figure and not an individual. Sorge's dramatist in *Der Bettler* is not the individual Reinhard Sorge, but the dramatist who has been typified out of the whole world of dramatists flowing through Sorge's ego. The individuality in the character is that which can be likened unto Sorge himself; but, owing to the distortion that has been wrought by typification, there is no pure autobiography. Again, in Hasenclever's *Der Sohn*, the son is a symbol of all sons, the only son in the world; and the character of the father must be viewed likewise. In Werfel's *Bocksgesang* we might feel more certain of encountering individuals since the dramatis personae carry individual names. Examination, however, reveals types. Juvan is not just Juvan, one among many students; he is *the student*. Stanja is not merely a daughter of the rich; she is *woman*. Furthermore, the monstrosity is clearly not a curiosity to be packed away in a museum, nor just a terror for the superstitious; it is the *ur*-man who is totally unqualified by any *affects* of a Culture World. The monstrosity is a symbol for *Seele*, and consequently the object of worship for the landless.

Individuality is also a matter of psychology, a matter of the physical sciences. Expressionism, however, is not comparable to science, and instead of many items it wants *the one thing*, the essence of reality. The ego radiates this essential reality of the cosmos and is not at all concerned with numbered individuals in society, nor with the social *affects* qualifying individuality.

Typification is a necessity in expressionistic drama and is consequent on subjectivity, on *Ausstrahlungen des Ichs.*

A hasty glance at several dramas indicates from the list of dramatis personae the usual run of expressionistic characters. In Fritz von Unruh's *Ein Geschlecht* [9] we have the following: " Mutter, Altester Sohn, Feiger Sohn, Jüngster· Sohn, Tochter, Soldatenführer " and the like.   In von Unruh's *Platz,*[10] the second part of the proposed trilogy, the *Jüngster Sohn* is qualified by an individual name; nevertheless he is the *type* youngest son of both the family and the human race, and the whole drama flows through his soul as it is enacted on the stage.   In Sorge's *Der Bettler* the characters have names like " Der Dichter, der Vater, die Mutter, die Schwester, das Mädchen, der ältere Freund . . . Gestalten des Dichters " and others similarly differentiated.   In many other dramas the dramatis personae are quite similar. Indeed, one often finds characters like " 1st Banker, 2d Banker, 3d Banker," or 1st Sailor, 2d Sailor, 3d Sailor," and so on. Even when one finds characters with individual names it is not wise to jump to the conclusion that they are necessarily individuals.   This is most aptly illustrated in Werfel's *Bocksgesang* in which the characters with individual names are essentially types.   The characters in this drama might well have been given as follows: " First Landowner, Second Landowner, Wife of First Landowner, Son of First Landowner, Daughter of Second Landowner, Student, Rope-Walker " and the like.   On the other hand, one must always exercise caution in judging typification according to the dramatis personae; it is necessary to read each drama to render a critical opinion.

Still other elements coming from *Ausstrahlungen des Ichs* are the monologue and the aside, elements that fell greatly into disrepute in the naturalistic period.   This inner drama does not seek to reproduce observed reality but rather to project imme-

---

[9] Written 1915–16, produced 1918.   [10] Produced 1920.

diately the inner experience, the objectification of the subjective. Consequently, both the monologue and the aside are quite legitimate and genuine elements of expressionistic drama. The inclusion of these two elements is determined by a philosophy of drama, whereas their exclusion is occasioned by the attempt to reproduce observed objective reality, a mechanics of drama. It is not surprising that writers of " Ich-drama," released from the mechanics of drama, go to extremes and sometimes give us three and four solid pages of monologue. In Sorge's *Der Bettler* [11] the monologue in Act V, containing something like eight hundred or a thousand words, begins on page 151 and is concluded on page 157. Likewise von Unruh is not above having Dietrich speak about one hundred lines with no one else on the stage.[12] Hasenclever's *Der Sohn* [13] also has a monologue, in the second scene of the first act, which contains about seventy lines.

This element *Ausstrahlungen des Ichs* actually is the main qualifying element of expressionistic drama. It is only too clear that factors like the Unconscious, Inner Experience, *Seele* and the relation to music are well included within the radiation of the ego. Yet, for convenience, it seems wiser to consider the elements separately with regard to the special contribution of each. Here, at least, *Ausstrahlungen des Ichs* determines autobiographical character in expressionistic drama, demands typification and allows monologue.

THE UNCONSCIOUS AND INNER EXPERIENCE

THE radiation of the ego has a tendency to give more emphasis to the unconscious than other forms of drama, since it demands the objectification of inner experience. Characters often become

[11] Sorge, *Der Bettler,* Fischer, Berlin, 1919, 5. Auflage.
[12] Von Unruh, *Platz,* Wolff, München, 1920, Part I, Scene 23.
[13] Hasenclever, *Der Sohn,* Wolff, München, 1917.

68   *Strindberg's Dramatic Expressionism*

shadows, figures that are not even types. They are like the specters that course in and out of our dreams, hardly to be recalled in consciousness by any other quality besides action. Moreover, not simply in characterization, but also in the technique of the drama this dream-form appears. Toller is especially fond of *Traumbilder*. In *Die Wandlung*[14] Toller explains that "Die Bilder 'Transportzüge,' 'Zwischen den Drahtverhauen,' 'Die Krüppel' . . . sind schattenhaft wirklich, in innerlicher Traumferne gespielt zu denken." In *Masse Mensch*[15] we have only one scene, the first, that even confesses to clear objectification; the other scenes alternate from the second through the seventh (the last) between "Traumbilder" and "Bilder in visionärer Traumferne." Moreover, in other expressionistic dramas, there is always an atmosphere of things happening in a dream, of "Bilder in visionärer Traumferne." Von Unruh's *Ein Geschlecht* and *Platz* have an atmosphere of nightmare alternating with ecstatic dream, even when the stage events are very similar to those which have not been digested by a radiating ego. Kornfeld's *Die Verführung*[16] and *Himmel und Hölle*[17] are not simply psychological naturalism emanating from the works of Dostojevski; they are dramas of a dream character, though probably not as pure "soul drama" as Kornfeld would have us believe. Even Kaiser's *Von Morgens bis Mitternachts*[18] is cast in a dream form. The plays of Kokoschka[19] step back from the vividness of dreams into the more shadowy recesses; and Mombert's trilogy *Aeon*,[20] completed before Sorge's *Der Bettler* ap-

---

[14] First written in 1917; "die endgültige Form wurde in der Haft des Militärgefängnisses im Februar und März 1918 vollendet." Produced 1919.

[15] Written 1919.   [17] Produced 1920.
[16] Produced 1918.   [18] Written 1916, produced 1917.

[19] Oskar Kokoschka: *Mörder Hoffnung der Frauen* (1907); *Der brennende Dornbusch* (1911); *Hiob* (1917); *Orpheus und Eurydike* (1918).

[20] Written 1907–11 (Part I, *Aeon — der Weltgesuchte;* Part II, *Aeon und die Frauen;* Part III, *Aeon vor Syrakus*).

peared, is several dream-thicknesses within a dream. Likewise, Werfel's *Bocksgesang* is the portrayal of inner experience. The objective experience of revolution was transmuted into inner experience which in turn was objectified into drama. It is not just a drama giving social conflict, nor a drama given to mysticism and expressing itself in nebulous symbols; it is a drama in which essential reality is given meaning through the symbolic objectification of intuition. Dream character is consequent on such drama. In the *Bocksgesang* the monster forces the dream character on the drama.

It is no wonder that dramatists lacking restraint produced plays that overwhelm us with the vertigo of ecstasy or else deliver us into a purgatory of nightmare, though at the same time these plays contain the more familiar elements of psychological naturalism, social realism and symbolism. Yet, even with the restraint that Werfel exercises, an expressionistic drama seems at first to be a jumble, especially a dream-jumble. This, of course, can be laid only to objectified inner experience, for expressionism never merely reports nor reproduces observed reality.

Dream character, inner experience, accounts largely for the element of distortion in expressionistic drama just as it determines the distortion in expressionistic painting. In the first place, continuity of action and of time [21] is lost or ignored. Action is nearly always that of dream action, in a plastic state of becoming, in duration unqualified by time. And, as in dreams, any action may without warning drop into oblivion and another

[21] In studying Spengler's *Der Untergang des Abendlandes* one may raise serious questions regarding dramatic time; i.e., its function as magnitude, as destiny and as the absolute (Ibsen's *Ghosts,* Shakespeare's *King Lear,* Mombert's *Aeon*). In expressionistic dramas time has no mathematical function; it is never magnitude. Consequently, unity of time, as commonly understood, cannot be maintained. Apropos of the problem of time see also P. D. Ouspensky's *Tertium Organum* (Knopf). Howsoever fanciful this book may be in details, it nevertheless offers excellent challenge to the concept of time.

one take its place with the same quality of eternal duration and with the same absence of time and space elements. This distortion also has its effect on the dramatic form, for the division of dramas becomes somewhat arbitrary: there may be acts with a large number of scenes; there may be parts, each having many scenes or tableaux; or, there may be stations, as Toller divides some of his plays. These, of course, are largely concessions to the objectifying of the inner experience and are not exact reproductions of this " absolute which is in constant play in the magic crystal of the ego."

The factors of time and place become nearly as shadowy as in dreams. Kaiser, who is only on the border-line of expressionism, nevertheless splits place in *Von Morgens bis Mitternachts:* " Die Kleine Stadt W. und die grosse Stadt B." In Toller's *Die Wandlung* " Die Handlung spielt in Europa vor Anbruch der Wiedergeburt." In von Unruh's *Ein Geschlecht* " Die Tragödie ist an kein Zeitkostüm gebunden; ihre Handlung spielt vor und in einem Kirchhof auf Bergesgipfel." In Hasenclever's *Die Menschen* [22] the time is " today " and the action takes place in " the world." Zweig has both a specific and a shadowy place in his drama *Ritualmord in Ungarn:* [23] " Ort: Ausserhalb des irdischen Raums und in Südungarn. Zeit: Ausserhalb der irdischen Zeit und von April 1882 bis Mai 1883." Finally, Hanns Johst's *Der König* [24] plays in " Die Zeit der Legenden oder des Rokoko." There is in the majority of expressionistic dramas no particular concern for time and place. The jumbling of these elements is a natural result of the objectification of inner experience.

Action becomes so strong an element that sometimes language becomes less and less necessary and pantomime more and more functional. It is, as in dreams, close to drama without words. The result is that in some expressionistic dramas we have an approach to film-drama; for instance, Hasenclever's *Die Men-*

[22] Published 1918.   [23] Produced 1919.   [24] Published 1923.

schen. This style of paucity of language is technically called telegram-style. It is, however, not wholly dependent on the dream character of drama, but is strongly linked with the element of *Seele* that conditions telegram-style with *Schrei.*

In the demand for types, inner experience also contributes another element of distortion. There is no such thing as a type-character in observed reality; all are individuals, differentiated each from the other.[25] The type is really a kind of plastic surd in drama; it is functional only as an entity, and its plasticity comes from its infinite value which allows all other elements in kind to be part and parcel of it without being the same. Typification, let it be repeated, is essentially distortion of observed reality. It is a genuine product of inner experience.

Distortion is the order of life, the law of existence. Outward reality reproduced must suffer distortion, and

> Wie Schönheit schrumpft,
> auch Flut verebbt. Frühling in Gossen stirbt,
> Johannes Mut in Pharisä'rn kalkte
> und Christus endete im Papst, so wird
> Karikatur das Ende jeder Tat.[26]

But the unconscious, with all its distortion of outward reality, at least possesses potentialities for the representation of truth. The psychoanalyst can integrate dreams into meanings; so can the dramatist gather the inner experiences from the unconscious and integrate them into a dramatic form that points to the essential reality behind objective experience.

The element of the unconscious, pointing the way to a dream-form drama, demands the hand of a genius if an art-product is to result from inner experience. Too many expressionists have apparently seen an escape from the difficulties of ordinary dramatic form, rather than an opportunity to create a finer quality

[25] See Spengler, *Der Untergang des Abendlandes,* I, 27 (English translation, I, 21) on "men" and the abstraction "mankind."
[26] Von Unruh, *Platz,* Part I, Scene 23.

in art. Typification has too often yielded marionettes whose guiding strings are twisted, or has produced speaking-trumpets instead of dramatic characters. Likewise, the absence of a well-defined plot and the timeless, spaceless character of expressionistic drama offer too many dangers along with the opportunities for realizing a higher form. A general formlessness has been credited too often with virtue, when as a matter of fact the expressionist himself would not admit that he desires to stress formlessness for its own sake. He really is seeking the most unobtrusive form, the one that will allow the maximum of opportunity for the objectifying of inner experience. His emphasis is essentially positive; it is placed on the realization of content, form notwithstanding.

SEELE

THE cry for more *Seele,* even to the exclusion of *Geist,* is also responsible for much that we have included under the *Unconscious;* for *Seele* minus *Geist* never projects into consciousness with more force than untranslatable intuition. There are, however, some factors that are largely determined by *Seele.* The appearance of verse, for instance, in the portions of exaltation in expressionistic drama, is due to *Seele* rising more and more out of the confines of *Geist.* In the second scene of the first act of Hasenclever's *Der Sohn,* the son occupies the entire scene with a monologue that is given in verse. The psychic state of the character is clearly given by two of the stage directions. In one of them " Er kniet nieder mit ausgebreiteten Armen " and in the other " Er taumelt, von grosser Erregung übermannt, rückwärts ins Zimmer."

Seele not only breaks forth in verse but also in ecstasy. In the fifth act of Sorge's *Der Bettler* the poet has a long monologue in which he becomes more and more ecstatic. Close to the end of the monologue the tension becomes increasingly greater:

"... Oh Träne! Träne! ... Glückseligkeit! ... DAS EWIGE LEBEN!!! Und es nicht leben können! Ich weiss ja, ich kann es nicht leben — oh Fluch! oh Fluch! zum Wort verdammt sein! Ja, ich bin zum Wort verdammt! Ich muss Bildner werden der Symbole, muss dem Priestertum entsagen ... Künstler ... Halbheiliger nur ... Schein-Heiliger ... Lass sinnen ... sinnen ... Symbole ... (*Jäh empor, mit Händen aufwärts*) Oh Trost des Blitzes ... Erleuchtung ... Schmerztrost des Blitzes ... SYMBOLE DER EWIGKEIT ... Ende! Ende! Ziel und Ende! Wenn mich das Blut, die Summe der Unwirklichkeit, des Lärms, des Lärmen-Wollens in mir ... in meinem Blut, wenn dieses verdammt, in Symbolen zu reden, so gilt es: DURCH SYMBOLE DER EWIGKEIT ZU REDEN.
(*Erschöpft*) "

In this scene ecstasy rises higher and higher until the character is exhausted, but at no time does the character completely lose all sense of restraint and break forth in wild yell. The ecstasy is contained, furthermore, within the limits of a monologue; a form which does not permit conduct too close to that of a babbling madman, unless we insist that this is the madness of ecstasy.

Fritz von Unruh, in the thirteenth scene, first part, of *Platz*, gives us a little warning of what we may expect to find later in the play. Schleich has just been swearing friendship to Dietrich forever and the latter has indulged himself in sarcastic comment on the word " forever."

> *Schleich.* Aussprichst Du Witz! Staatshirn verdeckend mächtig!
> Zusprecher Dir! Neuordner, Sekretär!
> Aufrufer Volks! Vollstrecker, Rechthand, komm. ...
>
> *Dietrich.* Welche Sprache redet man hier? Können Sie mir
> zu einer neuen Grammatik verhelfen?

Very often one needs not only a new grammar but also a new dictionary if all the meaning is to be gathered from expression-istic works. Von Unruh, however, has the saving grace of con-sciousness that his dramas are rather formless. Yet in this very same scene we have need for some interpreting book, whether it be grammar, dictionary or whatsoever you please. Schleich, re-leased wholly from the restraint of *Geist*, has a long speech that more closely approaches yell than it does anything else. In the

nineteenth scene of the second part there is also a combination of
telegram-style and incipient yell.

Dietrich (gläsernen Blickes). Wer bist du?

Schleich. Ich! Dein innerstes Gesicht!
Kennst mich?

Dietrich. Nein.

Schleich. Auge!

Dietrich. Spiegle mich?

Schleich. Ich!

Dietrich. Ich?

Schleich. Erraten?

Dietrich. Ich?

Schleich. Du?

Dietrich. Ich?

Schleich. Du! Du! — Gespräch unendlich!

Dietrich. Wirklichkeit?

Schleich. Wahrheit!
Ward Kraft dir umzubilden: Ich in du?
Dann: Dämme! Jeden Schritt belasten dir!
Sollst aller Menscheit Pein, Tagelend tragen,
bis knieknickst du! Todwinselnd.

Dietrich. O. . . .

Schleich. Ja! O. . . .
Kreis, Einheit? Tau von: Ich zu du? Ha, ha
Seiltänzer, schwindelfrei? Neuzwang? Neuzwang?
Volk unten gafft mit, ach und o . . . ? Irrsinn!
Ein Gott in Wolken? Überhöht den Märkten?
Ameisgewimmel unten? Oben, du?
Al ha Yat: Sonne? Ankerb dir dies Tau.
Hindonn're pflasterspritzend! Ohnmacht! Ohn-Macht!
Herz raus. Kopf ab. Ethischer Dunst vom Giebel . . .

Hyazinte. (tritt vor).

Schleich. Wir treffen uns allein zur Nacht?
(stösst sie zu Dietrich)
Da —

Hyazinte (lächelnd). Nein. . . .

Schleich. Nein? Ich könnte dich besitzen? Ich? Ich fühl's.
Du würdest dich nicht rühren, wenn ich dir
das Röckchen höbe . . . ? Ja, die Achse rückte. . . .

Hyazinte. Vom Mann. . . .

Schleich. Vom Mann?

Hyazinte. Die Hose fort! (*wirft sie weg*) Mannszwang!
Ich: Einheit.

Schleich. Einheit: Ich! Weib aus dem Kreise!

Hyazinte. Lust ist kein Drachen . . .

Schleich (höhnend). Blick ins All?

Hyazinte. Schleich, taumelnd!
Den Leib so breiten, bis mich Lust, ach, Lust —
wo ich im seidensten, zum Rasen bringt. . . .

Schleich. Schleich: Weib?

Hyazinte. Weib: Schleich! Uralter Vampyr: Mann!

Throughout the entire drama *Platz* there is material of much
the same kind, overflowing *Seele* that sometimes is restrained in
a spiritual ecstasy and sometimes is allowed to break forth in
wild yell. Yet it is from Schleich, the unqualified *ur*-man out of
Dietrich, that the wildness comes and it is rather fitting that his
language should so overflow the bounds of comprehensive expression. In fact, this yell is so nicely contained within the Schleich
character that one is at times tempted to believe that Fritz von
Unruh may be satirizing the all too general and uncritical use
of *Seele*, as well as the cry for it. Clearly, the only use of the
unqualified *ur*-man in drama should be that of suggestion. In
Bocksgesang Werfel builds all around the *ur*-man but he neither
lets him be seen nor heard. Too much *Seele* results in mad cry:
yell!

In Hasenclever's *Die Menschen* we have a combination of
telegram-style, pantomime and cry that at times is little short
of yell. The following is from scene three of the third act:

Das Mädchen (wankt ins Aufnahmezimmer, tastet an der Wand, bricht zusammen).

Die Krankenschwester (schleppt die Bewusstlose zur Entbindungsstation, legt sie ins vierte Bett).

Der Arzt (tritt ins Aufnahmezimmer).

Die Krankenschwester (kommt zurück). Entbindung.

Gilda (dehnt die Arme). Tanzen!

Thea. Der Arzt! *(Sie verstecken die Sachen.)*

Der Arzt (tritt ein, geht zum Mädchen, sieht Blut). Schweinerei!

Das Mädchen (schlägt die Augen auf, sieht den Arzt, schreit). Tier!

Der Arzt. Die Maske.

This is *Seele* trying to reach expression under restraint of the pantomime form that emanates from dream character drama. But this type of drama is obviously so close to the film that it depends on *Seele* finding an outlet in a dialogue carried on by one or two words. It becomes, in fact, little more than a *Schrei-film*, a drama that could easily be adapted to the modern talking movie. Only once, the fifth scene of the third act, do we get relief from the form. *Das Mädchen* sings a rhymed lullaby to her babe, a lullaby that somehow harks back in its last two lines to Robert Greene's poem *Weep Not, My Wanton*. Otherwise this film drama reminds one of wild cries coming out of a cage or a chamber of torture.

Seele also accounts for the *ur*-man and the *ur*-ish qualities of expressionistic drama.[27]   As already stated, Werfel handles this element in *Bocksgesang* with great delicacy, building around it, putting it on the stage in unbodied form. Other dramatists, however, have tried to characterize the bodied *ur*-man; or, what is hardly likely, to satirize him.[28]   The *suggestion* of *ur*-man brings out the contemplative qualities of *ur*-ishness, the duration

[27] Is it possible that the expressionists are unconsciously crying out for the eternal feminine, the cosmic? See the Spengler reference in note 5, Chapter V.

[28] Fritz von Unruh in *Platz.*

of unbodied *Seele* in man; the actual characterization in bodied form, however, tends largely toward regression, and the primitive man appears before us. Schleich, in von Unruh's *Platz*, is the savage let loose. The Cashier, in Kaiser's *Von Morgen bis Mitternachts*, is a combination of primitivity and temporary insanity, with emphasis on the latter. Bitterlich, in Kornfeld's *Die Verführung*, uses the comprehensible language of cultural man, but otherwise he is pure soul unqualified by any of the restraints imposed upon men by a Culture World. In Werfel's *Bocksgesang*, the *ur*-man is a monstrosity whose shadow alone falls across the stage. The appearance of the primitive instead of the *ur*-man is responsible for much of the naïveté, the childishness and trivialities that are presented at times with dynamic urge.

Again we find ourselves face to face with chaos and formlessness whenever *Seele* is presented in bodied form on the stage. It also shares with telegram-style in the responsibility for *Schrei* which sometimes is a lyrical ecstatic cry and often nothing more than a wild yell.

THE RELATION TO MUSIC

The effect of the parallel with music has been dual in dramatic literature. In the first place, music tends to give lyrical qualities to expressionistic drama and joins with *Seele* in demanding verse for moments of ecstasy. Verse naturally appears when a character so realizes *Seele* that he must breathe forth the *Bewegung* in *Seele*, in rhythm if not in rhyme.

The second effect of music is that dramas include music in the staging itself. The music is employed according to the demands of the scene, much as we find it used in the presentation of films. Mombert's *Aeon* not only has music and dance in the drama proper, but is also called a "Symfonisches Drama."[29] Von Unruh's *Platz*, Hasenclever's *Der Sohn, Die Menschen, Jenseits*,

---

[29] Bab thinks that "lyrische Symphonie" would be more apt; "Expressionismus," *Das deutsche Drama*, p. 757.

Barlach's *Die Echten Sedemunds*,[30] Zweig's *Die Umkehr*,[31] and others employ music. Toller, in the fourth tableau of *Masse Mensch,* makes use of the harmonica! " Der Namenlose beginnt auf einer Harmonika zu spielen. In aufpeitschenden, bald sinnlich sich wiegenden, bald stürmischen Rhythmen."

THE RELATION TO RELIGION

THE search for God gives a savoring of religious character to expressionistic drama, or a mystical atmosphere, or else a touch of mythology. Mombert's *Aeon,* Sorge's *Christos* [32] and Zweig's *Ritualmord* are permeated with such material. Goering's *Seeschlacht* also pictures man as battling against the " Powers." It is much like the uneven battles in which the characters of Greek dramas engaged: man struggles, storms the heights, but man cannot win. The expressionist, however, is determined not to yield; though baffled, though apparently defeated, he still reaches out for that which perhaps cannot be attained. To see God face to face is the realization of reality for the expressionist, for then one is God.[33]

THE WORTH OF MAN

THE stress on the worth of man again brings us in contact with type characters, with pathos, with a social point of view, with simplification (the sloughing of decorations of social rank) and most of all with the presence of realism in drama that is so filled with symbolism. This realism may be laid to the door of war experience, or to the long rule of naturalistic drama, but must also be recognized as an element of the dream character of expressionistic drama, even as our dreams are at times decidedly

[30] Published 1920.
[31] Published 1927.
[32] *Der Sieg des Christos,* dramatische Vision, published 1924.
[33] The religious element is more predominant in expressionistic lyrics and in critical material than in drama. See also above, pp. 57–58.

true to observed reality. Moreover, the stressing of a social point of view, in the sense of a spiritual brotherhood, is a natural outcome of expressionistic drama in its search for all that lies behind the materialistic mask. With the emphasis on *Ausstrahlungen des Ichs*, the expressionist is most certainly interested in a re-creation of human values before he can be concerned with anything else. Where else could he turn to realize cosmos in himself?

Von Unruh's *Platz* closes with the emphasis on the worth of man.

> *Tochter.* . . . Ich sehe
> tief in das Herz der Welt, da deine Kraft
> aus neuer Liebe neue Menschen schafft.

Toller, more than others, put a decidedly social content into the expressionistic drama. *Die Wandlung,* " Das Ringen eines Menschen," is a long cry for the revolution of man, for the re-creation of human values. *Masse Mensch* and *Die Maschinenstürmer* betray by their very titles the social content.

" The world begins in man," said Werfel. Expressionistic drama may be said to begin and end with emphasis on human values, on love, on a spiritual brotherhood. It is perhaps an esoteric socialism of the soul, a means of realizing essential reality in man himself.

CHAPTER VII

CONCLUSION

CONTROL factors have now been established. In compact arrangement these factors appear as follows:

1. *Ausstrahlungen des Ichs,* solipsism, objectification of inner experience, struggle of opposites, autobiographical tendency, typification, monologue, the aside

2. The Unconscious, *Einfühlung,* intuition, distortion, dream character, pantomime, telegram-style

3. *Seele, ur*-ishness, feeling, ecstasy, *Schrei,* music

4. Music, objectification of inner experience, lyricism, pure soul, verse, optical counterpoint

5. Religion, the search for God, realization of God, battle with the " Powers," the supernatural

6. The Worth of Man, social-political framework, an esoteric socialism, a spiritual brotherhood, realism, re-creation of human values.

The first item in each group should be considered the norm or control factor; the other items are given for fuller explanation.

Expressionistic drama is mainly characterized by *Ausstrahlungen des Ichs* which obviously resolves itself into a number of minor factors, both in theory and in practice. It is not drama that seeks to escape from this world into a more beautiful one either by embellishing the present world or by looking at it through half-closed eyes. Nor does expressionistic drama care to reproduce man in his situations of life as nearly as these may be imitated. It is not concerned with dramatic unities, nor primarily with art itself. It is first and foremost engaged in searching for the essential reality in our universe; it is a *Weltanschauung* and not a program for the arts.[1]

Consequently, we have no known categories of manners, sensibility, humors, discussion, or of comedy and tragedy into which expressionistic drama may be fitted. All these are conditioned by the *affects* of life, are indeed manifestations of observed reality. Expressionism would go behind the mask and seize upon the one essential reality that holds our cosmos in unity. Thus, one cannot call this drama tragic or comic, or anything else that is current in dramatic terminology. Even if the characters are pursued and defeated by the " Powers," as in Greek and Roman plays, the interest of the drama does not lie merely in pursuit and defeat; it lies in the attempt to grasp the heart of reality from all these manifestations of our complex being.

One can almost appreciate why Pfister, after having endured the double strain of scientific investigation and aesthetic criticism, suddenly becomes sentimental at the very close of his book. His last section is entitled " Nobler Life Theory " and is concluded with clear signs of exhaustion: " Art at its best is always a wordless fervent prayer: ' Thy Kingdom Come.' "

Though I do not desire to admit the play of exhaustion in this conclusion, it nevertheless seems well to administer a slight corrective to portions of this study that may have been unkind to critics or to dramatists. Expressionism has been more of a lofty gesture than the realization of a *Weltanschauung* in an artform. As a result both the critics and dramatists have often gone astray in attempting to interpret the gesture or to transmute it into an art-product. One needs only to consider the subject of romanticism, its products and its critics, to understand what has occurred in expressionism.

---

[1] Granted, of course, that many self-styled expressionists looked upon the new movement as an aesthetic program and even as a fine spring-board by virtue of which one might clear the buttocks of Pegasus and land high in the saddle.

One can say of expressionism, even with its art-products lying close at hand, that it was certainly a *lofty* gesture, that its aims were sound, and that its frailties were no more than one might expect. Indeed, it is surprising that in the field of drama so many good plays have been produced, even though no work of outstanding genius rises far above all the others. Again, this type of drama is the product of very *young* men, and Bab is probably right in pointing out that the world might experience some difficulty in flowing through the egos of these " knaben "-dramatists: childishness and dilettantism are quite natural effects.

We hasten back to our thesis, away from this digression. We set out to establish norms, irrespective of their aesthetic validity, and this work has been done. The problem of the aesthetics of expressionism is out of our immediate province.

PART II

EXPRESSIONISM IN STRINDBERG'S
DRAMAS

Ungerechtigkeit und Schmutz werfen sie nach dem Einsamen: aber, mein Bruder, wenn du ein Stern sein willst, so musst du ihnen deshalb nicht weniger leuchten!

— NIETZSCHE, *Also sprach Zarathustra*

Mit Bucklichten darf man schon bucklicht reden!

— NIETZSCHE, *Also sprach Zarathustra*

CHAPTER I

INTRODUCTION

THE problem before us has already been stated. The factors that have been determined in the first part of this study will now be used as norms in the discussion of Strindberg's dramas. We shall proceed chronologically, except when a particular type of drama demands association with an earlier item or group. *The Dance of Death* which was written in 1901 will be considered with the so-called naturalistic dramas, even though it was written more than a decade after *The Father* and *Miss Julia*.[1] Likewise, *The Great Highway* which appeared in 1909 will be associated with the *To Damascus* trilogy,[2] owing to the immediate similarity of form and content. The dramatic fragments will also be discussed out of chronological order after the completed dramas have been studied.

The text used is that of the *Collected Works*[3] edited by John Landquist and appearing from the press of Albert Bonnier, Stockholm, from 1913 to 1924 in fifty-five volumes. In addition, there are two volumes of posthumous works edited by Professor Carlheim-Gyllensköld.[4] The editor of the *Collected Works*, John Landquist, has done a painstaking piece of work and has compared all earlier editions. Furthermore, he has made note of all changes in the text and given them in an appendix to each volume, so that the critic has all textual data before him. The Landquist

[1] *The Father* was written and published in 1887; *Miss Julia,* written and published in 1888.

[2] Written 1897–1904.

[3] Strindberg, August, *Samlade skrifter.* References to this work will hereafter be given as in the following example: Strindberg, XXXIX, 211.

[4] Strindberg, August, *Samlade otryckta skrifter,* Bonnier, Stockholm, 1918. " Första delen, dramatiska arbeten " is the volume used in this study.

edition is, in fact, the authoritative text and is used constantly
by the outstanding Strindberg scholar, Professor Martin Lamm.[5]
Citations from the German translation will be made from
"August Strindbergs Werke, übertragen von Emil Schering,
München, Georg Müller" (copyrights 1908 to 1928). The
Deutsche Gesamtausgabe has thus far reached forty-nine volumes which are grouped in eight sections. Of these forty-nine
volumes five are either just off the press or still in preparation.
In the section devoted to letters one of the volumes, *Briefe an
Emil Schering, 1894–1912,* does not appear in the Swedish edition
by Landquist. The English text used is that of the four series
of plays translated by Edwin Björkman (Charles Scribner's Sons,
1912 to 1916), and consisting of eighteen of the sixty-five extant
dramatic items. The use of the Björkman translation will be
very limited. While much credit is due to Björkman for his
pioneering work in making the English reading public aware of
and familiar with Strindberg, some opprobrium must also be
heaped on his head for toning down the stark passages and not
permitting Strindberg to repeat in English what he has written
in Swedish.

LIMITATIONS OF THE SUBJECT

It is obvious that this study cannot pretend to discuss Strindberg's complete dramatic works apart from the subject of expressionism, nor will it define dramatic categories apart from the
expressionistic. When we refer to a class of drama, *naturalistic,*
for example, we shall follow the classification of Professor Martin
Lamm, unless our study assigns the group, or any item therein,
to the expressionistic category. We shall hold ourselves responsible only for the establishment of one classification, that
of expressionism.

[5] Lamm, Martin, *Strindbergs dramer,* förra delen, 1924; senare delen,
1926, Albert Bonnier, Stockholm. This work will be referred to hereafter
as Lamm, I, 26, or Lamm, II, 28.

Furthermore, this study cannot take space to explain individually why each of a large number of dramas has been excluded without mention. All the dramas have been read and carefully studied, and those that yielded nothing have been ignored as not pertinent to the subject. There is even one group containing expressionistic elements that has been omitted, the historical dramas. These dramas demand a careful study of sources if one is to note whether Strindberg has subjectively distorted his material, and, if so, to how great an extent. Such a study is clearly out of our range, both with respect to availability of source material [6] and the practical matter of book space.

Again, this study will not discuss expressionism in Strindberg's poems, novels or short stories. As a matter of general interest, however, the reader's attention is called to all the so-called autobiographical novels, and especially to the *Interview* which Strindberg wrote for his first autobiographical novel, *The Son of a Servant*.[7] The novels of the Inferno period and later would need especial consideration, with one eye on the scientific investigations of Jaspers [8] and Rahmer,[9] and the other on Pfister's book on expressionism.[10] The most promising of the poems seems to be *Nights of Sleepwalking in Broad Daylight*,[11] a poem in free verse written in 1883; for the very title inspires curiosity and also suggests possibilities of expressionism. This by no means exhausts the available material, but merely indicates that Strindberg's expressionism unquestionably involves a field somewhat larger than the one we are investigating.

---

[6] Scholarly work on Strindberg will continue to be handicapped until letters, documents and literary remains are either published or the various private and national archives are thrown open to scholars. Even Professor Lamm has apparently not had access to everything.

[7] Strindberg, XVIII, 452–458.

[8] Jaspers, Karl, *Strindberg und van Gogh*, 2 ergänz. Aufl.

[9] Rahmer, Sigismund, *Strindberg, e. patholog. Studie.*

[10] Pfister, O., *Expressionism in Art.*

[11] *Sömngångarnätter på vakna dagar*, Strindberg, XIII, 205–295.

AMONG all the articles and books discussing Strindberg's dramatic works, none has given *definitive* treatment to a single drama from the standpoint of expressionism. Diebold [12] and Soergel [13] have given general discussions; Marcus [14] and Lamm [15] have not employed norms of expressionism. The general character of investigations carried on thus far is well illustrated by Dr. Paul Landau's article in *Die deutsche Bühne.*[16]

Landau considers six dramas: *Easter, Advent, To Damascus, A Dream Play, After the Fire* and *The Ghost Sonata.* He also mentions *The Pelican, The Thunderstorm* and *The Great Highway.* The question that Landau attempts to answer is this: " Welches sind nun die Elemente des dramatischen Expressionismus, den Strindberg in diesen Werken ausgebildet hat? " Landau generalizes without analysis of the dramas: (1) There is no objective presentation of reality, but on the other hand a limning of " rein subjektiver Seelenzustände "; (2) All the characters in these dramas are " Ausstrahlungen seines Ichs "; (3) The scenes and tableaux are comparable to visions and phantasies in which inner experience is portrayed; (4) Typification goes hand in hand " mit dieser Subjektivierung des ganzen Weltbildes "; (5) The action seems unreal even when there is an obvious presentation of everyday milieu — dream character predominates; (6) The compositions are much like certain paintings, schematized contrapuntally and thus comparable to music; (7) " Zeit und Raum sind gleichgültig geworden."

So sind diese Dramen Strindbergs echte expressionistische Kunst, Ausdruck einer seelischen Notwendigkeit ohne Rücksicht auf die Natur, Schöpfungen einer neuen Phantasiewelt, Stücken einer gewaltigen, ganz

---

[12] Diebold, Bernhard, *Anarchie im Drama*, pp. 147–232.
[13] Soergel, *Dichtung und Dichter der Zeit*, pp. 176–204.
[14] Marcus, Carl David, *Strindbergs Dramatik.*   [15] Lamm, I–II.
[16] Landau, Paul, "Strindberg als Dramatiker des Expressionismus," *Die deutsche Bühne,* May 24, 1920, pp. 371–374.

persönlichen und zugleich überpersönlichen Konfession, die ihre Finale finden in jenem Epilog der *Grossen Landstrasse,* auf der der ewige Wanderer und Sucher, der dieser Dichter war, noch einmal die Bilder und Gestalten seiner inneren Vision an sich vorüberziehen lässt.

It is the object of this book to give evidence to prove or disprove the validity of such generalizations as the ones above, not simply with regard to the few plays mentioned, but the complete dramatic works, excluding the historical dramas. The evidence, of course, must be largely internal, drawn from the dramas themselves, if conclusions are to be established.

AUTOBIOGRAPHICAL NATURE OF STRINDBERG'S WORKS

EXPRESSIONISM calls for the supersubjective individual. When we consider Strindberg's works, we shall have to bear in mind constantly that these works are products of a supersubjective individual. They are, in a sense, autobiographical documents. Laura Marholm early recognized this fact: " Strindbergs sämmtliche Werke sind eigentlich nur biographische Beiträge zur Losung seines Ich-Räthsels." [17] Note well that this statement was made in 1895, just before the beginning of the Inferno period, and also before Strindberg wrote the dramas usually characterized as expressionistic by German critics.

Much more recently Martin Lamm has discussed the autobiographical character of Strindberg's works:

> When one has limned Strindberg's personality one has already given a descriptive account of his authorship. In world literature there are assuredly very few writers in whom life and literature so wholly intertwine. If his personality is nothing else than the disemboguement of his violently vital and intense temperament, then his literary product is essentially nothing more than the image of this temperament on paper. The explanation of the powerful influence that he has exercised both among us and in foreign countries rests in no small degree in his astonishing immediateness. To read him is the same as to live with him.[18]
>
> Strindberg's entire output is grouped around the great autobiographical works. It is really nothing else than a gigantic self-incarnation. Those

---

[17] Marholm, Laura, *Wir Frauen und unsere Dichter,* p. 166.
[18] Lamm, I, 19.

works of Strindberg are easy to reckon in which he does not appear in some disguise or other, in which some person or other has not received the author's features. And even in those works which are apparently quite foreign to Strindberg's own sphere of life, the dialogues throughout carry his accents, everything is seen and depicted with his unique intensity, everything is so plainly stamped with his temperament, that even for the most absurd situations one finds himself tempted to guess at an autobiographical background.

The main part of his production has also received its inspiration from his own experiences in life. In the first decade of his activity as an author, conflicts from his childhood home appear in more or less disguised form in his writings. Later, his first marriage furnishes him a nearly inexhaustible source for motifs, and during the last decades of his life he practically wears out the mystic experiences of his Inferno period. By 1887 [19] Strindberg has already written so much about himself that he complains in a touching letter to Lundegård that for him literature and life have been mixed to such a degree that he seems to live a shadow-life.[20]

It would seem at first glance that practically every work by Strindberg must be expressionistic, since the autobiographical element so pervades all his writings. That this is not wholly true is evidence again of the fact that subjectivity in expressionism is of a peculiar kind, and the form-and-content mould into which it is poured also differs from other art-forms.

[19] Lamm gives the date as 1888, but this is evidently a typographical error, for the letter is dated the 12th of November, 1887, in Lundegård's book, *Några Strindbergsminnen knutna till en handfull brev*, pp. 49–66. See below, p. 100.

[20] Lamm, I, 21.

CHAPTER II

THE SO-CALLED NATURALISTIC DRAMAS

A STUDY of the eleven dramas [1] written before *The Father* [2] fails to reveal any promising material for our study. True enough, if the dramas were put into the press of expressionistic criticism various pertinent elements might be squeezed from them, especially the ever present autobiographical factor. Indeed, we are told by Strindberg himself that family history was included in his first drama, *A Name's-day Gift*.[3] Yet, to exploit such material without sufficient and convincing data, is obviously to manufacture evidence.

There is only one work that demands a slight halt before proceeding to the discussion of *The Father*. This is the *Postludium* to the verse edition of *Master Olof*.[4] In his autobiographical work *Inferno* [5] Strindberg implies that he has been punished by the invisible powers for having written a miracle play into *Master Olof*. The miracle play is given within the framework of the *Postludium* and is interesting because in it the dramatist has stepped aside from the general trend of drama and dipped a bit into mysticism and mythology. Lamm says [6] that Strindberg most certainly has taken the play from a sixteenth century miracle play, but he has also moulded into the tiny drama his reactions to Hartmann's *Philosophy of the Unconscious*.[7] More-

---

[1] See list of Strindberg's dramas below, pp. 215–220.
[2] Written and published 1887.
[3] Strindberg, XVIII, 340. *A Name's-day Gift* was sent to a theater and lost. It is interesting to note that in this very first play Strindberg used a theme that was to occur repeatedly, reconciliation to life through woman.
[4] Written 1876; Postludium, a fragment, written 1877.
[5] Strindberg, XXVIII, 204.   [6] Lamm, I, 169.   [7] Published, 1869.

over, he has cast into the play his own reflections on the powers
of good and evil.[8] In *The Author,* the fourth book of *The Son of
a Servant,* Strindberg himself says, apropos of this miracle play,
that he could no longer believe in a God who personally inter-
feres with all the trivial affairs of human beings, so in his play
he created another power, " The Eternal One," to rule above the
evil power *God* and the good power *Lucifer.*[9]

The miracle play has the title *De Creatione et Sententia Vera
Mundi.* The theatre is divided into three parts: heaven, earth,
and hell. " Personae Dramatis quatuor sunto: scilicet," The
Eternal One (Invisible); God, or the Evil Power; Lucifer, literally, the Light-bringer, or the Good Power; also, Michael, or,
the Evil Angel. The play, which in subject-matter harks back
to *Prometheus Bound* and to *Paradise Lost,* deals with the struggle between Good and Evil, crystallized into gods, God and
Lucifer. The expressionist would say that somewhere between
the two lies the heart of reality, but Strindberg put the heart of
reality into " The Eternal One " who is not between the two
since he is so far removed that he visits them only once in a
myriad of years.

It would not be wise to attempt to force evidence from the few
pages of this miracle play. As it stands, however, the little
drama is interesting as a kind of prologue to later expressionistic
tendencies.

" THE FATHER "

THE critic in search of expressionistic drama might naturally
be expected to cast aside the so-called naturalistic dramas as
obviously irrelevant material. Yet anyone who has read carefully *The Father* or *The Dance of Death,*[10] or attended a perform-
ance of either, must have been impressed by the terrific struggle
of the characters, and especially by the demonic ecstasy in the

---

[8] Lamm, I, 171.   [10] Written and published 1901.
[9] Strindberg, XIX, 158.

second play. Furthermore, even in *The Father* there is a sense of the unreal and the mystic that should not escape the critic's attention.

Émile Zola was highly impressed by *The Father*, but he was not fully satisfied with it as an example of naturalistic drama. In his letter of December 14, 1887, he writes: [11]

MONSIEUR ET CHER CONFRÈRE!
   J'ai de bien grandes excuses à vous faire, pour mon long silence. Mais si vous saviez quelle existence est la mienne, que de travail et que de tracas! Je ne voulais pas vous renvoyer votre manuscrit sans l'avoir lu, et je viens enfin de trouver le temps nécessaire.
   Votre drame m'a fortement intéressé. L'idée philosophique en est très hardie, les personnages en sont très audacieusement campés. Vous avez tiré du doute de la paternité des effets puissants, troublants. Enfin, votre Laure est vraiment la femme dans son orgueil, dans l'inconscience et dans le mystère de ses qualités et de ses défauts. Elle restera enfoncée dans ma mémoire. En somme, vous avez écrit une oeuvre curieuse et intéressante, où il y a, vers la fin surtout, de très belles choses. Pour être franc, des raccourcis d'analyse m'y gênent un peu. Vous savez peut-être que je ne suis pas pour l'abstraction. J'aime que les personnages aient un état civil complet, qu'on les coudoie, qu'ils trempent dans notre air. Et votre capitaine qui n'a pas même de nom, vos autres personnages qui sont presque des êtres de raison, ne me donnent pas de la vie la sensation complète que je demande. Mais il y a certainement là, entre vous et moi, une question de race. Telle qu'elle est, je le répète, votre pièce est une des rares oeuvres dramatiques qui m'aient profondément remué.
   Croyez-moi votre bien dévoué et bien sympathique confrère.
                                                                    ÉMILE ZOLA

Zola, while appreciating the work as a powerful drama, feels nevertheless that *The Father* does not measure up to all the requirements for drama, naturalistic drama, of course. The thought is bold, the characters are audaciously drawn; but Zola has little use for abstraction. He wants the characters in a play like the ones we elbow every day, people who are in a plane with the rest of us mortals. The Captain, for instance, has not even a name! The other characters also fail to give Zola the feeling of reality that he demands; they are creatures

[11] Strindberg, XXIII, 422–423.

of reason and not of flesh and blood. The French naturalist, either to lighten his criticism with polite evasion, or else admitting that he could not understand the drama, put the blame on the racial differences between himself and Strindberg.

Martin Lamm, in concluding his study of *The Father*,[12] discusses the play in relation to naturalism. He considers Ibsen's *Ghosts*[13] and Björnson's *Beyond Human Power*[14] as steps toward naturalism, and *The Father* as an additional step in the same direction. Lamm, however, realizes that *The Father* is after all not a naturalistic drama, as Palmblad well indicates in his review of Lamm's books.[15] " Nothing could better illustrate the keen insight of a critic or the artistic achievement of a writer who built better than he knew than Lamm's interpretation of the title character of *Fadren*. When he tells us that the Captain's suspicions are really the products of his own brain, and that Laura merely ' whispers in his ears ' what he already ' thinks darkly,' our first impulse is to say that he has failed to grasp the meaning of the play. But a closer study of the character shows how well his interpretation fits. We may be sure that the dramatist never intended to endow his hero with this predisposition for suspicion. That the assumption of its existence harmonizes so well with the general portrayal of the character is, of course, due to the fact that the Captain is to a large extent a projection of Strindberg himself." It is obvious that some knowledge of expressionism would have permitted Lamm to see clearly what he now discerns faintly through the obsidian lens of naturalistic criticism: to wit, there are elements in *The Father* that are wholly foreign to naturalism but entirely native to expressionism.

The Father does not meet the requirements for naturalistic

[12] Lamm, I, 300.
[13] Published 1881.
[14] Part I published 1883.
[15] Palmblad, review of Martin Lamm's *Strindbergs dramer, Scandinavian Studies and Notes,* November, 1928, pp. 115–117.

is much autobiographical material în *The Father*. One cannot possibly read the autobiographical novels of Strindberg without discovering that they are excellent sources for the dramas. Lamm has drawn lines to *The Father* not only from *Le plaidoyer d'un fou*,[20] but also from letters written by Strindberg during the 'eighties.[21] Lamm clearly indicates the autobiographical nature of *The Father* without, however, making immediate identifications of specific incidents of the play with specific incidents in Strindberg's life.[22] Situations are similar, but they must often be translated and not directly transferred from Strindberg's life to his works.

Strindberg was living at Lindau in Bavaria at the time he was writing *The Father*. Obviously enough, the military environment influenced Strindberg in selecting a *captain* for his main character. It is likewise clear that this captain is the mouthpiece of the dramatist. At the time of writing *The Father*, Strindberg was greatly concerned with his own state of mind, and feared that insanity would eventually overtake him;[23] and he also felt that his wife was doing her best to get him out of the way. The quarrel in the Strindberg family centered about the education of the two daughters, the elder of whom was six years of age. Siri von Essen [24] wanted the daughters to be actresses,[25] whereas Strindberg demanded that the girls be given a practical educa-

[20] Strindberg wrote this work in French. It was later translated into Swedish under the title *En dåres försvarstal* (Strindberg, XXVI); into German as *Die Beichte eines Toren;* and into English as *The Confession of a Fool*. The last two titles are not accurate, for the content of the book, as well as the original French title, demands a title that carries the meaning " The Defense Plea of a Madman."

[21] Lamm, I, 264–301.

[22] It must be remembered that the autobiographical novels *are* novels.

[23] See Karl Jaspers, *Strindberg und Van Gogh*.

[24] Siri von Essen was Strindberg's first wife. One should read Karin (Strindberg) Smirnoff's book *Strindbergs första hustru* for a view of Siri von Essen that helps to balance other accounts.

[25] Greta Strindberg actually became an actress; her career was cut short when she was killed in a railway accident in 1912.

tion.[26] Strindberg was also suspicious that his wife had not
been faithful to him, for he was not positive that the son born in
1886 was actually his own child.[27] Situations are the same in
Strindberg's own life and in *The Father;* but the details, of course,
are different in each case. The autobiographical material has
been distorted for the sake of the art-form.

Critics are rather fond of using Strindberg's works either to
make the author sully his own fame or that of his wife.[28] The
result is that one finds in print some stuff like the following:
" One cannot speak of August Strindberg with much *gusto*. The
most broadminded critic will find himself under necessity to dis-
approve of him as a man and to condemn so many features of
his production that almost one might question his fitness as a
subject of literary discussion." [29] This statement probably is
best answered by a letter from Strindberg to Björnson which
carries the following recommendation: " Read my works and
then you will learn something." [30] One who has *read* Strindberg's
works may get into difficulties of interpretation, but he can never
question Strindberg's " fitness as a subject of literary discussion."

Thus if one reads Strindberg's works and the letters that are
available one will learn not to identify individual features of
his life with individual features of his artistic work unless one
has conclusive evidence. A reading of the *Interview*,[31] in the
appendix to the first volume of *The Son of a Servant*, should warn
one to exercise some care in the evaluation of the material presented in all Strindberg's works. In this *Interview* the author is
being questioned concerning the nature of his new book. He
replies that it is " The History of a Soul's Development, 1849 to

---

[26] He suggested that they be given training in midwifery!
[27] This suspicion is strongly limned and much handled in *Le plaidoyer
d'un fou.*
[28] Any one of the three wives.
[29] Heller, Otto, *Prophets of Dissent*, p. 71.
[30] Krogvig, A., *Bøker og mennesker*, Strindberg letter of October 14,
1884.   [31] Strindberg, XVIII, 452–458.

1867," the *evolution of a soul*. As the dialogue proceeds we learn that this new work is not just a novel, not even a physiological novel, not an apology, not a confession; it is an attempt " in the literature of the future." The author also declares that he considers Zola the literary master of Europe for the time being, but he believes that Zola overestimates the influence of milieu. " Furthermore," says the author, " I believe that one person's life depicted fully is more truthful and more enlightening than a whole family's. How can one know what is occurring in the brains of others, how can one know the involved motives of another's deed, how can one know what this one and that one said in a confidential moment? Yes, one constructs. But thus far the science of man has been little cultivated by authors, who with scanty knowledge in psychology have tried to sketch the soul-life which is practically hidden. One knows only one life, his own. The advantage of sketching his own is this: one deals with a sympathetic person, isn't that true, and then one always looks for the motive for his deeds." The author goes on to say that he limns the other characters of his book in their relation to himself. He considers this as the literature of the future and assures the interviewer that even as a very young writer he had made plans for a literature in which he would present the history of the soul. This *Interview* is specifically a statement demanding a literature of the soul. The emphasis, to be sure, is on psychology, but a psychological study of oneself would inevitably lead to the field of psychoanalysis. It is important to note that as a history of the soul this " literature of the future " is *not* autobiography according to the established standards.

This *Interview* was written in May, 1886, a year before Strindberg wrote *The Father*. It seems reasonable to believe, with the evidence that Lamm [32] has furnished regarding biographical

[32] We must keep in mind that Lamm *translates* biographical data and does not make gross identifications unless his evidence is complete.

data, that the drama belongs to this " literature of the future."
The struggle of Strindberg and Siri von Essen is taken out of the
individual status and put into the typical. The experiences are
indeed Strindberg's, but by the time they have become a part of
the soul and have later been objectified in an art-form they have
also gone through a process of distortion. The Captain is Strindberg's mouthpiece, but cannot be identified with Strindberg *in
detail*. Laura is *not* a mouthpiece for Siri von Essen, nor is she
Siri von Essen drawn true to life. She is Strindberg's reaction to
his wife and becomes thereby a distorted version of Siri von
Essen. The dramatist is not presenting other people's souls, but
is objectifying what passes through his own soul.

No wonder, then, that Strindberg should write the following
letter:

> It seems to me that I am walking about in my sleep, as though fiction
> and life were blended. I don't know if *The Father* is fiction or if my life
> has actually been so; but it seems that all this will evanish for me in a
> given moment which is soon approaching, and then I shall collapse with
> insanity and tortures of conscience or else commit suicide. Through much
> writing my life has become a shadow life. I no longer seem to be treading
> on earth but rather to be hovering without weight in an atmosphere not
> of air but of darkness. Should any light penetrate this darkness I would
> tumble down crushed. Peculiarly enough, an oft recurring dream at night
> is that I feel myself flying, without weight, find it quite natural. Likewise,
> all concepts of right, wrong, true, false, disappear; and, whatsoever happens,
> no matter how unusual it is, strikes me as quite fitting.[33]

And Strindberg was unconscious of the manner in which he
built *The Father?* That may still be a moot question. One
thing, however, is certain: the author of the letter just quoted,
of the *Interview*, and of *The Father*, most assuredly will not
give exact reports of objective experience. His works will be
born of inner experience, of *Ausstrahlungen des Ichs;* so much so,
in fact, that the author himself will be unable to determine
whether his work is fiction or actually a report of his own life.

[33] Lundegård, Axel, *Några Strindbergsminnen knutna till en handfull
brev*, p. 66; letter of November 12, 1887.

The struggle of the sexes, paternity,[34] motherhood and the immortality of the flesh have taken on concepts in the dramatist's mind. These concepts were developed from observations in the material world and from Strindberg's own immediate experiences. Yet when these same concepts are objectified in an art-form they have been transformed to such an extent that the material in art cannot be identified immediately with any of the observations or experiences. Such a transformation, or distortion, is quite obvious in *The Father*. It is a drama that radiates from the ego of the author.

Strindberg's drama *The Father* is not naturalistic in the sense that the author is making a scientific experiment in drama, nor realistic in the sense that he is reporting what he has observed, nor autobiographical in that he is giving the facts of his own life. Nor is it " life seen through a temperament." The play cannot be considered merely as a dramatic portrayal of a woman's success in driving her husband insane by suggestion; it is not just the report of the psychologist. This play presents an elemental struggle of opposites, male and female in their *ur*-status, that has burned itself into the soul of the dramatist and taken new shape there with new significance. The dramatist has fashioned the play not with his eyes on the objective experiences, but with his eyes turned within himself, focussed on his own ego. The drama is not therefore " life seen through a temperament," but life flowing through a soul. It is Strindberg's world and Strindberg's ego flowing together in a supersubjective self.

The drama has, indeed, the characteristics of expressionistic drama: typification, an elemental struggle of opposites, *Ausstrahlungen des Ichs* with its consequent distortion, autobiographical background and a suspense that erases all concept of time

[34] See Otto Weininger, *Geschlecht und Charakter*, p. 300, apropos of the illusion of fatherhood, and his note on p. 557 regarding Strindberg's *The Father*. See also *Fadren*, Strindberg, XXIII, 55–56.

and place even though the dramatic unities are nicely maintained. *The Father* is clearly not satisfactory as a naturalistic drama for the very simple reason that it is *not naturalistic!* The setting of the drama is not in the milieu of everyday life, but in the plane of sleepwalker realism that characterizes expressionistic drama. The drama has been a misfit in the naturalistic group but now can take up its rightful place in expressionism.

" MISS JULIA "

THE play *Miss Julia*,[35] labeled " A Naturalistic Tragedy," is especially convenient for study since we are given an author's preface which purports to explain the type of drama to follow. In this preface, Strindberg implies that he is giving us a new form of drama, and new ideas for drama as well. At the same time, however, he protests that he is really not doing anything new!

> In the following drama I have not tried to do anything new — for that cannot be done — but I have tried to modernize the form in accordance with the demands which I thought the new men of a new time might be likely to make on this art. And with such a purpose in view, I have chosen, or surrendered myself to, a theme that might well be said to lie outside the partisan strife of the day: for the problem of social ascendancy or decline, of higher or lower, of better or worse, of men or women, is, has been, and will be of lasting interest.[36]

Again, he shouts what we already know so well: " I find the joy of life in its violent and cruel struggles, and my pleasure lies in knowing something and learning something." [37]

Regarding the cause for Miss Julia's tragic fate, Strindberg declares that there is a combination of causes that forces the issue of the drama, a combination that points to elements far back of the drama as well as circumstances within the dramatic

---

[35] Written and published 1888.
[36] Strindberg, *Plays*, Björkman translation, 2d Series, p. 97.
[37] *Ibid.*, p. 98.

frame. " Thus I have neither been one-sidedly physiological nor one-sidedly psychological in my procedure. Nor have I merely delivered a moral preachment. This multiplicity of motives I regard as praiseworthy because it is in keeping with the views of our own time." [38] If Strindberg's drama follows the preface it will surely be difficult to determine motivation, for that will be complex rather than single and readily discernible. But a critic may also fall into the error of taking too much stock in an author's preface.

" In regard to character-drawing I may say that I have tried to make my figures rather ' characterless,' and I have done so for the reasons that I shall now state." [39] Strindberg objects to the term " character " because too often it has been applied on the stage to one single element of the soul, whereas souls are actually complex.

My souls (or characters) are conglomerates, made up of past and present stages of civilization, scraps of humanity, torn-off pieces of Sunday clothing turned into rags — all patched together as is the human soul itself. And I have furthermore offered a touch of evolutionary history by letting the weaker repeat words stolen from the stronger, and by letting different souls accept ' ideas ' — or suggestions, as they are called — from each other.

Miss Julia is a modern character, not because the man-hating half-woman may not have existed in all ages, but because now, after her discovery, she has stepped to the front and begun to make a noise. The half-woman is a type coming more and more into prominence, selling herself nowadays for power, decorations, distinctions, diplomas, as formerly for money, and the type indicates degeneration.[40]

And then Strindberg puts further limitations on the character of Miss Julia. " But *Miss Julia* is also a remnant of the old military nobility which is now giving way to the new nobility of nerves and brain." [41]

It is clear, then, that Strindberg intends Julia to be a type character. She is a representative of the upper class, and also

[38] *Ibid.*, p. 99.
[39] *Ibid.*, p. 100.
[40] *Ibid.*, p. 101
[41] *Ibid.*, p. 102.

of the "man-hating half-woman" group. She is not, however, just woman, or just female. Strindberg has not given universality to this character, for he has qualified Julia by a particular social rating and a peculiar attitude toward the male! Julia is decidedly more an individual than Laura; and, with the dual qualification of class and attitude, she cannot be representative of a very large group. Laura is Lilith, Adam's first wife and the mother of demons; Julia is after all Julia, a member of a particular sector of upper society and also a particular sector of the female sex. Even Julia's tragic experience is an individual case and not a typical situation, as the author himself suggests in the preface,[42] for he selected the theme from real life.

Jean is more of a type than Julia, for he comes from a larger class, the servants. Yet he too is limited to a specific minority among servants, to those aspiring to climb out of the lower class. Strindberg, however, undoubtedly felt that both Julia and Jean are qualified by individuality, since he refers to the minor characters as people "without individuality, showing only one side of themselves while at work."[43] After the discussion of *The Father*, one is at first sorely tempted to force the evidence and regard Julia and Jean as types, but both the drama and the preface warn against any such distortion of facts.

In his discussion of dialogue, pantomime and monologue, Strindberg stirs up renewed suspicion that after all this drama must contain some expressionistic elements.

In regard to the dialogue, I want to point out that I have departed somewhat from prevailing traditions by not turning my figures into catechists who make stupid questions in order to call forth witty answers. I have avoided the symmetrical and mathematical construction of the French dialogue, and have instead permitted the minds to work irregularly as they do in reality, where, during conversation, the cogs of one mind seem more or less haphazardly to engage those of another one, and where no topic is fully exhausted. Naturally enough, therefore, the dialogue strays

---

[42] Strindberg, *op. cit.*, p. 97.
[43] *Ibid.*, p. 105.

a good deal, as, in the opening scenes, it acquires a material that later is worked over, picked up again, repeated, expounded, and built up like the theme in a musical composition.[44]

This musical-theme dialogue actually does occur in *Miss Julia,* but with a rare degree of frequency if one makes comparisons with the post-Inferno dramas. Not only is the idea that Julia is wild ("komplett galen") on Midsummer night well illustrated by her conduct preceding the sex act, and also immediately preceding suicide; but, in addition, there are definite references to her condition in the dialogue. Comments are made by Jean, Kristin and Julia herself.[45] Likewise, there are several references to the fact that after all there is not a great deal of difference between upper class folks and the servant class.[46] Similarly, before the sex act, Jean repeatedly warns Julia to be careful, and afterwards taunts her with the reminder that she did the bidding in spite of his warnings.[47] There are also others ideas repeated once or twice. All in all, however, this is rather meager evidence for musical-theme dialogue in spite of the author's preface.

Strindberg further informs us that he has abolished acts in the hope of better maintaining the illusion for the spectators. These should be able to sit through a play lasting about an hour and a half. Yet, though there are no intermissions there are rest periods for players and spectators. "In the meantime I have resorted to three art forms that are to provide resting-places for the public and the actors, without letting the public escape from the illusion induced. All these forms are subsidiary to the drama. They are the monologue, the pantomime, and the dance, all of them belonging originally to the tragedy of classical antiquity. For the monologue has sprung from the monody, and the chorus has developed into the ballet."[48]

[44] *Ibid.,* pp. 105–106.   [45] Strindberg, XXIII, 117, 124, 164, 165, 166.
[46] *Ibid.,* pp. 120, 140, 151, 153, 169.
[47] *Ibid.,* pp. 122–123, 129, 131, 132, 134, 135, 141, 143, 153.
[48] Strindberg, *Plays,* Björkman translation, 2d Series, p. 107.

Strindberg also mentions that he has asked the musical director to make a careful selection of the music used in the play, so that the illusion may be maintained and not be distorted by incompatible moods. It is well for us to remember that, while pantomime, monologue and music are employed in expressionistic drama, we must exercise care not to grant too much significance to these elements. Strindberg himself calls attention to the fact that the music " is amply warranted by the Midsummer Eve's dance." [49]   He is not employing music, as he did in the post-Inferno period, with the primary purpose of establishing a mood, or different moods, throughout the drama. Here music is used because of necessity; it is a requirement of a particular milieu.

The autobiographical element is also clear. Strindberg, the " son of a servant," captures Siri *von* Essen, the daughter of the noble class.[50]   This autobiographical material, however, is so completely engulfed by the " theme from real life " that the parallels of Julia to Siri von Essen, and Strindberg to Jean, are very superficial. *Ausstrahlungen des Ichs* by no means qualifies *Miss Julia.*

All in all, the play cannot be considered as expressionistic, nor as manifesting any strong expressionistic tendency. The entire play answers the description of " life seen through a temperament "; and, instead of being the new form that Strindberg mentions in his preface, the play is an excellent example of thoroughgoing naturalism. The dialogue, arranged with regard to musical composition, is apparently more in the intention of the author than in his practice. There is no struggle of true opposites in this drama, and the situation is an individual case and not a typical one. The characters likewise are almost completely individuals. The autobiographical element wholly dis-

[49] Strindberg, *op. cit.*, p. 108.

[50] Lamm, I, 312.   Note also that in the *Starkodder Skald* fragment (Samlade otryckta skrifter, I) Storverk, the son of dark Loki, ravishes the daughter of the sun.

appears into the " theme of real life " without being integrated
into it; there is no dynamic resurgence of Strindberg's own experiences, but only a superficial and practically inconsequential
parallelism between Strindberg's life and the events of the drama.
Likewise, the use of pantomime, dance and music offers no evidence that could either compel or induce a critic to remove this
drama from its naturalistic category.

" THE DANCE OF DEATH "

CHRONOLOGICALLY, *The Dance of Death* [51] belongs in the post-
Inferno period, and could be discussed in a later chapter that
deals with dramas between *To Damascus* and *A Dream Play*. In
subject-matter, however, the drama is immediately related to the
so-called naturalistic group, and is especially close to *The Father*.
Lamm declares that *The Dance of Death*, with its bitter tones,
its rank naturalism and harsh matrimonial hate, appears like a
ghost out of the 'eighties.[52] Certainly the sex struggle is even
sharper than that of *The Father*, and the battle in the first part
of the play is pitched exceedingly high because it is more even
between husband and wife. The " rank naturalism," however,
is a qualification that this study will remove.

In *The Dance of Death* we encounter two primitive creatures [53]
who remind us of *ur*-man and *ur*-woman. Soon after Kurt's
entry Alice informs him that the Captain gets into a bad humor
if he is contradicted; [54] and a little later the Captain tells Kurt
that Alice has a " satanic temper." [55] It is not, however, until
the Captain has the first heart attack that we get a glimpse of
Alice's animal nature: primitivity more than *ur*-ishness. Alice
enters the room, views her stricken husband calmly, and offers
to play the piano to awaken him.[56] After the Captain has re-

---

[51] Written and published 1901.   [54] Strindberg, XXXIV, 35.
[52] Lamm, II, 222.   [55] *Ibid.,* p. 36.
[53] *Ibid.,* p. 82.   [56] *Ibid.,* p. 41.

gained consciousness and has gone out, Alice tells Kurt that she has always hated her husband and now has such a boundless hate for him that she would shriek with laughter the day he died.[57] Kurt, commenting on the relations of Alice and Edgar,[58] says, as though to himself, " It is called love-hate and is born of the abyss." [59] This love-hate is well illustrated by the rest of Part I of *The Dance of Death*. The Captain enters, after having attended to army duties, and remarks to Kurt sardonically that Alice has now had time to make her complaints: " Isn't she unhappy . . . . what? " [60] Shortly afterwards, Edgar has a second heart attack and Alice sighs hopefully — he may die this time.[61] When the Captain once more comes to his senses he asks for a drink of water.

> *Captain.* Will you give me a glass of water?
> *Alice.* I suppose I have to!
> *Captain.* How amiable! [62]

When the Captain receives flowers from the soldiers and fellow-officers, Alice remarks that she does not quite understand the situation and wonders if these are expressions of joy that the Captain is sick. The Captain retorts with one word only — " Hyena! " [63] Later Edgar informs Kurt that Alice is angry with him for not dying on the previous day, but Alice replies, " No, because you didn't die twenty-five years ago, because you didn't die before I was born." [64]

This element of love-hate seems hardly to justify the use of the word " love " when we read *The Dance of Death,* for it is hate that streams on and on through the drama. Yet there is a tiny fractional element of affection, if these two creatures are really capable of· it. For some reason or other they have never

---

[57] Strindberg, XXXIV, 43.
[58] The Captain's name is Edgar.
[59] Strindberg, XXXIV, 46.
[60] *Ibid.,* p. 50.

[61] *Ibid.,* pp. 51–52.
[62] *Ibid.,* p. 53.
[63] *Ibid.,* p. 77.
[64] *Ibid.,* p. 80.

been able to part from each other, though they quarreled as lovers and battled constantly throughout the twenty-five years of their marriage.[65] Alice also recognizes that Edgar has had no easy path in life, that he has in fact constantly struggled against heavy odds.[66] She has even found the man to be tender at times [67] and she admits that he is really to be pitied.[68] In the pantomime scene, the Captain shows tenderness for his children, and — for the cat! [69]

But these two people are also wild beasts in human form. Alice, especially, shows almost no soft emotions. Only toward the end of Part I, after Kurt has departed with the farewell greeting that she might go to perdition, does Alice seem to have some concern for her children, for the shame that she may bring upon them.[70] But she is cold and harsh in the early part of the play, well illustrated in the short dialogue with Jenny the maid.[71] After the advent of Kurt, Alice grows in wildness and passion until she is no less than a female demon.[72] The Captain also belongs to this type. Once he pushed his wife into the sea:

Kurt. . . . Why did you push her into the water?

Captain. I don't know. It merely seemed quite natural to me, as she was standing on the pier, that she ought to be in the water.

Kurt. Have you never regretted it?

Captain. Never!

Kurt. That's strange!

Captain. Of course it is! So strange that I cannot realize that I am the man who has been guilty of such a mean act.[73]

Alice says that no laws exist for the Captain, but he himself stands over the entire world.[74] The references to the Captain's vampire nature also point to his primitive qualities, primitive in

[65] *Ibid.*, p. 43.
[66] *Ibid.*, pp. 33, 70.
[67] *Ibid.*, p. 71.
[68] *Ibid.*, p. 82.
[69] *Ibid.*, pp. 101–102.
[70] *Ibid.*, pp. 116–119.
[71] *Ibid.*, p. 18.
[72] *Ibid.*, pp. 62, 70, 80, 84, 94, 97–100, 104–106, 114.
[73] *Ibid.*, p. 112.
[74] *Ibid.*, p. 79.

the sense of beastlike.[75] The Captain and his wife certainly are
not people who have been disciplined in life, but are two wild
beasts in chains. Just enough convention restrains them so that
they suffer no worse punishment than isolation from everyone
else on this little island which is nicknamed " Little Hell." [76] The
qualification that Alice gives to her husband applies to her
equally well:

> *Kurt.* What kind of human is this?
>
> *Alice.* It's a demon and not a human being! [77]

The relation of this pair is expressed by the love-hate combination
in which each element is ungoverned physical passion. It is the
primitivity of the beast that is enraged or in rut that qualifies
both partners of this sex struggle.[78]

   In the earlier sex battle, *The Father,* responsibility for the
matrimonial hell is placed on the " Powers "; [79] but not in *The
Dance of Death,* I, unless we accept Alice's statement that the
family seems to belong to a cursed race.[80] In the latter play
practically everything seems to grow out of the characters themselves, out of their selfishness and out of their ungoverned pas-
sions. The responsibility is apparently placed on the primitive
element in the human being, on that which bursts out in us in
spite of aesthetic, intellectual and emotional refinements.

   Diebold, however, seems dissatisfied with this conflict as an
elemental sex struggle.[81] The woman, in Diebold's opinion, is
too closely related to the emancipated type, and the man too
much engaged with womanly weapons of attack, " dialektischen

---

[75] Strindberg, XXXIV, 82, 88, 91, 97.

[76] *Ibid.,* pp. 96, 99.

[77] *Ibid.,* p. 96.

[78] It should be borne in mind that this primitivity has apparently as
much, if not more, duration than the more desirable and poetic *ur*-ishness
of the expressionists.

[79] Strindberg, XXIII, 93.

[80] *Ibid.,* XXXIV, 47, 59.

[81] Diebold, *Anarchie im Drama,* p. 157.

Guerillakriegs." Yet Diebold is apparently overlooking the fact that definite limits are placed on drama. Primitive brutality must be given partially in a battle of words, and must be given in the atmosphere rather than in deeds on the stage. Furthermore, it should be noted that in Part I Strindberg has carefully avoided a tragedy in which death eliminates one or both of the combatants. Here we have an *unending conflict*. Not only the whole twenty-five years of this particular matrimonial struggle live in the play, but the passionate struggle of the sexes surges through all time in the warfare of the Captain and his wife. " Everything repeats itself," says Alice,[82] and the play well illustrates that the struggle repeats itself without beginning and without end; it is a kind of plastic motion that seems to move and yet remains fast in its own material stuff. The Captain declares that death means the end of everything.[83] Each of the mates looks forward to the death of the other as the way to freedom;[84] but in *The Dance of Death*, I, there is no end, no death, no freedom. There is only the vicious repetition of the everlasting sex battle. The Captain and his wife are typical of the animal in humanity, and their struggle is decidedly elemental. " The final scene not only rounds out the drama artistically, but also gives it an infinite perspective. The unceasing, meaningless grim struggle in which the two battle against each other becomes a symbol of life itself." [85] Even Strindberg gives a little cue that he was generalizing in this drama, if not giving a necessary and elemental conflict. When Alice and Edgar are left alone after the latter's second heart attack there are two remarks casually dropped that are pregnant with meaning.

The Captain. . . . I wonder if everybody's life is just the same?

Alice. Perhaps, though they don't talk about it as we do! [86]

---

[82] Strindberg, XXXIV, 59.

[83] *Ibid.*, p. 9.

[84] *Ibid.*, p. 43.

[85] Lamm, II, 235.

[86] Strindberg, XXXIV, 56.

The necessity of the conflict springs from the sex opposition; it is elemental because it involves not individuals but types, involves the race of mankind from its beginnings to the present time; perhaps the conflict will survive as long as mankind propagates male and female.

This drama naturally has its autobiographical background. Kurt is easily identified as Strindberg's mouthpiece,[87] and Alice has the features of Strindberg's first wife.[88] Moreover the dramatist's own experiences in marriage made him limn the Captain more sympathetically than Alice.[89] The play as a whole is Strindberg's attempt to give universality to his own experiences in the matrimonial struggle. He has succeeded in remoulding his own experiences into a dynamic struggle that is elemental and endless, a struggle that is consequent on sex opposition. The dramatist, however, has exercised more control in this drama than in *The Father* with the result that he is almost neutral in his presentation of the pair.

Music, as sound, does not play an important part in *The Dance of Death*, I. We hear it in the distance coming from the Doctor's ball.[90] Alice plays on the piano while the Captain dances,[91] and throughout the one long pantomime scene music is played softly.[92] With the exception of the pantomime scene the music fits into the respective situations very naturally.

Musical theme dialogue,[93] on the other hand, appears with great frequency and is an important element in this play. The drama opens and closes with a discussion of the coming silver wedding of Edgar and Alice, and throughout the entire drama we are reminded of the twenty-five years of marriage.[94] A number of other ideas also weave in and out of the dialogue: the Captain's

[87] Lamm, II, 223.
[88] *Ibid.*, p. 228.
[89] *Ibid.*, p. 224.
[90] Strindberg, XXXIV, 14.
[91] *Ibid.*, p. 51.
[92] *Ibid.*, p. 101.
[93] Also called contrapuntal form of dialogue; see below, pp. 148–153.
[94] Strindberg, XXXIV, 9, 15, 28, 42, 73, 80, 87, 97, 121, 122.

habits of drinking and smoking; [95] the Doctor's ball; [96] the tele-
graph instrument; [97] the children of the Captain and Alice, who
never appear in the drama; [98] Kurt's family difficulties; [99] the
Captain's financial troubles; [100] and the element of hate.[101] We
should note also that in each repetition we do not have simply a
bald return to the original idea. In the midst of the opening
wrangle the Captain sounds a rather pleasant note by mention-
ing the approaching silver wedding, but Alice at the same time
dashes in a remark about twenty-five years of misery; [102] Alice
remarks that it seems strange that Kurt should be coming to
them just at the time of their silver wedding, and she adds quickly
" whether it is celebrated nor not "; the Captain tells Kurt that
the latter brought the former and Alice together in marriage
twenty-five years earlier; Alice says that to her Edgar is a
stranger, just as strange as twenty-five years earlier; Kurt im-
plores the Captain to make provisions in his will for the one who
has kept house for him for twenty-five years; Alice is angry with
the Captain because he did not die twenty-five years ago; Alice
tells Kurt that she has lived in the fortress for twenty-five years
and asks him if he knew that the place had once been a prison;
Alice says that the Captain has beaten her for twenty-five years;
the Captain declares that he feels sure they will celebrate their
silver wedding in three months, and he reminds Alice of a certain
silver wedding in which the bride had to wear her ring on the
right hand because the groom in a tender mood had cut off the
ring finger on her left hand; and the play comes to a close with
the Captain speaking seriously of the coming silver wedding. The

[95] *Ibid.,* pp. 8, 16, 17, 43, 61, 76, 78, 87, 89, 96.
[96] *Ibid.,* pp. 11, 14, 17, 23, 27, 60.
[97] *Ibid.,* pp. 22, 39, 44, 55, 59, 102, 103, 107, 111, 114, 116, 118.
[98] *Ibid.,* pp. 13, 22, 30, 46, 60, 65, 71, 77, 83, 88, 95, 114, 117.
[99] *Ibid.,* pp. 15, 28, 30, 36, 44, 75, 83, 91, 97.
[100] *Ibid.,* pp. 10, 21, 22, 24, 35, 38, 80.
[101] *Ibid.,* pp. 43, 45, 46, 77, 81, 88, 97.
[102] Page references are given in note 94 above.

same idea occurs with different associations all through the drama, though even the " different associations " are all variations on the theme " twenty-five years of misery." The early association of the silver wedding and the twenty-five years of misery stamps every later mention of twenty-five years with the coördinate images of silver wedding and domestic misery.

This contrapuntal form of dialogue is given added significance by Alice's statement, " Everything repeats itself." [103] The Captain also makes his comments on the continual recurrence of things.

> *Alice.* . . . Do you think it's nice for you to yawn in your wife's presence?
>
> *Captain.* Well, what can you do about it? . . . Haven't you noticed that we say the same thing every day! When you just made your good old rejoinder " in this house, at any rate," I ǀshould have replied with my old one: " It isn't just my house alone." But when I have answered that way for five hundred times, I just have to yawn instead. My yawn may then signify either that I am too lazy to reply, or else: " You are right, my angel"; or, " Let's quit." [104]

The frequency of the contrapuntal form of dialogue in *The Dance of Death*, I, is probably occasioned by the period in which the play was written: post-Inferno, and between *To Damascus*, I, II, and *A Dream Play*. Even if Strindberg had written a perfect naturalistic drama during this period, this element of technique would undoubtedly have been present.

The Dance of Death, I, makes considerable use of pause [105] and also has one remarkable pantomime scene.[106] Reading the play, one has the sensation that this pantomime will soon wear itself into boredom, that one person can neither create nor hold suspense for any length of time while remaining silent. On the

[103] Strindberg, XXXIV, 59.
[104] *Ibid.*, p. 23.
[105] *Ibid.*, pp. 8, 9, 12, 14, 21, 29, 47, 50, 52, 66, 67(2), 83, 90, 91, 107, 109(2), 112, 120, 121(2).
[106] *Ibid.*, pp. 101–102.

stage, however, the pantomime has a power that grips and holds, and there is no feeling that the dumb-show is out of place or that it is tiring. Instead, the pantomime, with an emotional support of music, gives clear evidence that language at times is either superfluous or else unable to express certain emotions as well as action alone. A monologue would have spoiled the effect. What should the Captain say when one by one he regards and then throws out of the window his deck of cards, his whiskey and cigars, and finally his spectacles? when he tears to pieces his wife's portrait, kisses the portraits of his children, burns his love-letters? and, finally, when he affectionately strokes the cat? The action in this pantomime speaks effectively, and words could only break the magic of the situation.

From our discussion it is clear that this so-called naturalistic drama *The Dance of Death*, I, has qualities that definitely remove it from the old classification. The struggle of sex is elemental, and the two primitive creatures might well fit into any drama of German expressionism. The whole drama is the reflection from Strindberg's ego, not a Strindbergian imitation of observed reality. Furthermore, the autobiographical material is typified and universalized, and not moulded into an individual situation enacted in a particular milieu.

In addition, certain elements of technique lend more evidence to justify the reclassification of the drama. The time element has a dream character. The play opens and closes with the same reference to the coming silver wedding and the drama itself becomes a vision of the twenty-five years of misery which Alice mentions in the opening scene. The place of this drama likewise is not simply a little island. The island, called " Little Hell," is the world of men. Time is essentially all time and the place is none other than the world. Besides time and place, the use of pause, pantomime and contrapuntal dialogue strengthen the conclusion that this play is expressionistic.

The Dance of Death, II, is much the same type of drama. Here, however, the Captain is completely a vampire and sucks the very existence out of Kurt. The play is also somewhat relieved by the presence of Kurt's son and the Captain's daughter Judith. Yet here, too, there is a definite feeling, if not excellent evidence, that " everything repeats itself." Judith and Allan will marry and dance " the dance of death " as all their ancestors have danced. The second part of *The Dance of Death* offers much the same kind of evidence as the first part and does not need individual discussion. We may qualify the double-drama as expressionistic.

CHAPTER III

THE "TO DAMASCUS" TRILOGY

BETWEEN *Miss Julia* and *To Damascus,* I,[1] there are eleven plays of which only one has any relation to our subject. This is *The Keys of the Kingdom of Heaven,* or *Saint Peter Wanders on Earth,*[2] which was composed just before Strindberg wrote a number of one-act plays of the naturalistic type.

This play is a rather peculiar one with unusual characters: the Smith, Doctor All-knowing, Saint Peter, Don Quixote, Sancho Panza, Bluebeard, the Mistress, and shadows. Among these shadows are Hamlet and Ophelia, Othello and Desdemona, Lady Macbeth as the wife of Bluebeard, and then Romeo and Juliet, old and the parents of five children who accompany them! Such a list is almost certain to excite curiosity.

A reading of the play dismisses the suspicion that it can be classified definitely as expressionistic, though our attention is directed toward certain factors. It has plenty of autobiographical background. Lamm says that Strindberg was experiencing a great longing for his children just before the writing of this drama.[3] The play has Strindberg in the rôle of the Smith searching for the children who have become " dead " for him. Doctor All-knowing, who can " troll," takes the Smith through all sorts of fantastic dream scenes and finally gives him back the children with the injunction not to exchange reality for dreams.

Lamm bases his opinion largely on two letters written by Strindberg. The first was written on the 9th of July, 1890, to Geijerstam: " Living completely a phantom life in my fictitious work and in the little lives of my children, I am indeed quite an

---

[1] Written 1897–98.   [2] Written 1891–92.   [3] Lamm, I, 378.

117

impossible figure in society. Disharmonies without solution compel me to work out a single new self which in the imagination can escape from the mountain in which I am held and which I neither dare nor desire to leave, for one also learns to cherish his hell." The second letter was written in October, 1891, to Birger Mörner: " My children are now my idée fixe, and I am writing a saga-play for them just now. . . ." Lamm further declares that it was undoubtedly with the intention of writing another *Lucky Per* drama that Strindberg conceived *The Keys of the Kingdom of Heaven.* A reading of the play justifies this association with *Lucky Per's Journey.* Both plays have auto-biographical background and both are mechanically operated by fairies or by magicians of the Doctor All-knowing type.

There is one little dialogue in the first scene of the second act that is significant for us. In this scene the Smith and Doctor All-knowing are seated at a table before the registry in a hotel:

> *The Smith* (*writes*). Well, there's my name, occupation, et cetera! Now it's your turn to write!
>
> *The Doctor.* You write it down for me; it's all the same.
>
> *The Smith.* What is your name?
>
> *The Doctor.* Anonymous!
>
> *The Smith.* An unusual name! Your occupation?
>
> *The Doctor.* My occupation? I have several! — Put down *doctor!*
>
> *The Smith.* Where from?
>
> *The Doctor.* The womb!
>
> *The Smith.* Where to?
>
> *The Doctor.* The grave!
>
> *The Smith.* Always mystical! Who are you, odd fellow, who now have my fate in your hands? What do you wish of me?
>
> *The Doctor.* You'll know that later when you are ready!
>
> *The Smith.* When shall I be ready?
>
> *The Doctor.* When, like myself, you have learned to know yourself!
>
> *The Smith.* Always self! What is this self you are so constantly preaching?

The Doctor. It is the fixed point for which Archimedes sought, the point by which he thought he could move the world. It is your ego which is not another, the midpoint in your horizon. . . .

The Smith. Who am I then?

The Doctor. For the time being a lad of forty years, ore and slag in the mixture, as sensitive as a child and equally ready for sorrow and joy! Most certainly life's simple joys still lure you:
a well set table, a brim-ful glass,
a dance with maidens on the green. . . .[4]

This section reminds us strongly of the " Gyntish self " in Ibsen's *Peer Gynt*, but it is also representative of the Strindberg self. Not long afterwards Strindberg was to battle terrifically for the maintenance of this self. The drama *The Keys of the Kingdom of Heaven* is not expressionistic, for it is obviously mechanically motivated and is in part a fairy play for children. Yet the play, with its strong autobiographical element, with its search for the self, the fixed point in the universe, is so close to expressionism that it deserves the little space we have assigned to it.

" TO DAMASCUS "

It is in the *To Damascus* trilogy [5] that we encounter a drama generally acclaimed as the first expressionistic play.[6] The critics, however, have been too much given to interpretation and too little to careful analysis from the standpoint of expressionism. Diebold does point out one or two important factors: " In ' Nach Damaskus ' steht mit dem ' Unbekannten ' zum erstenmal der Monologist des expressionistischen Dramas auf dem Theater. Jener im Kerne eher lyrische als dramatische Ankläger der Menschheit und Ausschreier seiner Schmerzen, wie Sorges ' Bettler,' Hasenclevers ' Sohn ' und Kornfelds Bitterlich, deren meiste Gegenspieler weniger Vertreter von wirklichen Gegen-

---

[4] Strindberg, XXV, 138–140. (See also Ibsen's *Peer Gynt,* Archer translation, Charles Scribner's Sons, 1907, pp. 132–133.)

[5] Written 1897–1904. [6] Acclaimed by German critics, of course.

willen sind als Materialisation ihrer eigenen Seelen." [7]   But Diebold does not give us much more.

In *To Damascus* we are face to face with a drama that completely frustrates any attempt to assign it to any known category.
" Nach Damaskus ist kein Drama im alten Sinne. Es enthält
keine Willenshandlungen, es hat kein Geschehn, das sich steigert,
anschwillt und abstürzt; es ist als Traumspiel nicht der Psychologie der wachen Wirklichkeit unterworfen; es spielt ja gar nicht
in ihr, so wirklich und alltäglich, allkläglich oft die Geschehnisse
— Eheleid und Geldverlegenheit — auch sind; es spielt auf einer
andern Ebene, wo alles Bild und Gleichnis ist, wo die Menschen
des Diesseits schon fast zu mythologischen Wesen werden oder
werden sollen. . . ." [8]

If this drama really answers the qualification of expressionistic
art it should stand the test of the norms set forth in the first part
of this book.   It should not only make it possible to generalize
with occasional reference to the work but even to plow right
through the work and turn up furrow after furrow of expressionistic factors.   The following sections will point out that the internal evidence is far more complete than critical literature has
thus far indicated.

AUTOBIOGRAPHICAL DATA

IN VIEW of what has already been said regarding the autobiographical character of Strindberg's works, it is almost superfluous to explain that *To Damascus* is immediately rooted, and
deeply rooted, in Strindberg's life.   We encounter material that
has already been given in the so-called day-book *Inferno* [9] which
records some of the most tempestuous of Strindberg's experiences.

[7] Diebold, *Anarchie im Drama*, pp. 165–166.
[8] Soergel, *Dichtung und Dichter der Zeit*, p. 192.
[9] Strindberg, XXVIII, originally written in French, 1896–97. A Swedish
translation was published in October, 1897, while the French original was not
published until 1898.

For further authority on the autobiographical character we refer to other critics [10] as well as to the direct comparison of *Inferno* with *To Damascus*. What is important for us is that the drama is not a day-book, though practically everything in the play can be traced back to Strindberg's own life. The drama has distorted the autobiographical material for the sake of the art-form. Situations are very similar and even individual incidents may be identified; but it would be entirely false to state that the drama reproduces the objective experiences of the author. The play gives Strindberg's inner experiences. It is autobiography consciously conditioned by the psyche and not a transcription of an object's activities in the empirical world.

TYPIFICATION

THE list of dramatis personae gives at least a superficial indication of the use of type characters: the Unknown, the Lady, the Beggar, the Doctor, the Sister, the Old Man, the Mother, the Abbess, and the Confessor. In addition there are subordinate characters and "shadows." The qualifications are general (sex, profession, social or family status) with no glimmer whatsoever of individuality.

The Unknown is a most shadowy figure if we draw any conclusions from his name, for he is clearly an *x* in a mathematical problem. Yet every reader of Strindberg recognizes the Unknown at once as the dramatist himself. He is Strindberg and is unknown to himself. He is the Smith in *The Keys of the Kingdom of Heaven* who does not yet know what Doctor All-knowing wants of him, for Strindberg has not learned to know himself.

The Unknown, however, is more than Strindberg, even as the Dramatist in Sorge's *Der Bettler* is more than Reinhard Sorge.

[10] Lamm, II, 52; Marcus, *Strindbergs Dramatik*, p. 231; Diebold, *Anarchie im Drama*, p. 162; Erdmann, *August Strindberg*, p. 710; Soergel, *Dichtung und Dichter der Zeit*, p. 190.

The Unknown is man battling with the " Powers," wondering when he will be ready to know his fate, and striving to know himself. The Unknown is characterized by all the hate and all the love that a human may possess; he has the extreme of pride and humility, the desire to search endlessly for truth and the longing to find repose at any cost; and he shows himself to be both a stark realist and a complete mystic! The Unknown is Strindberg plus all that has passed through the Strindberg self. He is Strindberg's concept of man in combat with his fate and man in search of himself.

The Unknown is the main character of the drama, and to some extent is the only character. It is *his* struggle with the " Powers " that the play represents; and the other characters are scarcely more than reflections, than *affects* of the Unknown. The struggle with the " Powers " is rather abstract since the " Powers " are invisible; so the concrete symbols that appear on the stage are the Unknown's concept of the " Powers." There is the struggle with the opposite sex, the struggle of the individual against the whole of society, the struggle with the church and its idea of resignation, the combat of science and religion, and the struggle of the individual with his several selves. If we throw out the Unknown, not only do we destroy the fabric of the drama, but we blot out the entire play. It is the Unknown's play from beginning to end, and all the characters emanate from his mind as symbols of the " Powers " with whom he is in combat.

The Lady, though fashioned after Strindberg's second wife in Parts I and II, and after his third in Part III, is nevertheless woman, the representative of her entire sex. She is a daughter, wife,[11] lover, mother, sly female and the ideal feminine, the one through whom man hopes to be reconciled with life. To say that the Lady is Frieda Uhl [12] entirely, or Harriet Bosse,[13] is ridicu-

[11] Wife several times: to the Doctor, the Confessor and the Unknown.
[12] Strindberg's second wife.   [13] Strindberg's third wife.

lous; for Strindberg, married to any woman of superior intelligence, would have found the same qualities present in the woman
and available for the type woman. The very fact that the Lady
is transformed from a likeness of Frieda Uhl to one of Harriet
Bosse, and for a moment in Part III [14] to a likeness of the Unknown's Mother, is evidence *ipso facto* that we have a type character and not an individual.

The other characters become still more shadowy until the
dream type is reached. What is the Beggar but a finger pointing
at the Unknown all the time — his own finger; the Doctor, but a
reminder of the Unknown's guilt both as a schoolboy and as a
wife-robber; the Confessor, but a representative of the church
and also a concrete symbol of the " Powers "? The mother-in-
law not only typifies her sex, but also appears like the shadow
of the Unknown's first wife, the one he deserted! Caesar [15] and
the other characters of the Asylum scene have already been
placed by the author in the category of subordinate figures and
shadows. These creatures receive material shape as they are
projected from the conscience-stricken mind of the Unknown.

THE MONOLOGUE

FROM the usual interpretation of the monologue the *To
Damascus* trilogy only rarely avails itself of this dramatic form.
From the expressionistic point of view, however, the whole play
is a dramatic monologue,[16] the monologue of the Unknown, since
the other characters are merely manifestations of his " self."

[14] Strindberg, XXIX, 308.
[15] Caesar is undoubtedly the shadow of Nietzsche. See Strecker,
Nietzsche und Strindberg, mit ihrem Briefwechsel, pp. 90–94. In one letter
of December, 1888, Nietzsche signs himself " Nietzsche Cäsar "; in another,
" Der Gekreuzigte "; and Strindberg's answer to the first is signed " Strindberg (Deus, optimus, maximus)." Nils Erdmann also relates *Caesar* and
Nietzsche; see his *August Strindberg,* p. 711.
[16] Diebold discusses *To Damascus* under the caption *Der Monologist
von Damaskus; Anarchie im Drama,* pp. 165–171.

This study is completely interwoven with the discussion on *Ausstrahlungen des Ichs*, the section immediately following, and will there find amplification.

THE whole play is so evidently a radiation of the ego that nearly all its elements may be included under the one caption. The expressionistic elements are so interwoven and mingled with *Ausstrahlungen des Ichs* that they hardly can be discussed separately. If one attempts to separate these dependent factors one is too likely to find oneself equipped with a handful of varicolored threads, fit to be used for a tassel, a duster, or a mop, but quite useless for a work of art. We shall, therefore, thread our way through the drama with an open eye for all that points to *Ausstrahlungen des Ichs*, the Unconscious, dream character and the objectification of inner experience. Other elements like the dramatic unities, the relation to music and " the worth of man " are independent enough to warrant individual treatment.

The very first lines in the drama dispel any illusions that one may have regarding the possibility of naturalism in *To Damascus*. The Unknown stands on a street corner undecided regarding the direction he will take. The Lady enters and is greeted by the Unknown: " See, there you are. I almost knew that you would come." [17] The Lady replies that the Unknown was calling for her, " Yes, I felt it." Were we to jump to conclusions without further evidence we might even now declare that the Lady is no more than a projection of the Unknown's consciousness on the stage, a materialization of his wish. But there are plenty of bridges in this drama, so the strenuous sport of jumping need not be followed.

A little later in the drama,[18] the Unknown tells the Lady that

[17] Strindberg, XXIX, 7.   [18] *Ibid.*, p. 9.

solitude is what he fears most of all, for when one is alone one encounters somebody! The Unknown says that he is not sure whether it is really someone else, or whether it is just a manifestation of himself that he apprehends. But " in solitude one is not alone. The atmosphere becomes close, it grows, and there come into being creatures that are invisible, but nevertheless possess life and can be apprehended." The Unknown further qualifies this statement by an explanation that not long since he simply observed objects and events, forms and colors, but now he sees thoughts and significances. " Life, which before was a monstrous nonsense, has taken on meaning " and where the Unknown formerly saw chance he now sees a purpose. He is not certain whether this comes out of his own ego or whether he has awakened to new truths, for he is evidently " hesitating at a street corner " in his mental life even as he stands on a street corner in material form. He is convinced, for example, that the Lady, whom he met for the first time on the preceding day, has been sent to him for one of two extreme purposes: either to save him or to crush him. The Lady is clearly an instrument of the " Powers," she typifies her sex, and she has been called into being by the Unknown's own desire.

When the Lady asks the Unknown if he has ever had visions he replies in the emphatic negative.[19] It is an obvious indication that this is not to be a drama of the experimental type indicating researches in the realm of psychology; it is not a drama consciously built on hallucinations which are to be interpreted by a scientist. It is constructed with a clear sense of the validity of the inner experiences, notwithstanding the fact that these experiences may possibly be the result of the " Powers " juggling with the ego of man.

The Unknown talks about himself and then suddenly turns to the Lady with the request that she tell him a few things about

[19] *Ibid.,* p. 11.

herself. She replies that there is nothing to discuss. The Unknown's comment is significant.

> *The Unknown.* Peculiarly enough, I also would rather think of you as impersonal, nameless — I only know the half of your name — I should like to give you a name myself — let me think what you shall be called! Yes, you shall be named Eve.[20]

The name Eve has two obvious interpretations: she is the type woman, the representative of the eternal feminine; and she is also the creature through whom sin came into the world.[21] She is like the flower that she wears on her bosom; it signifies meanness and slander, but has been known to heal insanity.[22] The naming of the Lady is a clear gesture of *Ausstrahlungen des Ichs.* Even as Minerva sprang from the brow of Jupiter, so Eve in *To Damascus* radiates from the ego of the Unknown. Whatsoever qualities she has also come from the Unknown. He names her Eve, gives her an age of thirty-four years and a good character. Without further characterization he turns again to himself.

In the midst of his tale the Unknown suddenly asks: " Do you think I am insane? " and the Lady replies in the negative.[23] With such a statement coming out of the drama one may be tempted to agree with Böök that " impressions of reality are transformed after having passed through a confused intelligence and a sick sensitiveness." [24] Böök admits the element of distortion and puts the blame on Strindberg's state of mind. If, however, we study the drama as literature, without focussing our attention too much on the autobiographical data, we should bear in mind that the Unknown is a *character* in the drama. The question of Strind-

---

[20] Strindberg, XXIX, 13. (Note also *Lilith* in the fragment *The Hollander,* Samlade otryckta skrifter, I.)

[21] *Ibid.,* pp. 87–88, offers further evidence.

[22] *Ibid.,* p. 20.

[23] *Ibid.,* p. 15.

[24] Böök, Fredrik, *Sveriges moderna litteratur,* p. 342 (the passage quoted refers directly to the novel *Svarta fanor,* but also indirectly to *To Damascus, A Dream Play* and the *Chamber Plays*).

berg's sanity is another matter which has been carefully considered, if not completely solved, in the studies of Jaspers and
Rahmer.[25] What is important for us is the dramatic figure, the
Unknown. He is actually bridging the gap between subject and
object, and has by no means lost his mental balance. He is
aware that this new phase of his life has distorted former views,
and he knows that strange things are occurring. The Unknown
struggles to keep himself in balance as he battles throughout the
entire situation, and he is not to be dismissed lightly with a
gesture that implies " another imbecile."

The Unknown's talk with the Beggar [26] discloses a most unusual type of beggar, and something more. In his conversation
with the Lady [27] the Unknown tells her to look at a scar on his
forehead. He explains that many years ago his brother hit him
with an axe. Later, when the Unknown asks the Beggar what
sort of scar he has on his forehead, the latter replies that he
received it at the hands of a close relative! [28] The Unknown
becomes somewhat frightened and feels of the Beggar's arm to
determine whether or not he is really of flesh and blood. The
significance of the scene lies in the question of the Beggar's
reality. Clearly, he is another creature from the Unknown's
mind; he is indeed one of the Unknown's several selves.

After the Beggar departs, the Unknown is alone and yearning
for companionship. The Lady comes immediately, like the fulfilment of the Unknown's wish. The Unknown cries out, " See
there! It is peculiar that I can't open my mouth and say something before I am immediately forced to recant." [29] In this same
conversation we get a little glimpse of the Unknown's concept of

[25] Notes 8 and 9, Part II, Chapter I, of this book.
[26] Strindberg, XXIX, 16–19.
[27] *Ibid.,* p. 13.
[28] *Ibid.,* 18.
[29] *Ibid.,* p. 20 (the Unknown has just been cursing the long Sunday
afternoon when it is impossible to meet a friend, when the Lady enters).

reality. The Lady has reminded him that he has forgotten that she is married, that her husband is a doctor and an admirer of the Unknown's works. The Unknown replies that he has done everything possible to forget just those facts and has so rooted them out of his memory that they no longer possess reality for him.

Scarcely has the Lady left him and entered the church before the Unknown sits down on the bench and resumes his " writing in the sand." Then a scene is presented that cannot possibly be interpreted as anything apart from a projection of the Unknown's mind, even though Strindberg gives no assistance in the stage directions. From the beginning of the play to the present scene a funeral march has been heard, now near at hand and then at a distance, but always in the atmosphere. After the Lady's departure, there enter six funeral assistants dressed in brown, who sit down with the Unknown and a number of guests at the tables outside the tavern. Everything is distorted. The answers to questions are wholly contrary to expectations. The implication is made that the dead man was none other than the Unknown himself. He is qualified as having been a useless creature, one who indulged in strong drinks a great deal, a family man who let others provide for his wife and children.[30] During the conversation between the Unknown and some of the guests the Beggar enters. The Owner of the café notes at once that the Beggar answers the description of a man wanted by the police. He refuses to serve this guest and threatens to summon the police if he does not move along. The Unknown defends the Beggar. Then the Owner discovers that the Unknown also answers the description of the man wanted by the police, for the Unknown and the Beggar are so much alike. Subsequently, both the Unknown and the Beggar are ejected. Just as the Unknown is in great confusion the church bells ring and the Lady enters the

[30] Strindberg, XXIX, 25–26.

scene again. The further identification of the Unknown and the
Beggar points again to the latter as a materialization of one of
the former's selves. The Beggar has radiated from the Unknown's ego.

The Lady asks the Unknown why he called out to her. Later,
in the same scene, the Unknown explains that he did not call out
to the Lady, but just longed for her.[31] She came once more as
the fulfilment of his wish. The Unknown is also concerned
enough regarding the nature of the recent events to ask the Lady
if all these things around them are real. He wonders, too, if he
and the Beggar actually look very much alike. The Lady, however, dismisses both questions in the spirit of a mother soothing
her child.[32] The spectator of *To Damascus* would also be left in
somewhat the same quandary as the Unknown, wondering whether
all were real or not, whether this scene was meant as ordinary
observed reality or as a vision. The attitude of the Unknown
obviates all difficulties; the scene is vision and not ordinary
realism. In fact, the same qualification applies that Strindberg
used in a letter to Geijerstam: " Yes, this is unquestionably a
piece of literature with a fearful half-reality behind it." [33] It is
this " fearful half-reality " that is the disturbing factor for the
critic. The scene at first seems real, then visionary, and lastly
both real and visionary. The truth is that we have here the
type of reality that pervades practically all Strindberg's works
after the Inferno period. The characters are all in the plane of
" nights of sleepwalking in the broad daylight." The reality is
the half-reality of dreams; not indeed poetic dreams of beautiful
maidens, ethereal love and castles in the air, not dreams of escape

---

[31] *Ibid.,* p. 30.

[32] An apt illustration of Strindberg's views on woman. The Lady, as
woman, does not speculate on the reality of things; indeed, there is a
shade of contempt in her dismissal of the Unknown's queries. See also
note 5, Part I, Chapter V.

[33] Strindberg, XXIX, 367.

from the hard realities of life, but dreams in which the realities come to us in a distorted arrangement of observed reality.

In the second scene, "At the Doctor's House," there is less evidence of *Ausstrahlungen des Ichs*. Only one incident shows the fulfilment of a wish expressed by the Unknown.

> *The Unknown.* But he never leaves us, this terrible werewolf.
>
> *The Doctor* (*looking at his watch*). Pardon me, but I must go away for an hour on a call. Hope you won't find the waiting too long.[34]

Clearly the Doctor's statement is made in answer to the desire of the Unknown which is expressed to the Lady out of the Doctor's hearing.[35]

There are other incidents that partially indicate *Ausstrahlungen des Ichs*. The Unknown hears Mendelssohn's *Funeral March* and is convinced that this music is following him and persecuting him. The subject is dismissed when the Doctor explains that a young lady near by is playing the piano, and he further informs the Unknown that this piece of music is in great vogue. Nevertheless, in spite of explanations that point to observed reality, we have once more the half-reality of the dreamer in this scene. The Unknown is depressed not only by the music and the Doctor's presence, but also by the proximity of an insane man and of cadavers. The place seems to be filled with strange beings.

In the third scene of the play, " A Hotel Room," the Lady and the Unknown are given a room which each has previously occupied in company with someone else. The Unknown also declares that he felt in every step of the way that he was being driven to one particular room, number eight, despite the fact that he also withstood the urge throughout the entire trip. The following conversation in the hotel room is likewise pertinent material.

[34] Strindberg, XXIX, 44.
[35] *Ibid.,* p. 42 (the Doctor, who is the " werewolf," is somewhat deaf).

The Unknown. And there remains only one t̲ing for us. . . .

The Lady. Two!

The Unknown. Yes, but the other is impossible.

The Lady. What is the other one?

The Unknown. To go to your parents in the country.

The Lady. You are already reading my thoughts.

The Unknown. We can no longer have anything secret from each other.

The Lady. Consequently the whole dream breaks. . . .

The Unknown. Perhaps! [36]

It is only natural that the Unknown should read the thoughts of the Lady, for she is a product of his mind. Whatsoever she thinks, says or does has already been formulated in the Unknown's mind. Yet there is also a sense of reality in this conversation, for we know that people who are much together are able " to read each other's thoughts."

In the same scene, the Unknown and the Lady both have visions. The wall-paper pattern forms a picture of the Lady's husband, the Doctor. Then the Unknown is just making out a well-known face in the table-cloth pattern when he is interrupted by hearing once more Mendelssohn's *Funeral March*. On this occasion the Lady hears nothing and the Unknown answers that he must be " on the way " — toward insanity.

In the fourth scene, " By the Seaside," the two have spent three happy days together, but the scene opens with uneasiness creeping over the Unknown. He feels that " fate is spinning its plot "; and once more he hears " the mallet fall and the chairs pushed from the table — judgment has been pronounced," [37] as he heard earlier in the play.[38] He calls especial attention to the crochet work that the Lady has in her hands, and it fascinates him for a time. The Lady has been engaged in this needle-work rather

[36] *Ibid.,* pp. 49–50.   [38] *Ibid.,* p. 30.
[37] *Ibid.,* p. 53.

constantly [39] and now it gains expressionistic significance through
the Unknown.

> *The Unknown.* What is it you are working on so constantly; like one
> of the Parcae you sit there and draw the thread through your
> fingers . . . but do so! One of the most beautiful sights I can
> think of is to see a woman bent over her work or her child. What
> are you working on?
>
> *The Lady.* It is nothing, just a bit of fancy work. . . .
>
> *The Unknown.* It looks like a mesh of nerves and knots where your
> thoughts are fixed. I can imagine that your brain looks like that
> on the inside. . . .
>
> *The Lady.* If only I had half the thoughts you wish to ascribe to me;
> but I haven't any at all!
>
> *The Unknown.* Probably that is why I enjoy your company so much,
> because I find you so complete that I can't think of an existence
> without you! Now the cloud drew away! Now the heavens are
> high, the wind is soft; feel how it caresses! This is life! Yes, I live
> now, just now. And I feel my ego swell, expand, become thin,
> become infinite; I am everywhere, in the sea which is my blood,
> in the mountains which are my skeleton, in the trees, in the flowers.
> And my head reaches up into the heavens. I look out over the
> universe which is my Self, and I feel the Creator's whole power in
> me, for I am that One. I should like to take the whole mass in
> my hand and knead it over again to something more complete, more
> enduring and more beautiful. . . . I should like to see every
> created thing and every creature happy: born without pain, live
> without sorrow, and die in quiet joy! Eve! Will you die with
> me, now, in this very moment, since in the next one pain will
> sweep over us again? [40]

The Unknown, the mouthpiece of the dramatist, is clearly an
expressionist. Here is supersubjectivism, the world and ego
flowing together in the supersubjective individual, according to
the words of Marzynski. We recall also the statement, " The
expressionists . . . desire to reshape reality until the art-form
emerges from the nature-form." [41] Pfister's words, too, are
applicable to the Unknown's character: " The expressionist
creates out of the depths of things, because he knows himself to

[39] Strindberg, XXIX, 12, 37, 45, 51, 52, 54.
[40] *Ibid.,* p. 54.   [41] See above, pp. 12, 18.

be in these depths. To paint out of himself and to paint himself means to reproduce the intrinsic nature of things, the Absolute. The artist creates as God creates, out of his own inner Self, and in his own likeness." [42] The Unknown is certainly an expressionist and whatsoever world we find about him will be created out of his own being. It is only through him and in him that the other characters of this drama have existence.

In the same scene the Lady cautions the Unknown about speaking in such a fashion, for then he seems to be so much like the insane man back home, like Caesar! The Unknown is greatly perturbed by the likeness between himself and this insane man. The spectator or reader of this drama is reminded that for the third time the Unknown has been likened to some other character: to the Beggar, to the Dead Man and now to Caesar. These are nothing more or less than radiations from the Unknown's ego. They are three of his " selves."

A little later in the same scene the fancy work gathers added significance, and demonstrates to some extent that it actually is the " inside of the Lady's brain." The Unknown has just challenged the " Powers," to the great distress of the Lady.

> *The Lady.* May heaven never punish you. . . .
>
> *The Unknown.* The heavens are just as blue and just as mute; the sea is just as blue and stupid. . . . Hush, I hear a poem coming. . . . I call it that because when a motif begins to grow in my brain . . . but I hear the rhythm first . . . this time it is like the trotting of horses, the clang of spurs and the rattle of weapons . . . but there is a fluttering also, like the flapping of a sail; it is the flags.
>
> *The Lady.* No, it is the wind that you hear soughing in the trees. . . .
>
> *The Unknown.* Now they are riding over a bridge, but it is a wooden bridge and there is no water in the river, only flint-stone . . . wait! Now I hear the chanting of a rosary, men and women; the Angelus; but now I see — do you know where? — in your crochet work — a large kitchen, it is white, the walls are calcimined; there are three small but deep windows with lattice and flowers; to the left,

---

[42] See above, p. 20.

in the corner, is the hearth; to the right, the dining table with
pine benches; and over the table in the corner stands a black
crucifix; underneath, a lamp is burning . . . but the beams of the
ceiling are blackened with soot! . . . and on the walls there hangs
mistletoe, somewhat dried out. . . .

The Lady (terrified). Where do you see all this? Where?

The Unknown. In your fancy work. . . .[43]

The Lady is frightened by the seerlike powers of the Unknown,
especially when he continues in the same manner to describe the
people of the house. The Unknown suddenly awakens as though
from a trance and cries out that this was no poem. The Lady
answers that it was reality; it is her home, the home of her
parents, that the Unknown has described. As he sees all this in
the fancy work, it is clear that he either has the gift of second
sight or else is responsible for everything in the drama, even for
the home of the Lady's parents.

It is easy to recognize all this as a projection from the mind
of the Unknown, with the crochet work a symbol of the Lady's
mind. She actually has no thoughts of her own;[44] she is Eve and
impersonal[45] and there is really nothing to say about her.[46] She
is indeed nothing, but the Unknown intends to make something
out of her.[47] He reads her mind[48] and also declares that this
fancy work looks like her brain turned inside out.[49] The Lady,
then, is clearly a *tabula rasa* apart from the Unknown, and she
owes him whatsoever existence she possesses. Everything radiates from the Unknown's ego: The Lady, her fancy work and
the interpretation of the latter. This character, the Unknown, is,
as Diebold has already pointed out,[50] an expressionistic monologist, and not one among several other characters.

The seventh scene, " In the Kitchen," gives us more information

---

[43] Strindberg, XXIX, 58–59. [47] *Ibid.,* p. 16.
[44] *Ibid.,* p. 54. [48] *Ibid.,* p. 49.
[45] *Ibid.,* p. 13. [49] *Ibid.,* p. 54.
[46] *Ibid.,* p. 12. [50] Diebold, *Anarchie im Drama,* p. 165.

regarding Eve, the Lady, and also additional manifestations of
the radiating ego. The Mother asks the Unknown why he calls
the Lady " Eve," since her name is Ingeborg.

> *The Unknown.* By giving her a name of my own invention, I have
> made her mine, just as I intend to refashion her according to my
> own ideas.
>
> *The Mother.* In the image of yourself! [51] (*Smiles*) I have heard
> that the sorcerers in the country are in the habit of making a
> scarecrow image of the one they wish to bewitch; and then they
> baptize it with the name of the one they wish to cast a spell upon.
> It is so you have reckoned on doing with your self-made Eve —
> to destroy her whole family.
>
> *The Unknown.* The Devil you say! Pardon, you are my mother-in-
> law, but you are also religious. How can you conceive such
> thoughts?
>
> *The Mother.* They are yours.[52]

Once again thoughts are turned back to the Unknown as the
creator. Strindberg also gives us the comment of the country
folk on the character of the Unknown. The Old Man, grand-
father to the Lady, reports that the people are superstitious.
There is no doubt in their minds, that the Unknown is a Mephistophelian character. The boatman swore that the boat grew
lighter as the Unknown stepped in. Another declared that his
horse had shied at the newcomer. And still another had to bind
his dogs when the Unknown drew near. At that very moment, the
Old Man, partly inclined to superstition himself, declares that a
magpie just flew in through the closed window, through the window pane! [53] Strindberg allows this view to the credulous, but it
is clear throughout the entire drama that the Unknown is not a
Mephistopheles.[54] While far from being a Faust, the Unknown

[51] See above, pp. 20, 133.
[52] Strindberg, XXIX, 72–73.
[53] *Ibid.,* p. 76.
[54] The Unknown, however, may be compared to Aeschylus' *Prometheus,*
Milton's *Satan,* and Strindberg's *Lucifer* in the *Postludium* to the verse
edition of *Master Olof.*

is much closer to him in character than he is to Mephistopheles. Here is no witchery, no mechanical diablerie, but the half-reality of dream life that is found in " nights of sleepwalking in broad daylight." Everything is born in the Unknown's own soul.

The third act opens with the eighth scene of the play, " The Rose-room," with the Lady seated and busy with her fancy work. Through the door in the background one sees an ugly building, the poorhouse. The sun shines brightly into the rose-room, but the poorhouse in the background is an ominous symbol that evil is approaching. Likewise, the Lady's industry with the crochet work is a sign of the feverish working of the mind of the Unknown. In a conversation with the Mother, the Lady declares that the Unknown anticipates everything she says. There is nothing that he has not already heard even before she has spoken. Consequently, the two talk but little.[55] Yet the Unknown and the Lady seem to be living happily together.

The Mother urges her daughter to read the Unknown's last book. In spite of a promise that she would not do so [56] the Lady accepts the book from her Mother with the intention of reading it. Scarcely has she done so when she hears the Unknown coming.

> *The Lady (hiding the book in her pocket).* He is coming now! It's just as though he felt at a long distance that people were talking about him.

> *The Mother.* Would that he also might feel it when people suffer for his sake — at a great distance (*she goes*).

> *The Lady (alone for a moment; reads at random in the book; seems astonished; hides the book in her pocket).*

> *The Unknown (comes in).* Your mother was here; naturally you were speaking about me. I seem even now to hear the vibrations of her evil words; I feel how they lash the air and darken the sun's rays. I think that I can trace in this air the impression of her body standing in the room; and she leaves an odor behind her like a crushed snake.[57]

---

[55] Strindberg, XXIX, 80.   [56] *Ibid.,* p. 21.   [57] *Ibid.,* p. 81.

The Unknown soon learns that the Lady has read his book,[58] for his intuition spies out everything. The Lady, who thus far has been quite unmoral, without conscience,[59] now has her eyes opened; she sees how evil *the Unknown is!* [60] Paradise is consequently lost, so the Unknown departs.

The next scene in the third act, the ninth in the drama, takes place in the Asylum, a religious institution called " The Good Help." In the room there are characters recalling all who have appeared in the earlier part of the drama and some who have only been mentioned. In the stage directions, Strindberg says that the faces of these characters are a yellow waxlike color: they are like the faces of corpses. The whole group has not only a ghostly appearance but also a weird manner of behavior. The Unknown declares that all these people seem to be acquaintances of his, that he seems to see them as in a mirror. He even asks the Abbess if these people are real or if this is only a play being performed.[61] He sees one pair, for example, that reminds him of his parents. The Abbess calls the Confessor who comes to the Unknown and explains who these individuals are. They are much like the insane man " Caesar," the Beggar, the Doctor, the Unknown's parents and all the others. There is even one figure like the Lady, who is busy with fancy work. The Confessor, however, gives no hint that he is aware of any relationship between these people and the Unknown.

Here is a superb example of *Ausstrahlungen des Ichs.* The café scene in Act I is without question projected from the mind of the Unknown, but the dramatist gave us no direct assistance in making this decision. Here, however, there is no question; the stage directions, the speech of the Confessor, the attitude of the Unknown, the reading of the Deuteronomic curses, the action of the shadow characters, all reveal that the ego of the Unknown

[58] *Ibid.,* p. 85.
[59] *Ibid.,* pp. 69, 72.
[60] *Ibid.,* p. 87.
[61] *Ibid.,* p. 91.

is enstaged. All these people have arisen from the Unknown's evil conscience and are reading the Deuteronomic curses over him.

The Unknown is in need of blessings after all these curses. This time, as usual with Strindberg, the aspergillum is wielded by a woman instead of a priest. The Unknown starts back to the Lady, in search of mercy. And the rest of the eight scenes in Part I are the same as those preceding the Asylum scene, except that they are given in reverse order, the play ending at the street corner where it began.

The second half of Part I is much like the first, so we may be content with a few examples. In the last scene of the third act, the second kitchen scene, the Unknown says, " Afterwards I had to remain standing on the floor and see again the whole panorama of life unrolled, all, all . . . and that is the worst of it." [62] The Unknown has made the same observation twice before.[63] Indeed, it is rather clear through the play that past events are continually unrolling themselves before the Unknown. He also reminds his Mother-in-law that things occur in a strange fashion, even as he once saw that very same kitchen in — in an ecstasy, if she prefers to call it that.[64]

In the second scene of " The Hotel Room " the Unknown remarks that the panorama has become a cosmorama. At night he has had the terrible dream that the Doctor is about to marry his former wife and become the stepfather to his children.[65] That this is more than dream is revealed later in the play.[66] It is also in this hotel room that the Lady comes to the end of her thread and the crochet work is finished. The work is filthy, but it has the tale of the Unknown and the Lady in its pattern, colored by the filth of the highway, by tears and blood.[67]

This whole drama, *To Damascus*, I, teems with examples of

[62] Strindberg, XXIX, 107.   [65] *Ibid.*, p. 123.
[63] *Ibid.*, pp. 86, 100.   [66] *Ibid.*, pp. 131, 205.
[64] *Ibid.*, p. 110.   [67] *Ibid.*, p. 125.

Ausstrahlungen des Ichs, and reveals that the play *in toto* is one of the purest expressionistic dramas. It is rich with autobiographical data, though this is necessarily distorted; the play is enacted by type characters; and all the characters are projections from the mind of the one main character, the Unknown. Certainly in this drama one may well say that Strindberg is gazing in the magic crystal of the ego and selecting for his drama the elements that are in play in this wonder-glass. The drama as a whole radiates from the ego of Strindberg, even as the drama radiates from the ego of the Unknown.

THE " POWERS," *UR*-ISHNESS, DISTORTION AND REALITY

THROUGHOUT the drama the Unknown is obviously in a struggle with the " Powers "; and this combat presents an antithesis of the natural and the supernatural, the mortal and the infinite, the visible and the invisible. The characters of the play are projections from the evil conscience of the Unknown, and each one is a concrete manifestation of the " Powers." Through the Lady the " Powers " are offering an example of the struggle between the sexes. Also the Lady, as type woman, is an antithesis within herself. Through one woman sin was fastened on the human race; through another it was removed.[68] The Doctor is a reminder of guilt, a finger pointing at the Unknown and calling to his attention that he has sinned. With all his claims of having searched for the truth, of having tried to contribute to the well-being of himself and others, the Unknown nevertheless has made many miserable and is himself a wretched creature. The Beggar is the manifestation through which the " Powers " indicate to the Unknown that with all his learning, with all his pretensions to philosophic research, he is, nevertheless, a character in rags hunting cigar stumps in the gutter. Caesar, a very shadowy

---

[68] *Ibid.,* p. 88

figure in the first act, constantly calls to mind the Unknown's
dubious state of mind, and also the disastrous effect that the
Unknown's works have had on other people.[69]   The Mother is
employed by the " Powers " to indicate the struggle of the sexes
and also the Unknown's own guilt; the Mother was forsaken by
her husband even as the Unknown forsook his first wife and their
children.

The concept of the " Powers " points at times to something
Absolute that is in and over everything; at other times to a pur-
suing Nemesis.   Moreover, the " Powers " also arise from the
Unknown's own mind.   In the first " By the Seaside " scene, the
Unknown has expressed the idea that he is God, the Creator,
the whole universe; [70] and a little later in the same scene he cries
out against the " Powers."

> *The Unknown.* . . . Now the glove is cast, and you shall witness a
> set-to between big folk! (*He opens his coat and vest and casts
> threatening glances upwards.*)   Come!   Strike me with your thun-
> der, if you dare!   Scare me with your storm, if you can!
>
> *The Lady.* No, no! don't do that!
>
> *The Unknown.* Yes, just that! that!   Who ventures to disturb me in
> my love dream?   Who snatches the cup from my lips and the
> woman from my arms?   Ye envious ones, gods or devils!   Little
> burgher-gods who parry the sword with a thrust of the needle
> from behind; who don't meet in the field, but who answer with an
> unpaid bill at the kitchen in order to belittle the master before
> his servants.   Not to strike, to hew with naked metal, but to spit
> upon and to yell . . . fie!   Powers, potentates, princes, fie! [71]

It seems that the " Powers " themselves have scarcely more than
a " half-reality," the dream type of reality that comes from inner
experience projected into material form.   The " Powers " come
from the Unknown's ego as well as the visible characters.

The idea of " Powers " as an unalterable fate also runs through
the play.   At the very opening of the play [72] the Unknown is

---

[69] Strindberg, XXIX, 92 (see also note 15 of this chapter).
[70] *Ibid.*, p. 54 (see p. 132 above).   [71] *Ibid.*, p. 58.   [72] *Ibid.*, p. 8.

wondering if there are people already damned in life, and tells the Lady to look upon himself as an excellent example. In the first " Hotel Room " scene, he finds himself paralyzed and unable to do what reason dictates; it is as though Fate demanded an act of folly.[73] Again, the Lady says that no one can escape his fate.[74] At the same time she senses that the " Powers " have held consultation over her and the Unknown and come to some conclusion regarding their fate. Even the Unknown admits that he could actually hear the gavel fall, the chairs pushed away from the table and the messenger sent out. The idea that fate is unalterable occurs again and again throughout the drama, now from the lips of one character and then from another.[75]

Ur-ishness is more in the atmosphere than in the language of the play. The Lady, as Eve, is the *ur*-mother of us all and also the *ur*-sinner. The Unknown himself has early been called a " deliverer "[76] and apparently would free people from restraint. He tells the Lady that he could not bear to see people suffer, so he cried out, " Free yourselves and I shall help you." He told the poor not to let the rich sap their strength, the woman not to let her husband subjugate her, and children not to obey their parents when the latter were unjust; and, as a result, the Unknown had against him both rich and poor, husband and wife, parents and children.[77] The Doctor, in referring to the Unknown's capacity as a deliverer, says that it is probably well that people are fond of their shackles.[78] The Unknown, however, would deliver people from the bonds of convention in order that the injustice of civilization might be rooted out. In other words, the Unknown would inaugurate the reign of pure *Seele*.

We can gather an idea of the *ur*-ish qualities still more patently when the Lady asks, " Have we done wrong? " and the Unknown

[73] *Ibid.*, p. 50.
[74] *Ibid.*, p. 29.
[75] *Ibid.*, pp. 29, 32, 51, 53, 71, 72, 77, 84, 119, 133. [77] *Ibid.*, p. 15.
[76] *Ibid.*, pp. 15, 31, 37. [78] *Ibid.*, p. 38.

answers by asking another question, "What is wrong?"[79]   The
two are as unmoral as the *ur*-pair of the human race.   The
Mother also senses that her daughter is quite lacking in conscience,[80] so much so that she later says to her, "I don't know
whether you were born with all the wisdom of the world or
whether you are just simple-minded."[81]   A sharper emphasis is
placed on the *ur*-qualities when the Lady has read the last book
written by the Unknown.   Then she has eaten from the tree of the
knowledge of good and evil and has acquired a moral sense.[82]
Both the Unknown and the Lady are symbols of the *ur*-ishness
that persists within us and of the constant recurrence of the ideas
of good and evil.[83]

There is a further significance to the Unknown if we allow
ourselves to be tempted.   In the miracle play *De Creatione et
Sententia Vera Mundi* [84] Strindberg has portrayed Lucifer, the
Light-bringer, as the good power who is being persecuted by the
evil power, God.   Lucifer attempts to free the earth-people by
tempting them to eat of the tree and learn the difference between
good and evil that they might see how evil life is.   But God, the
Evil Power, conquers so completely, that the earth-people regard
Lucifer as the Devil, as the evil power.   Since Strindberg implies
in the *Inferno* [85] that he is being punished for having written the
miracle play, it seems inescapable that he should still have this
play in mind one year later when he was writing the first part of
To Damascus.   It seems very reasonable to call the Unknown a
typical man, the mouthpiece of Strindberg, and also the repre-

---

[79] Strindberg, XXIX, 60.
[80] *Ibid.,* p. 72.
[81] *Ibid.,* p. 80.
[82] *Ibid.,* p. 87.
[83] Note that the Lady is strongly qualified by *Seele* whereas the Unknown is *Seele* struggling in *Geist*. See above, note 5, Part One, Chapter V,
and pp. 72–77.
[84] Strindberg, II, 312–319 (see also above, pp. 91–92).
[85] *Ibid.,* XXVIII, 204.

sentative of the Good Power who is being mercilessly whipped by the Evil Power.

Elements of distortion are also closely bound with the elements of *Ausstrahlungen des Ichs,* as we have already seen, and with the concept of reality as well. The Strindberg letter to Geijerstam [86] declares that the drama has a " fearful half-reality behind it," but even without this letter the drama itself gives us enough evidence. In the first scene the Lady has cried out in horror that the Unknown is " playing with death." His reply gives us a cue to his concept of reality in life and in works of art.

> *The Unknown.* Just as I play with life — I was a writer. In spite of my inborn gloominess I have never been able to take anything seriously, not even my own great sorrows, and there are moments when I doubt that life has any more reality than my own writings.[87]

This is the kind of statement that not only lives in the play itself but also has a " fearful half-reality " about it. It leaps out of the play and fastens itself upon Strindberg's own character.[88] Critics who hasten forward to point out that Strindberg has this or that to say in a certain literary product must always face this dilemma: Strindberg's life and works are so intertwined that it is extremely difficult to determine whether his life is a gesture from his works or his works purely radiation from his life. Strindberg so lives in his literature and his life that his concept of reality in the one is conditioned by his concept of reality in the other.

It is here that we encounter distortion of observed reality because of inner experience. But even more than that Strindberg baffles us at times by presenting observed reality and inner experience in a combination that permits the spectator or the reader to see both at once. His works are by no means the result of " thoroughgoing introversion " in which the bridges between sub-

[86] *Ibid.,* XXIX, 367 (see also above, p. 129).
[87] *Ibid.,* p. 9.
[88] See also letter apropos of *The Father,* p. 100 above.

ject and object are completely broken. It is this " half-reality " that Strindberg presents, a standing *on the bridge* with complete uncertainty regarding the direction he will take, even as the Unknown stands on the street corner at the opening of *To Damascus*.

For the Unknown, reality has changed from the mere report of observations to a contemplation of meanings.[89] He no longer sees objects and incidents, but thoughts and meanings. Moreover, the whole universe ceases to be a chaos of chance objects and chance occurrences; it is now the manifestation of a purpose. If the Unknown is the mouthpiece of the author of *Inferno*, he will see meanings in chance scraps of paper, the message in a book that opens to a particular page as though some higher power were turning the pages; and he will be able to give a mystical interpretation to every movement of earth stuff.[90] If the Unknown goes back to *De Creatione et Sententia Vera Mundi*, he knows that the purpose of this life on earth is the diversion of the gods. In *To Damascus*, however, we must credit the Unknown with his own expressionistic nature; he seeks for the heart of reality behind the superficial objective manifestations.

There is also a little tale in the first scene that demands our attention. The Unknown tells the Lady that in his family there runs a story that he is a changeling, that he himself is actually an elf's child.[91] He admits readily enough that he does not take much stock in the story, but he thinks that there is an astonishing similarity between himself and an elf's child. When the Lady a little later refers to this story the Unknown hastily dismisses it with the careless explanation, " That was only a tale! " Nevertheless, he continues to refer to the elves until the Lady requests him not to distress her with further mention of the story. The

[89] Strindberg, XXIX, 10.

[90] Note that the title of the first chapter of *Inferno* (Strindberg, XXVIII) is " Den Osynliges hand," that is, " The Hand of the Invisible One."

[91] Strindberg, XXIX, 11.

Unknown replies, " To tell the truth, I don't believe in them, but just the same they are always coming back. Aren't elves cursed spirits which haven't received salvation? Well, then I am also the child of a troll." Later on in the drama, the Unknown now and then calls to mind the elf story. He does not have any particular faith in the tale, but even elves have this " fearful half-reality " about them. Besides, is there any more reality in life than in the author's works, or in stories about elves?

The first time that we encounter the Beggar in the drama we well ask with the Unknown what kind of reality this creature possesses. He is, of course, clearly a projection from the mind of the Unknown, and his reality is of the same kind that we meet in dreams, a sort of paradoxical real-unreal. It is distortion of observed reality, but as true a reproduction as possible of the inner experience that has been stimulated by objective reality. Even the Unknown himself is in a condition that is rather precarious for the maintenance of observed reality.

> *The Unknown.* . . . It seems as though I am lying all hacked to pieces in Medea's kettle and cooking slowly: either I shall be going to the soap-works or else arise rejuvenated from my own bouillon! All depends on Medea's proficiency.[92]

The figure of speech may be applied to the conditions of reality, whether or not Strindberg himself thought it out in this fashion: All the conditions of observed reality are hacked to fine pieces when poured into the unconscious; dependent on the proficiency of the ego, a new inner experience is born of the old objective one or else everything becomes mere refuse.[93]

The entire scene of the burial assistants and guests at the tavern is not only a dream scene but also an explanation of reality and distortion in the play. When the Unknown asks the guests

---

[92] *Ibid.*, p. 23.

[93] This is not offered as evidence, but as a reasonable interpretation employing expressionistic cant.

why they are dressed in brown instead of the regulation mourning color, black, the guests reply that they are actually dressed in black; but " if, sir, you so command, it shall be brown for you." [94] The Unknown then asks if the spruce-brash is possibly something else and receives the answer that it is part of a grape-vine. The scene is without question inserted by the author to stress the half-reality of this drama, its dream character, its conscious distortion of observed reality and its objectification of the inner experiences of the Unknown.

The first " By the Seaside " scene is another that beggars analysis unless it is just a mechanical device to create suspense. The Unknown, in ecstasy, describes the Lady's home, and he declares that he sees the whole vision in the pattern of the fancy work. When the Unknown subsides into his ordinary self he cries out, " This is not a poem," and the Lady declares, " It is reality." [95] We comment once more that it is the half-reality that is born of pure inner experience and of observed reality. The Lady, her fancy work, and the vision in the latter are all radiations from the ego of the Unknown. The scene is, in spite of the Unknown's declaration, a poem. It is a poetic observation on reality.

This state of half-reality is well illustrated once more in the first " At the Gorge " scene. Everything that the Unknown sees has a natural explanation for its appearance and yet bears something unreal about it. The Unknown cannot escape the conviction that things are bewitched, in spite of their apparent normality. He even sees the profile of the Doctor in the rock. The Lady points to the evil conscience as the source of the apparition,[96] more evidence of inner experience conditioning objective reality.

Likewise, the asylum scene is clearly a projection of the Unknown's ego, a distortion of observed reality which, like the stuff

[94] Strindberg, XXIX, 25.   [95] *Ibid.,* p. 59.   [96] *Ibid.,* p. 64.

of dreams, has been collecting in the memory for many years.
When the Unknown asks about the other people in the asylum
and wonders if they are actually human beings, the Abbess replies
with ambiguity, ". . . they possess a fearful reality. That you
probably see them somewhat awry is due to the fact that you
still have fever, or . . . to something else." [97] Indeed, throughout the whole play the concept of reality is cued with that early
statement of the Unknown regarding reality in life and in his
own works.[98]

THE RELATION TO MUSIC

A READING of the *To Damascus* trilogy reveals that music plays
an important rôle. Indeed, Strindberg took special pains to
arrange even for the music that was to precede each act,[99] as
well as for the music that is contained within the drama.

In the first scene of the drama a funeral march seems to be
approaching and then drawing away, to the discomfort of the
Unknown. When he has named the Lady " Eve " and joyously
cries out for fanfares, the funeral march responds.[100] Later, the
playing of the organ in the church serves as an announcement
that the tavern will soon be open and one may begin to drink
again.[101] When the Unknown is uncomfortably involved in the
tavern scene, taunted with being wanted by the police, he cries
out that it looks much like an intrigue. The vision is at once
broken by music. The church bells ring, and one hears the organ
playing and the choir singing as the sun comes out in brilliance.[102]
In the scene " At the Doctor's House " the Unknown hears once

[97] *Ibid.,* p. 91.
[98] *Ibid.,* p. 9 (see also p. 143 above).
[99] Hellström, Victor, *Strindberg och musiken,* p. 35.
[100] Strindberg, XXIX, 13.
[101] *Ibid.,* p. 22 (this is also an example of the kind of humor found in
Strindberg's works).
[102] *Ibid.,* p. 28 (is it possible that church bells function here as in
Ibsen's *Peer Gynt,* to scare away the trolls? See Archer translation of
Ibsen's Works, IV, 83).

more Mendelssohn's *Funeral March* and it seems that the music is persecuting him.[103]   Throughout the play music, as sound, contributes to the mood of the various situations.

Musical form also applies to the dialogue in *To Damascus*. We recall that in his preface to *Miss Julia* Strindberg speaks of dialogue written like a musical composition.[104]   This form of dialogue did not appear strongly in *Miss Julia*, but it is of great significance in post-Inferno dramas. If we also look at a later drama, *The Regent*,[105] we find a note referring to *To Damascus*. In this note Strindberg says that he is using the same device for scenic arrangement in *The Last Knight*[106] and *The Regent* that he used in the first part of *To Damascus*. " This contrapuntal form, borrowed from music, which I used in *Damascus*, I, carries this effect with it; the listener is reminded of the different places previously enstaged, and thereby the drama functions as though occurring far in the future with a great deal behind it. . . ."[107]

This so-called contrapuntal form refers specifically to the arrangement of the scenes. The drama begins at the street corner, passes to the Doctor's house, the hotel room, the seaside, the highway, the gorge, the kitchen, the rose-room and the asylum. The play mounts up and up until the asylum scene is reached as a climax; then the play falls away through the same scenes in reverse order until once more we have the Unknown seated on the street corner writing in the sand. This last part is quite comparable to dénouement, only here it is a scenic dénouement.

This polyphonic form would be rather superficial if it existed only in the arrangement of the scenes in three or four of Strindberg's dramas. But, with the statement of Strindberg's preface to *Miss Julia* in mind, we may study the dialogue itself for further evidence of contrapuntal form. An analysis proves that throughout the entire drama, especially Part I, which we are dis-

[103] Strindberg, XXIX, 38.   [104] See above, pp. 104–105.
[105] Strindberg, XLIX (an historical drama, written 1908).
[106] *Ibid.* (also an historical drama written 1908).   [107] *Ibid.,* p. 138.

cussing, there are not simply ideas coming again and again in new dress but also phrases that are nearly identical in form as well as ideational value.[108] Very early in the play [109] the Unknown informs the Lady that he has no more sins on his conscience than other people who walk about the streets unmolested by the police, except for one sin: " I didn't wish to be life's fool." It is woven into the drama once more when he says, " I did not want to be life's dupe "; [110] and again with the addition, " and therefore I became it! " [111] Even in the third part of *To Damascus* the idea is repeated in Father Melcher's discussion of Kierkegaard: ". . . because he did not want to be life's fool he wrote articles under different pseudonyms, representing each as a ' Station on the Road of Life ' . . . but the Lord of life made him the fool in spite of all his precautions." [112]

The Unknown also asks a question that heightens the mystic atmosphere of the play and likewise provides the sensation of something coming vividly out of the past. When the Unknown first meets the Doctor, he says, " Haven't we met before — in our youth? " [113] The same question is also put to the Confessor in the asylum scene.[114] In the third part of the drama, the Unknown asks a pilgrim the same question and receives the enlightening reply that the latter is none other than Caesar, the insane man of Part I.[115] Likewise, the same idea is employed in the first conversation between the Unknown and the Mother, though in a little different guise. The Unknown says, " I have seen this room before," to which the Mother answers, " And I have seen you before." [116] This last little dialogue is not only

---

[108] Some critics contend that Strindberg was carelessly and unintentionally repetitious, owing to hasty work. There is sufficient evidence to warrant the belief that the dramatist was repetitious for the contrapuntal effect.

[109] Strindberg, XXIX, 10.

[110] *Ibid.*, p. 102.

[111] *Ibid.*, p. 135.

[112] *Ibid.*, p. 357.

[113] *Ibid.*, p. 37.

[114] *Ibid.*, p. 92.

[115] *Ibid.*, p. 293.

[116] *Ibid.*, p. 71.

functional in the contrapuntal arrangement, but recalls once more *Ausstrahlungen des Ichs* and typification. It is worth a slight digression from our subject to note that this room is a typical one because the setting is typical, an unpleasant dialogue of mother-in-law and son-in-law. The Unknown has seen that room before because he has experienced the same kind of conversation before. Moreover, the Mother has seen the Unknown before because the latter is a typical man. The Mother's husband ran away, deserting wife and children; the Unknown has done the same. Indeed, though experiences seem to differ one from the other, they are after all variations on the same theme, they are only repetitions, and the type experience gathers all unto itself.

Another example of contrapuntal arrangement is found in the Unknown's request: " Tell a little about yourself now! " He says this twice to the Lady in the first scene [117] and once in the rose-room scene.[118] Each time also the idea is presented as a sharp break with the preceding material. Likewise, the significance of the Lady's fancy work is built up by frequent repetition of the image which is brought to mind either through stage directions, " the Lady crochets," or through the dialogue.[119] " The Lady crochets " becomes a constant reminder that the fates are busy making patterns of the lives of the dramatis personae. Similarly, the Unknown's writing in the sand has the effect of the reiteration of a musical theme,[120] and also alludes to biblical material.[121] An idea that becomes the leitmotif of *A Dream Play* [122] is given once in Part I of *To Damascus*,[123] and twice in Part II,[124] in a slightly modified form.

The Unknown also talked considerably about money during his

---

[117] Strindberg, XXIX, 12, 14.   [118] *Ibid.*, p. 87.
[119] *Ibid.*, pp. 12, 37, 45, 51, 52, 54, 59, 79, 93, 95, 121, 125.
[120] *Ibid.*, pp. 16, 19, 20, 24, 133.
[121] John 8:6.   [123] Strindberg, XXIX, 75.
[122] " Mankind is to be pitied."   [124] *Ibid.*, pp. 158, 195.

delirium in the asylum,[125] a subject that is in his mind throughout the play.[126]   In fact, it is this subject of money that has given whatever motivation this play possesses.   The Unknown's capricious behavior in refusing to call for a letter at the post-office led to his financial distress and consequently to the major portion of his troubles.   It is only at the end of Part I, when the Unknown is again on the street corner, that he obtains the letter and learns that money has been awaiting him all the time.[127]

Then there are other ideas that come in again and again like harmonies or dissonances sounded before: biblical allusions,[128] conscience,[129] hate,[130] insanity,[131] the " deliverer," [132] suffering,[133] the forsaken wife.[134]   Music as sound also threads its way through the drama.[135] We should likewise note that the idea of suffering becomes stronger and stronger throughout the second [136] and third [137] parts of the drama.

This analysis has been carried out still further in the preparations for the writing of this book, but a greater mass of detail is not essential to establish evidence.   In this same way one could trace the references to and appearances of the Beggar, the Doctor, and " Caesar "; the referential and concrete manifesta-

[125] *Ibid.,* p. 90.
[126] *Ibid.,* pp. 18, 22, 45, 49, 53, 57, 62, 65, 67, 73, 74, 77, 80, 83, 90, 101, 103, 113, 134.
[127] One cannot escape the suggestion that Part I is a day-dream which the Unknown has experienced while seated on the bench and writing in the sand with his cane.
[128] Strindberg, XXIX, 23, 56, 68, 86, 87, 90, 93, 102, 103, 110, 113, 116, 118, 119, 121, 128.
[129] *Ibid.,* pp. 10, 23, 65, 72, 85, 96, 107, 113, 119, 132.
[130] *Ibid.,* pp. 11, 13, 14, 33, 42, 82, 83, 99, 102, 103, 131.
[131] *Ibid.,* pp. 15, 20, 28, 33, 40, 50, 89, 98, 123, 129, 130.
[132] *Ibid.,* pp. 15, 21, 27, 30, 31, 37, 45, 52, 64, 93, 119, 124.
[133] *Ibid.,* pp. 23, 55, 69, 108, 119, 121, 124, 131.
[134] *Ibid.,* pp. 8, 26, 27, 60, 73, 93, 123, 131.
[135] *Ibid.,* pp. 7, 9, 13, 22, 28, 31, 38, 45, 66, 93, 116, 133.
[136] *Ibid.,* pp. 140, 157, 173, 176, 177, 206, 212, 214, 226, 227, 229.
[137] *Ibid.,* pp. 240, 242, 265, 280, 281, 284, 290, 291, 292, 294, 295, 301, 308, 310, 326, 347, 348, 362.

tions of the " Powers "; and so on, almost endlessly. The evidence already given, however, is complete enough to prove conclusively that Strindberg has fashioned the dialogue in the manner suggested in the preface to *Miss Julia*. What he failed to accomplish in the dialogue of *Miss Julia* [138] he developed to a considerable extent in the post-Inferno works. Though some repetition may be due to accident and hasty work, there is much that is planned and arranged contrapuntally.

There is still another illustration of the so-called contrapuntal method. The asylum scene is in itself the most remarkable of all the examples. It contains elements of practically everything that has appeared earlier in the drama, and even characters only mentioned in the dialogue are given material form. The brown-clad funeral assistants are there; a woman in mourning with two children represents the Unknown's first wife and children, and also declares through her dress that the Unknown is " dead " to her; a woman who looks like the Lady, but is not, though she too is crocheting; a man who looks like the Doctor, but is not; a Caesar likeness; and others who appear like various relatives of both the Unknown and the Lady. In the conversation between the Unknown and the Abbess, the latter says that the former was found with a broken cross in his hand threatening someone whom he imagined he saw in the clouds. This calls back to the readers the Unknown's struggle with the " Powers " in the scene mentioned earlier [139] as well as other occasions preceding the asylum scene.[140] On one of these occasions the Unknown cried out, " I should like to spit Fate in the face," [141] which is rather contemptuous of the Unseen One if not exactly threatening him. And just before the asylum scene the Unknown has declared, " I have heard that one can struggle with God, and not without

[138] See also Lamm, I, 320–321.
[139] See above, p. 140.
[140] Strindberg, XXIX, 48, 51, 58–60, 65, 82–84, 87.   [141] *Ibid.*, p. 83.

some success, but to battle with Satan — not even Job could do
that! " [142]

The Abbess also tells the Unknown that he was constantly
complaining of a pain in the hip even though examinations revealed no injury.[143] A later conversation between the Beggar
and the Lady gives a Mephistophelian hue to the hip injury.[144]
The diabolical character had already been given to the Unknown
in his own statement that he is one of the damned [145] as well as
in the conversations between the Mother and the Old Man.[146]

The entire asylum scene, in fact, presents a picture of events
of the past now gathered up and fashioned into a phantasmagoria.
It is the constant cry of Strindberg's later dramas, " Everything
repeats itself," that is both heard and demonstrated in *To
Damascus*.[147] The drama is gathered up in the eight scenes preceding the asylum, the elements are all combined in the one scene,
and then the drama unfolds itself gradually throughout the last
eight scenes. It is the so-called contrapuntal method in staging
and in dialogue. The staging is given in single counterpoint, and
the dialogue in manifold counterpoint.

THE DRAMATIC UNITIES

EXPRESSIONISTIC drama has been characterized as lacking or
ignoring the unities in time, place and action.[148] With respect
to place in *To Damascus*, I, we find nine so-called real scenes,
with no attempt whatsoever to regard unity of place unless the
dream framework be allowed for all these scenes. The element of
time is also of no significance. Scene nine is apparently three
months removed from scene eight,[149] but the whole drama is
rather indifferent to the element of time. The contrapuntal scene
arrangement makes the play seem relatively long as one struggles

[142] *Ibid.*, p. 87. [146] *Ibid.*, pp. 69, 76.
[143] *Ibid.*, p. 89. [147] *Ibid.*, pp. 86, 100, 107.
[144] *Ibid.*, p. 117. [148] See also above, note 21, Part I, Chapter VI.
[145] *Ibid.*, p. 8. [149] Strindberg, XXIX, 97.

from scene to scene in company with the Unknown. Yet when one finally returns to the original street corner one has the feeling that no time at all has passed. It seems as though the Unknown has been sitting day-dreaming, as though the whole drama were a materialization of what has taken place in the Unknown's mind.

There is no unified action in the drama unless one considers the play as a battle between the Unknown and the " Powers." The drama seems to gain impetus through the financial distress of the Unknown, occasioned by his refusal to get a letter from the post-office. The " Powers," of course, are responsible for all the difficulties. Since the Unseen One and the " Powers " are born of the Unknown's mind, any suggested motivation becomes flimsy at best.

The action of the play centers around the struggle between the Unknown and the Unseen One. The Unknown desires to grasp essential reality and the Unseen One demands humility and resignation. At one time the Unknown cries out that the devil is opposing him. To the Lady's question, " But why? " he answers in exasperation:

> *The Unknown.* Bang! That's why! Why is man born here as an ignorant creature, ignorant of laws, customs, conventions, which one breaks out of ignorance and then gets beaten for it? Why does one become a youth with noble views which he desires to realize, and why is one driven into all sorts of wretchedness which one loathes? Why? Why? [150]

The play is a prolonged *why*, with the Unknown constantly asking questions and never receiving acceptable answers. Note, for example, the concluding sentences in the second kitchen scene:

> *The Unknown.* Have you noticed that just before the sun rises a shudder runs through a man. Are we the children of darkness since we tremble so in the light?
>
> *The Mother.* Do you never grow weary of asking?
>
> *The Unknown.* No, never! I long for light, you see! [151]

---

[150] Strindberg, XXIX, 83.   [151] *Ibid.,* p. 111.

Whether or not essential reality is precipitated from the struggle in *To Damascus* is a matter of individual judgment. The logical interpretation of the three parts of *To Damascus* is the one which a preacher proclaimed when he cried out so frequently, " Vanity of vanities, all is vanity," and yet persisted in teaching and in searching for truth. " ' Nach Damaskus ' ist ein Selbstgespräch ad infinitum; ohne Anfang und Ende; ein skizzierter Erlösungsversuch; eine Anregung." [152]

To Damascus has no concern for the so-called dramatic unities, for these are replaced by the contrapuntal method of staging and dialogue, and also by the dream-frame that holds the entire play together. Strindberg has not arbitrarily broken the unities for the breaking's sake; the unities are not functional in this type of drama and are consequently ignored. The drama must be judged by standards other than those already established, by its contrapuntal method and its dream character. In this study, however, we are not judging the drama aesthetically but analyzing it according to the norms of expressionism. The validity of the contrapuntal method is not within our province.

THE WORTH OF MAN

IN THE *To Damascus* trilogy there is no constant cry for the worth of man, but there is a resounding echo of it in many scenes. The Unknown, who is an author, has continually striven to free mankind from its various forms of slavery. Whatsoever his success has been, he at least has cried out for the good and the beautiful and has worked for the well-being of men. The evidence is by no means overwhelming, for the " worth of man " pervades the drama much as invisible dust sifts through the atmosphere.

The evaluation of woman is given more clearly. Woman holds positions as mother, as sex antithesis to man and as the one through whom he may be reconciled with his lot. As man's op-

[152] Diebold, *Anarchie im Drama*, p. 175.

posite she is a cunning but unintellectual creature, a relative of Laura in *The Father*. As Mother, woman is more an abstraction than a tangible form, as the Unknown tells the Lady early in the play.

> *The Unknown.* You receive an excellent character, for your voice sounds like my departed Mother's — by mother I mean an abstract concept mother, spoken 'mother,' for my Mother never caressed me but I remember that she beat me.[153]

We are reminded throughout the play that the Lady has a mission in the Unknown's life; through her, a woman, the Unknown is to be reconciled with life. Early in the drama the Unknown declares that once he thought reconciliation was nigh, " but no illusion was greater for then the seventh hell began." [154] This idea of reconciliation through woman occurs occasionally in Part I [155] and also in Part III,[156] but seems to be entirely absent from Part II. One might go even further and say that the first part of *To Damascus* holds out strongly the idea that man may be reconciled to his fate through woman; whereas the third part of the play shows that reconciliation through woman is impossible, for the Unseen One wills otherwise. Moreover, though the idea of reconciliation may be fairly strong in the mind of the Unknown, it certainly is not strong enough to remould the woman. As far as we can observe, woman as reconciler is as abstract in *To Damascus* as the concept of " mother."

PARTS II AND III

The second and third parts of *To Damascus* have received very incidental discussion in the preceding material. To proceed

---

[153] Strindberg, XXIX, 13.

[154] *Ibid.,* p. 14.

[155] *Ibid.,* pp. 14, 20 (in the symbol of the flower), p. 88 (in the symbols of Eve and Mary, mother of Jesus), p. 97 (when the Unknown leaves the Asylum and goes to Woman for mercy).

[156] *Ibid.,* pp. 279, 309, 314, 320.

with the same type of analysis, however, would only mean repetition without much gain for this particular book. Moreover, it would demand a single volume for this drama alone. The last two parts of the trilogy are not so beautifully constructed as the first part, but they show nevertheless the same general characteristics with variations in details. The second part pitches the sex battle a little higher, and also exploits Strindberg's researches in alchemy. Likewise, the battle with the " Powers " is carried on with renewed zest. In the third part the Unknown has become weary and longs for repose at any cost. It is curiously enough filled with at least one antithesis which the author undoubtedly did not consciously develop. The element of hate seems to become stronger at the same time that biblical allusions appear more frequently. One is tempted to go back to *The Father* and quote the Captain's speech to the nurse apropos of her religious zeal: " It is certainly remarkable that as soon as you begin to talk about God and love, your voice becomes hard and your eyes so full of hate." [157] But the Unknown has a cosmic weariness in his soul, and religion is for him little more than a mechanical device to give relaxation.

Parts II and III of *To Damascus* are so similar to Part I that they may be placed in the expressionistic category without further discussion.

" THE GREAT HIGHWAY "

THE last drama that Strindberg published is *The Great Highway*,[158] though Lamm is not without evidence that points to an earlier date of composition.[159] This play comes to us as a fourth part of *To Damascus*· both by the nature of its form and its content. The main character, the Hunter, speaks for Strindberg; and, as the Unknown in *To Damascus*, the Hunter speaks almost endlessly.

---

[157] *Ibid.*, XXIII, 34.   [158] Published in 1909.   [159] Lamm, II, 429.

"Strindberg calls his literary epilogue *The Great Highway,* 'A Wander-drama with Seven Stations.' This subtitle at once reminds us of the *To Damascus* series, and *The Great Highway* is essentially the last part. As in the trilogy Strindberg has here scorned every form of disguise. In the character of the Hunter he appears as both plaintiff and defendant in his own case. *The Great Highway* is also a monologue drama in which the remaining characters are simply shadows without individual existence, now doubles of the hero and now his opposites. The dialogue is simply an echo of the Hunter's monologues which from time to time are broken and filled in by the conversation of others. It is a drama without conflicts and without suspense; and the only action that holds the play together is the Hunter's descent from the Alpine regions on the dusty path of life and his subsequent resolution to mount again, to seek once more the mountains and solitude. This action is simply a repetition of the Indra-motif in *A Dream Play.* With almost a monomaniacal one-sidedness this action circles around the one question: Strindberg's relations to his fellow men and to his ego." [160]

With our study of *To Damascus* and this paragraph from Lamm, we may safely assign *The Great Highway* to Strindberg's expressionistic dramas. No one can read the play without coming immediately to such a conclusion.

[160] Lamm, II, 428. See also Lamm, II, 366; and Marcus, *Strindbergs Dramatik,* pp. 428–435.

CHAPTER IV

BETWEEN "TO DAMASCUS," I, II, AND "A DREAM PLAY"

OF ALL the plays written between *To Damascus*, I, II,[1] and *A Dream Play* [2] there are only six that merit our attention: to wit, *Advent, There are Crimes and Crimes, Easter, Midsummer, Swanwhite* and *The Bridal Crown*.[3] None of these plays is decidedly outstanding in expressionistic characteristics and yet each one demands some attention.

" ADVENT "

" ADVENT," [4] described as " ein Mysterium," draws from Andersen, Maeterlinck, Swedenborg and Dickens as well as from Strindberg's own experiences.[5] It is in some respects a fairy play, in others a " Mysterium," and in many ways an expressionistic drama. The autobiographical element carries back to Strindberg's second marriage, especially to his parents-in-law of that period. The Judge and his Wife are moulded on these parents-in-law; Amalia, on Frieda Uhl; and Adolf, on the dramatist himself. That they are distortions of their originals is a condition of the Strindbergian method, as well as that of expressionism, and not a result of pure malevolence.

The characters are of the type one finds in expressionistic drama: The Judge, his Wife, Amalia, Adolf, the Neighbor, the Other One (also appears as the Franciscan Monk) and the like. Here, however, the types are not simply *man* and *woman* in op-

---

[1] Written 1897–98.   [2] Written 1901–2.
[3] For a study of *The Dance of Death*, see Part II, Chapter II.
[4] Written 1898.   [5] Lamm, II, 76–88.

position to each other alone, but also far more significantly in opposition to the " Powers." There is, furthermore, no one individual through whose ego the entire drama flows, except the ego of the dramatist apart from Adolf, his projected shadow.

There are, however, manifestations of *Ausstrahlungen des Ichs* in the drama. There is a procession of shadows that passes before the Judge and his Wife and brings forth the following comment from the Wife: " Are they shadows or ghosts, or our own sick dreams? " [6] Strindberg does not tell us clearly, but his method in *To Damascus* allows us to draw some conclusions here. The characters that appear in the procession can come only from the troubled conscience [7] of the Judge: Death, whom the Judge is facing; the White Lady, the first wife of the Judge; the Goldsmith with the counterfeit monstrance; the Beheaded Sailor, carrying his head in one hand; and so on, to the Magistrate with a rope around his neck, a character otherwise described like the Judge himself. Later, to the question of the Wife, " But what is this? Mist from the earth, or shadows from the trees? " the Judge answers, " No, it is we who see visions. There I am going and yet I stand here! " [8] And the Judge adds that if he could only get a night's sleep he would be able to laugh at the whole thing.

The scene that begins at the crossroads in the spruce forest and changes into the " Waiting Room " is likewise one that can only be projected from the mind.[9] In this scene, however, Strindberg has made use of a mechanical device, a witch who blows on a whistle and transforms the scene before the eyes of the spectators. The characters in this scene remind one of those in the procession; but this time they come from the mind of the Wife, for she alone appears among the shadow characters, the Judge

[6] Strindberg, XXX, 33.
[7] Note that *conscience* is an element in the contrapuntal arrangement: Strindberg, XXX, 8, 10, 15, 43, 48, 65, 83, 84.
[8] *Ibid.*, p. 34.
[9] *Ibid.*, pp. 68–82.

not being present. The Master of Ceremonies is none other than the Franciscan Monk, also known as the Other One, and clearly the Devil himself. The vision is a scenic comment on the vanity of the Wife, her belief that she has eternal youth.[10] The musicians at this " ball " tune and play their instruments, but not a sound is heard. The guests are cripples, beggars and night-hawks wearing black gloves. The seven deadly sins are also present and cluster around the throne. The dancing partner for the Wife is a hunchbacked prince who later proves to be the former's dead brother.[11] All these shadow characters reveal the sins of the Wife. She, however, shows no remorse whatsoever and becomes so vicious in her speech that the Master of Ceremonies finally brings the scene to an end with " Down, damned bitch! " [12] Once more the scene changes without a lowering of the curtain.

The " Waiting Room " scene occurs once more in the fifth act, this time with the Judge present as well as his wife. The Witch gives each a stereoscope, in which the past life of each is revealed. Thus the Judge and his Wife see in diminutive form what the spectators have already seen on the stage, the sins of the pair.

In the fourth act the scene of the Judge and the Ghost is clearly one of *Ausstrahlungen des Ichs*. The Ghost is given the same description as the Judge, except that his eyes appear like those of a plaster of Paris statue. There is, furthermore, no other character in the scene besides these two. It is obviously expressionistic monologue: a character is engaged in conversation with a shadow of his " self."

The play also employs elements like pantomime,[13] and makes repeated use of biblical allusions.[14] Likewise, there are symbols

---

10 *Ibid.*, pp. 9, 25, 64.
11 *Ibid.*, p. 79.
12 *Ibid.*, p. 81 (" Couche! fördömda hynda! ").
13 *Ibid.*, pp. 31, 32, 66, 70, 81, 82, 106 (all of short duration).
14 *Ibid.*, pp. 8, 11, 17, 18, 37, 51, 57, 58, 63, 68, 94, 99, 107 (Latin nativity song).

like the " sun cat," [15] and the silverware that cannot be cleaned.[16] The appearance of the supernatural is quite concrete in *Advent* and also brings us into direct contact with *To Damascus*. In the latter play [17] the Unknown and the Lady thought that they could hear the gavel fall and the chairs pushed away from the table, and the supernatural was allowed to remain more or less in the minds of the stage characters. In *Advent*, however, the inanimate things actually take part. At the opening of the scene between the Judge and the Ghost a bell actually strikes of its own accord, the gavel falls likewise, chairs are pushed at the same time toward the table and candles are lighted. A little later the bell on the table rings again and one chair is pushed away from the table; and, when judgment is finally pronounced, the gavel strikes and the chairs are pushed away from the table.[18] Throughout the entire play we note that the elements of the supernatural leave a wider trace of their passage than in *To Damascus*, for they gain existence not only through the dialogue but also through the movements of inanimate objects. In other words, the supernatural becomes mechanized and thus gives the drama an aspect that is somewhat similar to a modern mystery play.

Besides being a distorted medley of Andersen, Maeterlinck, Swedenborg, Dickens, a nineteenth century criminal proceedings and Strindbergian autobiography, this play also possesses distortion within itself. The procession scene and the ghost scene and the " Waiting Room " scene are clearly distortions of observed reality. In the second " Waiting Room " scene the Judge and his Wife see their lives in the stereoscope and see them distorted; even the fairest of memories seem to have become foul. Then the Judge and his Wife give further expression to their distortion of soul by comments on love. The Judge has been

[15] Strindberg, XXX, 19, 21, 23, 44, 50, 51, 52, 63.
[16] *Ibid.*, pp. 36, 39–40, 90.
[17] *Ibid.*, XXIX, 30, 53.
[18] *Ibid.*, XXX, 82–85.

endeavoring to find some light, some memory of joy in his past life. Eventually he fastens on the word " love."

Judge. ... Love! What was it!

Wife. ... What was it? Two cats on a backhouse roof!

Judge (foolishly). Yes, that's what it was! And three dogs on the edge of the sidewalk! How sweet it is to remember that!

Wife (presses his hand). So sweet! [19]

Here is distortion with a vengeance, especially when one remembers that of all animals Strindberg hated dogs as the most filthy manifestation of life.[20]

One could go further in the analysis of this play, but the gain would be slight. Lamm declares that this drama is in many respects a forerunner of *A Dream Play* and *The Ghost Sonata*.[21] At the same time, Lamm states that *Advent* well illustrates how little Strindberg was dependent on foreign movements in symbolism and expressionism, though these movements later pointed to Strindberg as a forefather. From the tone of the paragraph one gathers that Lamm means to imply further that *Advent* is quite unrelated to expressionistic drama. As if to clinch the argument, the Swedish professor points out that Strindberg built up this play on his own experiences of the Inferno period, and that he also used his old saga-play technique. Lamm is apparently eager to give Strindberg full credit for his " intuitive sense for color and form " and his " daring," and a mixture of credit and reproach for Strindberg's " childishness." In spite of his implications that *Advent* is by no means an expressionistic drama, Lamm offers no evidence to support the tonal character of his paragraph.[22] That Strindberg had nothing to do with the movements of his own day is assuredly no proof

[19] *Ibid.,* pp. 101–102.

[20] For examples see *Götiska rummen,* Strindberg, XL, 35 *et alibi* regarding " Fylax," the " skvättmaskin "; *Ensam,* Strindberg, XXXVIII, 137 *et alibi.*

[21] Lamm, II, 88.   [22] See also above, p. 94.

that he did not father a movement of a later day. Furthermore, the relation of *Advent* to *A Dream Play*, *The Ghost Sonata* and *To Damascus*, and its basis in Strindberg's own experiences should be enough to startle the unbeliever into suspecting that expressionistic elements may actually be found in the play. Moreover, Lamm's declaration that Strindberg made "noteworthy attempts in modern expressionism" in *A Dream Play* and in the *Chamber Plays*[23] should have led him to suspect that other plays of the post-Inferno period also contain elements of expressionism.

Advent is, indeed, a mixture of fairy lore and expressionism. The evidence given above, however, indicates the necessity of including this play within the limits of Strindberg's expressionistic dramas. We need not insist, indeed should not, that *Advent* is thoroughgoing expressionism, but we must grant that it contains very pronounced elements of expressionism.

" THERE ARE CRIMES AND CRIMES "

FROM the standpoint of Diebold[24] the play *There are Crimes and Crimes*[25] is a counter gesture to *To Damascus;* it is a wave of the hand and the author's laugh. " Strindberg lächelt! und er lässt Mutter Cathérine laut und herzhaft in ihr Taschentuch lachen. Das soll ihm hoch angerechnet werden, dass er das ' Crux, ave spes unica ' hier mit der gebührenden Rücksicht auf seine eigene Konstitution behandelte und wahr blieb. Denn die Komödie ' Rausch ' — das ist der letzte Trumpf des ' Unbekannten ': das ist der wahre Schluss von ' Nach Damaskus.' Was Resignation und Mönchseinmauerung! Welch Schauspiel für den Theatraliker! Aber, ach, ein Schauspiel nur! . . . Also um acht Uhr ins Theater — um neun Uhr in die Kirche." If this play is a gesture then there is the possibility that a great deal in Strind-

---

[23] Lamm, I, 25.   [25] Written 1898–99.
[24] Diebold, *Anarchie im Drama,* 178.

berg's life and works must be interpreted as artistic pose, and a number of the works must be termed caricature. Then *To Damascus* is also caricature, and so is the oaken cross on the dramatist's grave; still more so, the inscription on the cross, " O Crux, ave spes unica."

Investigation may some day reveal that *There are Crimes and Crimes* is a hearty laugh, that *To Damascus* is a caricature, and that Strindberg's grave is his last good joke, but for the present Diebold has given us only an opinion and not a critical judgment based on sound evidence. The following letter would give Diebold a little support, but very little. Strindberg himself writes of the play to his German translator, Schering: [26]

Also " Rausch " in Berlin! Nun aber möchte ich als Dichter bitten, dass man *einmal* auf mich hört, denn ich weiss, welchen Gefahren das Stück ausgesetzt ist.

Die grösste, an der wir schon gescheitert sind, ist das Predigen, das Moralisieren, trotzdem das Drama durchaus befreien will.

1. Henriette soll seelisch verführen; der Vampyr, der Seelen trinkt; und braucht keinen Körper zu haben. (Aspasia ist körperlos!) Sie weiss nicht, was gut und böse ist: " alles ist erlaubt." Da sie aber nicht berechnet, dass Handlungen Folgen haben, so ist sie erstaunt und wütet zuerst, dann entdeckt sie, dass nicht alles erlaubt ist — macht die Entdeckung aber mit einer flotten Resignation, ohne Reue, aber mit einer gewissen Wehmut! Uebrigens ist die Rolle ja gründlich gezeichnet; und die Schauspielerin muss genau wissen, was die anderen von ihr sagen, wenn sie draussen ist.

2. Maurice ist klar, in der Rolle.

3. Frau Cathérine ist gutmütig, nachsichtig; lächelt über die Schwächen, und, wohlgemerkt, straft nie!

4. Der Abbé ist am gefährlichsten. Er muss — genau wie Frau Cathérine sein — jedoch ohne läppisch zu werden! Mit Humor also und Laune. Besonders in der letzten Szenen schelmisch, nachsichtig; kindlich erstaunt über die ausserordentliche Freiheit von Vorurteilen, die sich hier gezeigt hat! — " Schrecklich ist es jedenfalls. . . ." (Gelübde zu brechen!)

Und dann: eine Zeichnung aus dem Alltagsleben, ohne " Räubergebärden!" Schwedisch: das heisst, eine leichte Skepsis hinter allem! Nicht norwegisch! Denn der Norweger kann nicht lächeln! Er ist hart, unversöhnlich.

Schliesslich: nicht Abgründe andeuten, die nicht vorhanden sind; noch Tiefsinnigkeiten, an die ich nie gedacht habe! Also nicht Ibsen!

10 SEPTEMBER 1902.

---

[26] Strindberg, *Werke*, Abt. 8, Bd. III, 80.

Strindberg's description of Henriette offers us a character that might well fit into expressionistic drama, but scarcely into a drama of laughing gesture. At the same time even Strindberg warns us not to see too much in the play. In spite of the fact that we have a creature who seduces spiritually, one who is without body, one who is as unmoral as the Lady in *To Damascus,* we are requested not to make this drama heavy with meaning. We must therefore lay bare whatsoever expressionistic elements can reasonably be ascribed to this play without pushing anything to extremes.

Certainly the autobiographical element plays its constant part.[27] Strindberg, like Maurice, had just enjoyed a Parisian success with a play, *The Father.* He had also had a fleeting affair with an English sculptress (Henriette in the play) whom he had met at Madam Charlotte's crémerie (Madame Cathérine in the play). Moreover, Strindberg's sketch *In the Cemetery*[28] gave him a living model for Jeanne. The death of Marie likewise has its counterpart in Strindberg's own life. He had tried, through the effects of suggestion on a photograph, to give his own daughter a mild illness! Even one of his companions in Berlin, the Polish author Stanislaus Przybyzewski, hovers in the shadow land of this drama. All the elements in the play have their basis in actual experience, but none of them is identifiable completely with the objective experience. Strindberg, as usual in his post-Inferno works, reshapes the material until an art-form emerges out of his experiences. Were this element of distortion closely applied, it would probably cover everything that Strindberg wrote, and much that countless non-expressionistic writers have contributed to literature. Yet the play *There are Crimes and Crimes* is conditioned enough by *Ausstrahlungen des Ichs* that we may include the autobiographical data as an evidence of expressionism.

[27] Lamm, II, 90–93.   [28] Written 1896. See XXVII, pp. 659–672.

There is also the supernatural aspect of the play. In a letter of February 24, 1899,[29] Strindberg says that it is wiser to let the work stand for what it is, " an event which is not the work of man."[30] Then, in a letter of March 22, 1899,[31] the author declares that " the last act is Swedenborgian with hell already on earth, and the hero, the intrigue-maker in the play is the Unseen One. . . ." Such material would furnish excellent evidence, if we could feel that the play justifies the statements in the letters. The play, however, does not measure up to the promise of the letters.

The contrapuntal form of dialogue is built into the drama to some extent: conscience,[32] hate,[33] jealousy[34] and suffering.[35] This gives us more evidence, but evidence that is only tempting and not compelling. *There are Crimes and Crimes* is only on the border-line of expressionism.

" EASTER "

LAMM declares that of all Strindberg's plays *Easter*[36] is the most difficult to analyze.[37] Certainly, if one should attempt to assign the play to the category of fairy plays one would feel dissatisfied. In this drama, as in *To Damascus*, the supernatural is felt and not manifested in the play of inanimate objects as in *Advent*. The drama is clearly not of the fairy play type, not a " Mysterium " and not romantic drama. By analysis we shall point out that it tends strongly toward expressionism.

The autobiographical element is clear if we are able to go with Lamm behind the scenes.[38] While the play in itself indicates no

---

[29] Strindberg, XXX, 226.
[30] *Ibid.*, pp. 169, 173, 179, 191 (repeated by the Abbé).
[31] *Ibid.*, p. 227.
[32] *Ibid.*, pp. 142, 143, 148, 163, 181, 183, 201, 206, 207.
[33] *Ibid.*, pp. 145, 160, 183, 205, 206, 212.   [36] Written 1900.
[34] *Ibid.*, pp. 117, 123, 129, 144, 145, 158.   [37] Lamm, II, 204.
[35] *Ibid.*, pp. 118, 131, 132, 149, 153, 158, 193, 220   [38] *Ibid.*, pp. 204–222.

particular locality for its setting, Lamm proves without a doubt that the setting is the city of Lund. Likewise, Elis' reactions to his environment are practically identical with Strindberg's to Lund during at least one visit. Eleonora may be identified with one of Strindberg's sisters who was committed to the asylum at Upsala. After the death of this sister in 1904 Strindberg sent her picture to Harriet Bosse with this message: " I simply want to show you the ' Easter-girl ' who suffered for others. . . ." In a letter written to Harriet Bosse three years earlier Strindberg makes almost the same statement that he does to Bergh in a letter written the 20th of January, 1901. Eleonora is " a girl somewhat related to Swedenborg's niece Seraphita, gloriously depicted by Balzac." Eleonora is thus possibly a composite picture formed in part from Strindberg's actual experiences with his sister and also from his book experiences with Seraphita. The leading male character Elis is, of course, very much like Strindberg.

The play exemplifies *Ausstrahlungen des Ichs* in its dream character. Kristina remarks that at times she has gone about as though in a dream.[39] Eleonora also announces that she has been with her father who is in prison, and with her sister in America; with them in her sleep.[40] We have, moreover, the characteristic of dream stressed by the frequent occurrence of the expression, " Everything repeats itself." [41]

Eleonora attracts our attention more than the other characters. She would undoubtedly be declared insane by alienists. While there is nothing in her action that need be judged harshly, it is nevertheless clear that she is either " beyond good and evil " or else lacking in concepts of both. Furthermore, as stated above, she is with her father and her sister while she is asleep, and she seems to have faith in her dream knowledge that her sister has

[39] Strindberg, XXXIII, 47.   [41] *Ibid.,* pp. 70, 77, 115, 116, 119, 124.
[40] *Ibid.,* p. 100.

sold a large quantity of goods in her shop. She also can sense when prison authorities are cruel to her father.[42] Still more pertinent is one of her speeches in a dialogue with Benjamin.

> *Eleonora.* For me time and space do not exist. I am everywhere and whenever I please! I am in my father's prison and in my brother's schoolroom; I am in my mother's kitchen and my sister's shop in far away America. When things go well for my sister so that she makes good sales, then I can feel her joy; and when things are bad for her I suffer, but I suffer most when she does not do right. Benjamin, you are called Benjamin because you are the youngest of my friends . . . yes, everyone is my friend. . . . If you will take me into your confidence I shall suffer for you also.[43]

Eleonora remarks further, apropos of time, that the clock in the house always went fast when misfortune was at hand but went slow when the house enjoyed good days.[44] Likewise at the end of the play Eleonora tears off the calendar sheets in order to hasten the passing of time.[45] For this girl, time and space do not exist and cannot exist. She is a creature of another plane. Eleonora would be very close to " reine Seele," an *ur*-creature idealized, were it not for the fact that she is too often the mouthpiece for Strindberg's post-Inferno theology. Had Strindberg allowed her to be free from religious as well as social convention he would have created a more perfect expressionistic character.

The Picardian idea of the struggle of opposites is not functional in this drama. There are no two forces of polaric value in struggle, although the Unseen One has his hand in the drama. On the other hand, we have a somewhat passive function of antitheses in *Easter*, a verbal recognition of opposites in constant play. Eleonora who is so unhappy can make others joyous;[46] misfortune soon treads upon fortune;[47] " Today the rod, and to-

---

[42] *Ibid.,* p. 63.

[43] *Ibid.,* pp. 61–62.

[44] *Ibid.,* p. 95.

[45] *Ibid.,* p. 127 (in *A Dream Play* there is a variation of the device to hasten the passing of time; XXXVI, 238).

[46] *Ibid.,* p. 73. [47] *Ibid.,* p. 75.

morrow the Easter-egg! Today snow and tomorrow thaw! Today death and tomorrow the resurrection! ";[48] " Elis and Kristina . . . like each other and yet hate each other ";[49] Eleonora, judged mentally unbalanced, is nevertheless wise;[50] good is rewarded with evil;[51] for the happiness of some another must suffer torment.[52] These opposites do not reign as elements of conflict in the play, but are dropped in like philosophical comments that are precipitated from the conflicts.

With respect to the dramatic unities time and place are well maintained. Action, however, is rather muddled. The shadow of Lindkvist the creditor hovers over the first part of the drama and becomes a flesh and blood bogy at the end of the play. Eleonora purchases an Easter lily in a most unusual manner with the result that the family momentarily expects the police or the attendants of the asylum to come for the girl. Benjamin fails in his Latin examination, and causes his tutor, Elis, mental anguish. And Elis quarrels with his fiancée, Kristina. The play actually seems to have a combination of motifs, of which none is independently functional.

It seems clear that all these elements of motivation are centered toward one purpose, the suffering of Elis. These elements are simply increments to the pain of the proud Elis. The play is thus one of atmosphere more than of action; it aims to give a picture of Elis' suffering during the Easter days, an intentional parallel to the suffering of Jesus.[53]

The atmosphere is created in part by the music played before each of the three acts. Haydn's *Sieben Worte des Erlösers* is given in three themes: Introduction, *Maestoso Adagio*, before the first act; Largo No. 1, *Pater dimitte illis*, before the second act;

[48] Strindberg, XXXIII, 96.
[49] *Ibid.*, p. 101.
[50] *Ibid.*, p. 105.
[51] *Ibid.*, p. 119.
[52] *Ibid.*, p. 123.
[53] Strindberg himself suffered during Easter days. See *Werke*, Abt. 8, Bd. III, 203, letter of April 1, 1907.

and No. 5, *Adagio,* before the third act. Here, says Lamm,[54] is
the first time that Strindberg has experimented with musical
composition. Lamm, however, may have forgotten or ignored
the use of music in *To Damascus,* especially the contrapuntal
arrangement of scene and dialogue. Even if Lamm refers solely
to the function of music in creating moods for the drama, there
is a question whether *Easter* or *To Damascus* furnishes the first
example. According to Victor Hellström,[55] Strindberg made
careful preparations for the music preceding each act of *To
Damascus* at the Stockholm première of November 19, 1900.
Whether this was conceived by Strindberg while writing *Easter,*
or earlier, is a matter that possibly defies solution.

The contrapuntal form of dialogue is not particularly outstanding in *Easter.* If there is a leitmotif, it can only be " Everything
repeats itself," [56] although this expression does not seem to carry
an exceptionally strong emphasis as, for example, " Mankind is
to be pitied," in *A Dream Play,* or " Ich erhoffe, ich erhoffe, dass
mir der Erlöser lebet," in *The Bridal Crown.*[57] The predominant
theme in the play is *suffering.*[58] The element of hate also has a
part,[59] though not a large one, in *Easter.* Besides the contrapuntal
dialogue there is also an atmosphere of rhythm and music that
surges through the entire drama.[60]

The play is by no means a perfect specimen of expressionistic
drama, but it certainly has enough elements to warrant the expressionistic qualification. Eleonora is the most expressionistic
of all the characters, but even the others are to some extent " sleepwalkers in the broad daylight." Even the staging gives some evi-

[54] Lamm, II, 218.
[55] *Strindberg och musiken,* p. 35.
[56] Note 41 of this chapter.
[57] See note 78 of this chapter.
[58] Strindberg, XXXIII, 40, 42, 44, 46, 52, 54, 60, 62, 68, 77, 90, 93, 96,
103, 105, 107, 109, 110, 123.
[59] *Ibid.,* pp. 41, 99, 101, 105.
[60] Lamm, II, 218.

dence of *Ausstrahlungen des Ichs.* When the mental difficulties are cleared away, then also the sun streams into the room.[61] This evidence is by no means unimpeachable, but it is of such validity that one may defend the inclusion of *Easter* in the expressionistic group.

" MIDSUMMER "

THE play *Midsummer*[62] contains a curious mixture of two Stockholm milieux: one, the Stockholm of the 'seventies; the other, that of the end of the century.[63] Strindberg was influenced by the powerful spirit of nationalism of his day and answered the demand for drama containing local color.[64] The play has autobiographical material, and also definite parellels with type characters in Holberg's dramas. But, apart from the fact that Ivar Lundberg is a fine Mons Montanus or Jean de France, he is both in spirit and name a representative of the University of Lund. As such he falls a victim to Strindberg's satire. Lamm also tells us that the play is directly related to Strindberg's short story " Compelled To " which is published in the volume *Married.*[65] The play, however, is not of interest to our study. It employs contrapuntal dialogue to some extent, but that element is not sufficient to qualify the play as expressionistic. It is a milieu drama that does not respond to expressionistic norms.

" SWANWHITE "

THE play *Swanwhite*[66] is most assuredly a fairy play, but it cannot be dismissed without some examination. The drama has considerable autobiographical background, Strindberg and Harriet Bosse, the third chapter in the dramatist's book of marriages. Lamm has no difficulty whatsoever in proving that, in spite of

[61] Strindberg, XXXIII, 110, 127.
[62] Written 1900.
[63] Lamm, II, 190. [65] *Ibid.,* p. 196. (See also Strindberg XIV, 104–130.)
[64] *Ibid.,* p. 193.   [66] Written 1901.

several sources for the play, the author has written much of his own experiences into it.[67]   Indeed, Lamm considers that the play has suffered through Strindberg's inability to resist inserting autobiographical material that is irrelevant.

Love is as fragile and delicate as a butterfly. When it comes in contact with earthly things it loses the silvery dust on its wings and then can no longer soar. This, according to Lamm, is the theme of the play.

The play is filled with music,[68] with dream character,[69] elements of the supernatural,[70] and pantomime sometimes mingled with monologue.[71]   The dream character, however, has the romantic desire for escape from this world of suffering into a more embellished world. The love scenes [72] refer to the land of dreams as the land of realization, but fear is expressed for earthly contacts. Realization, then, is not to be had in this world but in a dream land of perfumed clouds and fairy-touched skies. It is not the expressionist's demand for realization within this objective world, but the romanticist's provisions for escape from this world. If the drama fits into any of the modern -isms, it must be *impressionism*.[73]

Swanwhite is not an expressionistic drama. It belongs either in neo-romanticism or impressionism, two modern movements very closely allied.

" THE BRIDAL CROWN "

" THE BRIDAL CROWN " [74] is a folk-play, another response to the spirit of nationalism. One might expect to escape the auto-

[67] Lamm, II, 273–279.

[68] Strindberg, XXXVI, 161, 164, 181, 194, 208, 211.

[69] *Ibid.*, pp. 140, 155, 161, 164, 165, 167, 169, 170, 181, 184.

[70] *Ibid.*, pp. 147, 148, 150, 154, 155, 161, 172, 180, 182, 185, 205, 207, 208, 209, 211.

[71] *Ibid.*, pp. 133, 161, 164, 174, 179, 194, 207, 208, 211.

[72] *Ibid.*, pp. 165–171, 180–181.

[73] See plays of Hugo von Hofmannsthal and of Per Hallström. The latter's short stories are also good examples.   [74] Written 1901–2.

biographical element in a folk-play, but Hedén has pointed out [75] what every reader of Strindberg must see in the play: Strindberg and his first wife, Siri von Essen; the birth of their first child shortly after marriage,[76] and the death of this child while in the care of a midwife. The marriage " before God " of Mats and Kersti is the kind of marriage Strindberg had in mind for himself and Harriet Bosse. Likewise, the idea of the reconciliation between the Mewlings and the Mill-folk is taken out of Strindberg's own experiences. Strindberg has once more moulded experiences into an artistic form.

The drama exhibits the strongest tendency toward expressionism in the employment of music. As in almost no other play the element of music surges through scene after scene [77] until the play itself almost blends with music. Likewise, the song of the Watersprite, " Ich erhoffe, ich erhoffe, dass mir der Erlöser lebet! " runs through the play like a leitmotif.[78]

In general, however, *The Bridal Crown* scarcely qualifies as an expressionistic drama. One can *feel* expressionism in this play, but analysis fails to strengthen the feeling by the addition of evidence.[79]

---

[75] Hedén, Erik, *Strindberg: Leben und Dichtung,* pp. 283–284 (see also Lamm, II, 245–246).

[76] Before the marriage in *The Bridal Crown.*

[77] Strindberg, XXXVI, 8, 9, 11, 12, 13, 14, 25, 26, 30, 31, 38, 52, 58, 59, 63, 76, 77, 79, 80, 82, 83, 84, 93, 103, 106, 119, 120.

[78] *Ibid.,* pp. 25, 26, 30, 52, 80, 82, 83, 93, 97, 103, 119. (The German translation is given rather than the English. This leitmotif is very difficult to translate into acceptable English: either the rhythm is lost, or the spirit, or both.)

[79] This may be one case in which emotional reactions come closer to the truth than well-plotted scholarly analysis.

CHAPTER V

"A DREAM PLAY"

IN A letter to his German translator, Emil Schering, Strindberg declares, " Das *Traumspiel* ist eine neue Form, die meine Erfindung ist." [1] One month earlier Schering had undoubtedly been puzzled about *A Dream Play* and written for explanations, for Strindberg sent him the following letter:

> Das *Traumspiel* verstehen? Indras Tochter ist auf die Erde niedergestiegen, um zu erfahren, wie die Menschen es haben; und da lernt sie kennen, wie schwer das Leben ist. Und das Schwerste ist: andern Böses tun, wozu man gezwungen wird, wenn man leben will. Die Form ist ja im Vorwort motiviert: das Sammelsurium des Traumes, in dem es doch eine gewisse Logik gibt! Alles Unsinnige wird wahrscheinlich. Menschen tauchen an mehreren Punkten auf und werden skizziert, die Skizzen fliessen zusammen, dieselbe Person löst sich in mehrere auf, die wieder zu einer zusammenfliessen. Zeit und Raum existieren nicht, eine Minute ist wie viele Jahre, keine Jahreszeiten: der Schnee liegt in Sommerlandschaft, die Linde färbt sich und grünt usw.[2]

Unless one admits the dream character of this play, recognizes that one has before oneself the cinematic reeling of dream images, one can only agree with Robert Lynd's portrait of Strindberg: " The mirror that Strindberg held up to Nature was a cracked one. It was cracked in a double sense — it was crazy. It gave back broken images of a world which it made look like the chaos of a lunatic dream." [3] Why Lynd must qualify dream by *lunatic* is incomprehensible unless perchance he has never dreamed. The dream life compared with conscious life *is* crazy! It does distort

---

[1] Strindberg, *Werke,* Abt. 8, Bd. III, 75; letter of June 13, 1902 (*A Dream Play,* excluding the Prologue, was written 1901–02).

[2] *Ibid.,* pp. 74–75; letter of May 13, 1902.

[3] Lynd, Robert, *Old and New Masters,* p. 123.

the objective world and it gives back " broken images " of the world. It is quite childish to attack *A Dream Play* and a number of Strindberg's other literary works unless one challenges the validity of the art-form.[4]

In *A Dream Play* one may demand that critics give attention to the drama as a new form instead of trying to praise or damn the work according to standards of established categories. Exclusive of the Prologue, the drama gives us the dream dimness or dream sharpness of scenes floating swiftly before our eyes, scenes in which we are actors at the same time that we are seeing them as spectators. The scenes are sometimes nightmare in their vividness and horror, sometimes the paradisiacal world to which the romanticist would escape, and sometimes the world of Sheol which fades away into the shadows of an evening crepuscle. The frame of *A Dream Play* includes them all.

As an expressionistic work *A Dream Play* satisfies all the requirements, although the Prologue gives one a sense of artificiality. Yet one should remember that the Prologue was written more than four years after the drama proper was completed. A letter to Adolf Paul, written on November 18, 1911, may also furnish a clue regarding the function of this Prologue and its late addition to the drama. In this letter Strindberg says, " Spiele das Traumspiel mit Prolog und lass auf dem Programm das kurze Vorwort drucken, damit sie nicht denken, es sei verrückt." [5] In part, at least, this Prologue is a concession to the average playgoer, like Lynd, who would be certain to find a crazy world instead of this ordinary world distorted through dream imagery. Lamm also adds that the Prologue represents a change in Strindberg's own mood.[6] It was written in Septem-

---

[4] Of course Lynd may be justified for his distortion of Strindberg. Critics and reviewers, yes, even scholars, must sparkle at times, though it be at the expense of the Masters.

[5] Paul, Adolf, *Strindberg-Erinnerungen und -Briefe,* p. 231.

[6] Lamm, II, 335.

ber, 1906, a time when Strindberg would scarcely have cried out, as he did four years earlier, " Mankind is to be pitied."

Putting the Prologue aside we may take the drama as written in 1901–2 and examine it for expressionistic characteristics. The " Reminder " which Strindberg desired to have printed on the programs is enough to stamp the work at once as expressionistic.

> As he did in his previous dream play (the trilogy *To Damascus*), so in this one the author has tried to imitate the disconnected but seemingly logical form of the dream. Anything may happen; everything is possible and probable. Time and space do not exist. On an insignificant background of reality, imagination designs and embroiders novel patterns: a medley of memories, experiences, free fancies, absurdities and improvisations.
>
> The characters split, double, multiply, vanish, solidify, blur, clarify. But one consciousness reigns above them all — that of the dreamer; and before it there are no secrets, no incongruities, no scruples, no laws. There is neither judgment nor exoneration, but merely narration. And as the dream is mostly painful, rarely pleasant, a note of melancholy and of pity with all living things runs right through the wabbly tale. Sleep, the liberator, plays often a dismal part, but when the pain is at its worst, the awakening comes and reconciles the sufferer with reality, which, however distressing it may be, nevertheless seems happy in comparison with the torments of the dream.[7]

In this foreword the author has already committed himself as an expressionistic dramatist, but his drama even more convincingly brings to light the factors of expressionism. The whole play has this dream character, or framework, in which the " wabbly tale " is placed. It is a sequence of events in which time and space do not exist, in which also the various characters do not remain stable.

The framework demands the characterization which is given in the title of this drama, *A Dream Play.* Yet we find this relation to dream going beyond the framework itself. Taking details of the drama separately, we might well declare that the work is filled with realism, that it is very close to an itemized

[7] Strindberg, *Plays,* Björkman translation, 1st series, p. 24.

report of observed reality. It may be observed here, however, that realism plays a part in dreams and in expressionism; individual items of both may be identical with individual items in observed reality. It is in the relation and sequence of elements that we get our cue to the dream character and expressionistic nature of *A Dream Play*. The arrangement of elements is distorted and precludes any further comparison with observed reality.[8]

The keynote to this play has already been cited by Lamm [9] in the following quotation from the drama:

> *The Poet.* I fashioned that in a poem once!
>
> *The Daughter.* Then you know what poetry is. . . .
>
> *The Poet.* Then I know what dreaming is. . . . What is poetry?
>
> *The Daughter.* Not reality, but more than reality . . . not dreams, but wide-awake dreams. . . .
>
> *The Poet.* And the children of men think that we poets are only playing . . . fabulating and inventing.[10]

Lamm further declares that we must accept this as the basis of the dramatist's philosophy of dream play; otherwise we shall open " the secret door " and, like the " deans of the faculties," find nothing behind it!

Like everything else that Strindberg has written, *A Dream Play* has its background in the dramatist's own life. In fact, the play goes back not only to incidents recorded in the autobiographical novels, but even to scenes in Stockholm, to the dramatist's very home on Karlavägen.[11] Lamm also makes the statement that practically every detail in *A Dream Play* can be allocated to objective reality.[12] Moreover, the drama will call to mind again and again incidents from other plays: the love-hate complex in marriage which courses through a large number of

---

[8] See below, p. 179.

[9] Lamm, II, 315.

[10] Strindberg, XXXVI, 301.

[11] Lamm, II, 312.

[12] *Ibid.*, p. 313.

works;[13] the idea that " everything repeats itself ";[14] the feeling
that one has had earlier contacts with a person otherwise a
stranger, or with an experience that seems new.[15] Indeed, everything repeats itself in *A Dream Play:* old autobiographical
material that has appeared in other plays, and motifs likewise
that have been present in earlier works. The autobiographical
material in the drama lurks behind almost every word!

We recall that the importance of autobiographical data in
expressionistic literature lies in the transmutation of the objective experiences. In *A Dream Play* Strindberg has sometimes
taken his experiences bodily from their objective state, but has
placed them in a context or an arrangement that gives them a
transmuted value. The Officer's dream of school days and the
puzzling problem of two-times-two [16] is not simply Strindberg's
but is also a typical dream for adults.[17] It becomes no longer
individual in its function, but general. No matter how close to
objective reality an incident of *A Dream Play* may be, it is
nevertheless so ordered in the dream frame that it loses its objective value and significance.

The combination of all these objective experiences within the
dream frame reminds one strikingly of the type of expressionistic painting that is exemplified in Marc Chagall's *Ich und das
Dorf.*[18] There are elements of Strindberg's childhood and of his
adult days all put together on a canvas with no particular regard
for their original arrangement. The consciousness of the painter
orders Chagall's *Ich und das Dorf;* and the consciousness of the
dreamer, Strindberg's *A Dream Play.* The latter is no more
spun out of pure fancy than the former; both present objective

[13] See especially *The Father* and *The Dance of Death.*
[14] See *Easter;* also pp. 167–172 above.
[15] See *To Damascus;* also pp. 149–150 above.
[16] Strindberg, XXXVI, 274–275, 279–283.
[17] Lamm, II, 320; Marcus, *Strindbergs Dramatik,* p. 304.
[18] See p. 17 above.

experiences that are real, but are ordered by consciousness instead of being presented imitatively according to the arrangement gained through physical observation.

One of the most significant expressionistic features of *A Dream Play* is, then, the element of distortion. Read the play and note how characters, staging, time, place and action are all distorted! Just as the Unknown in *To Damascus* was present in several selves — the Beggar, the Dead Man and Caesar — so here the Officer shades into the Lawyer who in turn becomes the Poet. They are, furthermore, manifestations of the Strindberg ego; they represent three of his " selves." Note that even Indra's Daughter is apparently the daughter of the Glazier in the opening of the play,[19] but later on is recognized as the Daughter of Indra.[20] Yet she is more than the Daughter of the Gods: she is also the representative of her sex; she is the woman through whom man may be reconciled to life; and, finally, she has some features originally found in Harriet Bosse.[21] The characters in *A Dream Play* have lost all individuality. They are either shadows or else are typified by sex, professional, family or social status: for example, the Father, Mother, Officer, Portress, Bill-poster, Glazier, Teacher and others. None of the characters, however, is wholly stable. All glide in and out of this dream drama like figures in a vision. They may stand out sharply defined at times, and again may appear like ghosts without faces, like beings whose presence we apprehend but cannot fix objectively.

Staging, likewise, follows no system previously ordained for drama. The scenes glide into each other and fade into each other, like the " Changemang à vue " already used in *Advent*. Or, pitch darkness reigns while the setting changes, just like our dreams which change the setting without regard for logic or may have the scenes separated by gaps of oblivion, pitch darkness.

---

[19] Strindberg, XXXVI, 223 (note stage direction " to the father " — *her* father).   [20] *Ibid.*, p. 226.   [21] Lamm, II, 326.

The play opens with a forest of giant hollyhocks in the background and the gilded roof of a castle appearing above this forest. The scenes on the wings remain the same throughout the entire drama. They are conventionalized mural paintings which at the same time represent an interior, architecture and landscape. The Glazier and his Daughter have the first dialogue of the play. Soon " they go toward the background which opens slowly to the sides." [22] The stage then represents an humble room. A little later, voices are heard coming from behind a partition.[23] This partition is pulled away and the stage changes slightly once more. Not long afterwards the Father bids farewell and makes his exit right through the wall.[24] Likewise, all through the play changes in setting take place with no regard whatsoever for the logic of such changes in the empirical world.

There is absolutely no unity of time, no unity of place, and none for action. Once and for all these unities are thrown aside as measurements of physical observation; they are not functional in the life of the unconscious, in dream existence. " But one consciousness reigns above them all — that of the dreamer; and before it there are no secrets, no incongruities, no scruples, no laws." [25] The Officer shakes the tree and remarks that it is becoming green again,[26] but this does not prevent him, just a little later,[27] from saying, " I shall tell the Glazier to put in the double windows, for it is soon winter and I am freezing frightfully! " Again, time is wholly distorted when the stage is made light and then dark alternately.

> *The Officer.* What is that? (*he keeps time with the blinking of the light*). Light and dark; light and dark.
>
> *The Daughter (imitating him).* Day and night; day and night! . . . A merciful Providence desires to shorten your waiting, and therefore the days fly, chasing along the nights! [28]

---

[22] Strindberg, XXXVI, 222.   [25] See note 7 of this chapter.
[23] *Ibid.*, p. 224.   [26] Strindberg, XXXVI, 233.
[24] *Ibid.*, p. 226.   [27] *Ibid.*, p. 235.   [28] *Ibid.*, p. 238.

In the school scene the concept of time is brought up for immediate questioning when the Magister asks, " Do you think that time and space exist? " [29]

Throughout all, distortion holds sway. There is no fable for this drama, no direct line of action, unless one says that Indra's Daughter is wandering on earth to experience the lot of mankind. And even the Daughter realizes that all is topsyturvy on this earth.

> *The Daughter (standing by the organ).* Do you know what I see here in the mirror? . . . The world turned aright! . . . Yes, inasmuch as it is awry in itself!
>
> *The Lawyer.* How did it get awry?
>
> *The Daughter.* When the copy was made. . . .
>
> *The Lawyer.* There you said it! The copy . . . it was always my suspicion that it was a faulty copy . . . and when I would begin to remember the original images then I would become dissatisfied with everything . . . people called it discontentedness, the Devil's look in my eye, and something else. . . .
>
> *The Daughter.* No doubt it is crazy! . . .[30]

This quotation illustrates a fundamental principle of expressionism. One must not put all aside as dream stuff. Once more we call to mind the dialogue of the Daughter and the Poet; dream, reality and poetry are all mingled in one.[31] The expressionist says that reality cannot be apprehended by physical observation except as distortions,[32] and the Daughter of the Gods is the only one on earth who can look into the heart of reality; she alone can see the world aright. Indra's Daughter actually gives the secret of existence to the Poet: " The world, life and mankind are thus only a phantom, an apparition, an image out of a dream! "[33] All objective reality is a tangible nothing that consequently can never have independent existence. And mankind dreams not only when asleep, but also when wide awake! *A Dream Play* has much of this " wide-awake dreaming."

[29] Strindberg, XXXVI, 281.   [30] *Ibid.*, p. 249.   [31] *Ibid.*, p. 301.
[32] See pp. 15–17 above.   [33] Strindberg, XXXVI, 324.

The element of distortion also gives the effect of a dream within a dream. In an early scene of the play the Officer is clearly dreaming even within the dream frame itself; in fact, the Officer is consistently the most typical dreamer of all. In the scene just mentioned the Officer is talking with his father and mother, and yet in the latter's presence he can say: " Imagine that cupboard still standing there after twenty years . . . we have moved so many times and my mother died ten years ago! " [34] Throughout the drama there are numerous occasions when characters seem enfonced in the unconscious by several dream depths. " I have heard that voice before, in my dreams . . . ," says the Blind Man.[35] The poet cries out, " That's just what I heard once upon a time . . ."; [36] and, again, " It seems to me that I formerly. . . ." [37] Still later, when the Poet sees the Officer come in and cry out for Victoria, he remarks, " It seems to me that I have experienced this before. . . ." It was also the Officer's experience and not the Poet's in the early part of the play.[38] Clearly, the Officer is the Poet and in the guise of the latter is dreaming of himself as the former. Even awakening hardly seems more than a passing from one dream state to another, as though man is constantly dreaming within a dream.

> *The Daughter.* Have you always doubted?
>
> *The Poet.* No! I have had certainty many times; but after a time it went its way, just like a dream when one awakens! [39]

Certainty, consciousness of objective reality is unstable and practically lacks being. The dream state alone is functional, whatsoever the circumstances may be, and there are only transitions from one form of distortion to another, from one dream scene to another. " The puzzling sleepwalkers on the stage engage each other in real intercourse and at the same time they

---

[34] *Ibid.*, p. 227.
[35] *Ibid.*, p. 286.
[36] *Ibid.*, p. 299.
[37] *Ibid.*, p. 300.
[38] *Ibid.*, p. 232.
[39] *Ibid.*, p. 323.

dream about each other. In part these dreams agree with the spectator's, and the whole is twisted together in a single huge dream-tangle, our life's nightmare that cannot be disentangled. Just like the characters in the drama, we wander about in reality as though we were in the world of dreams, we refashion our life into a dream in order to deliver ourselves from reality's grim torment. . . ." [40] " It is this complex feeling that dream frees us from the weight of reality, and reality from the nightmare of dream, that makes *A Dream Play* in spite of its pessimism seem less unpleasant than Strindberg's pictures from actual reality." [41]

ANTITHESES

THE Picardian concept of the struggle of opposites toward each other is softened though by no means lost in *A Dream Play*. In dramas like *The Father* and *The Dance of Death* the opposites are represented by symbols of the most tangible kind. Type man and type woman are the opposites in the struggle, and the dramas literally burn with the terrific tension of the combat. In *To Damascus* we also have the struggle, but this time the manifestations in material form are merely indications of another battle, " Jacob wrestling with God." The Unknown struggles with the " Powers," with the Unseen One. In *A Dream Play* the typical marriage scenes of love-hate quality are present but the circumstances are by no means such that the tension of the struggle endures. The dream character of the play removes much of the sting from the scenes; and, again, since the woman in the play is Indra's Daughter as well as typical woman, one has far more patience with her, even if she is an uncommonly poor housekeeper!

Furthermore, the element of conflict in *A Dream Play* is rationalized and fixed; it is accepted so thoroughly that all argument is precluded. From the beginning of the play to the end

[40] Lamm, II, 316.   [41] *Ibid.,* p. 323.

these various antitheses are thrown out at us either fixed in comments or demonstrated in scenes of short duration. The dream
scene of the Officer [42] offers an opportunity for the Father and
the Mother to quarrel about a scarf which he gave her. In the
first " Fingal's Cave " scene, the Daughter asks the lawyer if there
is nothing at all in life that offers joy, and the latter answers:
" Yes, the sweetest which is the most bitter — love! A wife and
a home! the highest and the lowest! " [43] Even the staging itself
presents opposites. Fairhaven and Foulstrand are given together
in two different scenes.[44] In the first scene Foulstrand is in the
foreground with Fairhaven in the background; in the second
scene the arrangement is reversed. Here is this curious world of
contradictions that the Officer makes note of but does not struggle
against.[45] Likewise, two children in summer clothing are playing on the stage at a time when the scene represents winter.[46]

All the characters have accepted this world of opposites. The
Officer suffers agony when the woman whom he recognizes as
Victoria is at the height of joy.[47] The Husband tells his Wife
that he wishes to die when happiness is so great, because " right
in the midst of happiness there sprouts a seed of misfortune; it
eats itself like the flame . . . , it cannot burn eternally but must
die out; this presentiment of the end annihilates bliss right at
the high point." [48] The Blind Man also cries out stoically: " To
meet and to part; to part and to meet! That's life! " [49] The
Lawyer remarks that when he has a pleasant day and evening,
the next day is certain to bring him the torments of hell and an
evil conscience; and he also makes the paradoxical statement
that " to have talent is a mortal danger, for one may easily starve

[42] Strindberg, XXXVI, 225.
[43] *Ibid.,* p. 252.
[44] *Ibid.,* pp. 264–291.   [45] *Ibid.,* p. 269.
[46] *Ibid.,* p. 276.
[47] *Ibid.,* p. 275 (every bride or betrothed one is a ",Victoria ").
[48] *Ibid.,* p. 284 (see also *To Damascus,* Strindberg, XXIX, 54).
[49] *Ibid.,* p. 286.

to death!" [50]   When the Daughter cries out, " This is paradise," a coal-heaver, close at hand, offers the natural opposite, " This is hell!" [51]   The coal-heaver adds more material of the same kind when he says: " We who work the most eat the least; and the rich who do nothing have the most!" [52]

There is also the reiterated antithesis of the evil acts of the " right-thinking people."

> *The Daughter.* Why do they complain more than usual today?
>
> *The Lawyer.* Because the sun is shining here, because there is music here, dance, and youth! They feel their misery so much more deeply.
>
> *The Daughter.* We must deliver them!
>
> *The Lawyer.* Just try! One time a deliverer did come but he was hung on a cross!
>
> *The Daughter.* By whom?
>
> *The Lawyer.* By all the right-thinking people! [53]
>
> .   .   .   .
>
> *The Daughter.* Why is it that people do nothing to better conditions?
>
> *The Lawyer.* Well, but they do! But all the reformers end either in prison or in the insane asylum. . . .
>
> *The Daughter.* Who puts them in prison?
>
> *The Lawyer.* All the right-thinking, all the respectable. . . .
>
> *The Daughter.* Who puts them in the insane asylum?
>
> *The Lawyer.* Their own despair at seeing the hopelessness of the struggle.[54]
>
> .   .   .   .
>
> *The Daughter.* What boat can that be?
>
> *The Poet.* I believe that it's the spook-ship.
>
> *The Daughter.* What is that?
>
> *The Poet.* The Flying Dutchman.
>
> *The Daughter.* He? Why is he punished so severely and why doesn't he come ashore?

---

[50] Strindberg, XXXVI, 288 (Strindberg, and a whole host of artists, could well make the same statement and point to personal experiences as incontrovertible evidence).   [51] *Ibid.,* p. 291.   [53] *Ibid.,* p. 290.
[52] *Ibid.,* p. 292.   [54] *Ibid.,* p. 294.

The Poet. Because he had seven unfaithful wives.

The Daughter. Is he to be punished for that?

The Poet. Yes! All the right-thinking people condemned him. . . .[55]

.   .   .   .

The Daughter. Who is coming there?

The Poet. Walking on the water? There is only one who walks on
the water — Peter, the living rock, is not the one, for he sank like
a stone. . . .

The Crew. Christ Kyrie!

The Daughter. Is it he?

The Poet. It is he, the crucified one. . . .

The Daughter. Why — tell me, why was he crucified?

The Poet. Because he wished to deliver. . . .

The Daughter. Who — I have forgotten — who crucified him?

The Poet. All the right-thinking people.

The Daughter. What a curious world! [56]

The Deans of the four Faculties and the Lord Chancellor also
add to the antithesis in the little satire of which Strindberg has
made a dream scene. The Deans and the Lord Chancellor quibble
in their academic chatter until the Daughter of Indra cries out
in protest.

The Daughter. For shame, teachers of the youth!

Dean of Law. Lord Chancellor, representative of the government, chief
of instruction, prosecute this woman's misdemeanour! She said to
you " for shame! " That's an insult. And, in a derisive, ironical
manner she has called you the instructors of the youth, and that is
abusive language.

The Daughter. Poor Youth! [57]

Before long, the Dean of Law has also appealed to the " right-
thinking people " and the Daughter of Indra has received their
condemnation. Life is a series of antitheses, of contradictions,
of opposites in struggle, and essential reality seems quite in-

tangible. The Daughter of Indra voices such an opinion even at the very close of the drama, just before she is ready to leave this world.

> *Daughter.* O, now I sense the whole of mortal's pain,
> So is it, thus, to be of human kind. . . .
> One lacks what one has never cherished
> One has regrets for what was never broken. . . .
> One would go forth and yet would fain remain. . . .
> And thus the heart's each half is torn apart,
> And feelings rent as though 'twixt horses
> By contrast, vacillation and disharmony. . . .[58]

SYMBOLS

THE use of symbols is not necessarily expressionistic, but is nevertheless in accordance with the practice in expressionism. In *A Dream Play* there are four symbols which predominate: Indra's Daughter, the growing castle, the secret door and the shawl.

Indra's Daughter is a female figure of the pattern of Christ. She is a symbol of womanhood as well as a shadow of a particular individual, Harriet Bosse. The Daughter is further a symbol of Strindberg's hope that reconciliation to life would come through woman.[59] The hope was so strong in Strindberg that even after three unsatisfactory unions he contemplated a fourth marriage and actually proposed to the woman.[60]

The symbol of the growing castle is easy to interpret; it represents life itself, especially the physical being which imprisons the soul. At the end of the drama the Daughter enters the burning castle which shows a wall of human faces questioning,

[58] Strindberg, XXXVI, 329.

[59] In medieval Christianity, and still in Roman Catholicism, a woman also plays a similar rôle, Mary, Mother of Jesus. Indra's Daughter, however, is not modelled on Mary, for she is a product of Strindberg's life-long desire, not of Strindberg's post-Inferno theology and mysticism. Even in his first play, *A Name's-day Gift,* Strindberg sought reconciliation to his father through his stepmother.

[60] See Fanny Falkner, *Strindberg i blå tornet.*

sorrowing and thrown into doubt. As the castle burns the bud
on the top bursts into a giant chrysanthemum; in other words,
as the body disappears, the soul, formerly potential but im-
prisoned, is released and becomes beautiful. That this is more
than symbol for Strindberg is evidenced by the letter he wrote
to Carl Larsson on the 2d of November, 1901: " Life has become
more and more dream-like and inexplicable for me — possibly
death is really the awakening! " [61]

The riddle of life is symbolized by the secret door with the
trefoil opening.[62] When the door is finally opened there seems
to be nothing behind it, and the Dean of the Theological Faculty
cries out: " Nothing! That's the solution to the riddle of the
universe — Out of nothing God created Heaven and earth in the
beginning." [63] But Lamm adds a wise word: it is the Dean of
Theology who speaks and not the Daughter of Indra; and, inasmuch as the Dean is a subject of Strindberg's satire, it scarcely
follows that his words should be taken as the dramatist's own
opinion. The real answer is not given to Deans of Faculties! It
comes only to the Poet, when near the end of the drama the
Daughter says to him: " The World, life and mankind are thus
only a phantom, an apparition, an image out of a dream! " [64] If
this is the answer to be accepted, then neither the Glazier nor the
Deans can possibly find anything behind the door. None of
mankind can guess the answer to the riddle of existence, but the
Daughter of Indra may whisper the solution in the soul of the
Poet.

The shawl [65] is obviously the cloak of human misery, for it is

[61] Lamm, II, 315.

[62] Strindberg, XXXVI, 233, 238, 239, 241, 242, 243, 247, 267, 289, 310,
312, 316, 317 (see Lamm, II, 326: such a door was actually in the old
Dramatic theater in Stockholm and Strindberg was continually wondering
what was behind it when he was waiting for Harriet Bosse).

[63] *Ibid.*, p. 317.

[64] *Ibid.*, p. 324 (see also above, p. 182).

[65] *Ibid.*, pp. 231, 236, 237, 244, 245, 248, 327.

heavy with all the human woes that have come to the Portress during thirty years; and it seems to weigh down and burn the individual who wears it. In *To Damascus*, I, the Lady was constantly engaged in a bit of fancy work that became extremely dirty before the end of the wanderings, though the Unknown remarked that it could be washed.[66]   In *A Dream Play* the Lawyer desires to burn the shawl with all its miseries and sorrows, but the Daughter first wants it full before she disposes of it.[67]   A little later, however, she announces that she has actually washed the shawl.[68]   But even washing seems to be of no avail, for the shawl is burned at the end of the drama when the Daughter is preparing to forsake this world.[69]   Here the meaning is clear; when we forsake the body we also leave behind us the cloak of miseries and sorrows that covers our existence.

RELATION TO MUSIC

Music is used as a mood accompaniment to the drama rather frequently.[70]   In one scene there is also a musical antithesis in which Ugly Edith [71] plays on the piano Sebastian Bach's *Toccata con Fuga*, No. 10, in opposition to the waltz that is coming from the dance hall.   In the stage directions Strindberg gives a clear indication of the struggle: " The waltz from the hall is first heard softly but rises as though battling against Bach's Toccata. Edith, however, plays it down and brings it to silence.   The guests at the ball appear in the doors and listen to her playing; all on the stage stand attentively listening." [72]   Music accompanies the leitmotif in *The Bridal Crown*,[73] but not that in *A*

---

[66] Strindberg, XXIX, 125.
[67] *Ibid.*, XXXVI, 245.   [68] *Ibid.*, p. 248.
[69] *Ibid.*, p. 327.
[70] *Ibid.*, pp. 238, 248, 250, 270, 272, 277, 278, 297–300, 307, 330.
[71] Is an antithesis also implied in the situation itself. *Ugly* Edith has command of *beautiful* music?
[72] Strindberg, XXXVI, 278.   [73] See above, p. 174.

Dream Play. The sentence which is repeated so often, almost exclusively by the Daughter of Indra, is the main theme of the drama: " Mankind is to be pitied! " [74]

There are several elements of the so-called contrapuntal method that are perfectly obvious. The symbols, the leitmotif and the idea of suffering [75] weave in and out of the play. Then, again, there is the repetition of the scene in which the Officer calls for Victoria.[76] The Poet also adds to the warp and woof of the pattern by declaring that he dimly recalls living through that scene once before. There is also the shadow of a return to the style of staging given in *To Damascus*, I. The first and last scenes are identical in setting, and give the same impression that one gains from *To Damascus*, I; the whole drama seems like a paradox of fixed motion. There has been constant change and activity, but the return to the original starting point reminds one that the action has come from one's own imagination and like a dream has disappeared on awakening. Then, too, there is a rather clumsy passing in review of all the characters of the play.[77] The Daughter, Portress, Officer, Bill-poster, Glazier, Lawyer, Quarantine Master, Victoria, Ugly Edith and the Blind Man all pass over the stage and contribute something to the flames, at the same time that Don Juan rolls across the stage in a wheelchair! This is an attempt to manipulate again the contrapuntal staging of *To Damascus*, but is admittedly rather unsuccessful.[78] The contrapuntal turning point of the drama seems to be at the Fairhaven and Foulstrand scenes; but, according to Lamm, Strindberg apparently grew weary and hurried back to the original scene without too much regard for his method.

[74] Strindberg, XXXVI, 229, 231, 246, 249, 259, 276, 284, 318.

[75] *Ibid.*, pp. 219, 224, 226, 229, 230, 231, 237, 246, 249, 250, 252, 270, 275, 283, 284, 285, 289, 290, 299, 321, 329,

[76] *Ibid.*, pp. 232, 310.

[77] *Ibid.*, pp. 326–329,

[78] Lamm, II, 318,

There is, furthermore, another very striking appearance of contrapuntal style, the constant reiteration of antitheses.[79] The Officer's comment, " This curious world of contradictions," runs through the entire drama in various shapes and manifestations. With its manifold changes and yet constant progression this concept of antitheses becomes the most important in the contrapuntal element of *A Dream Play*. It establishes harmonies and discords throughout in its vertical contacts with the leitmotif, and the element of suffering. Yet, the antithesis, like the other elements, is also in constant horizontal progression.

It is impossible for drama to be as immediate as music in transmuting objective experience into feeling, but *A Dream Play* has certainly accomplished much within the limits of its art-form. The play not only employs music as sound to pitch the mood of various situations, but also uses the so-called contrapuntal method of dialogue. In this respect *A Dream Play* becomes fully rounded out as an expressionistic drama, for practically all factors are present.

THE WORTH OF MAN

THE leitmotif of *A Dream Play*, " Mankind is to be pitied," sounds also the expressionistic note of the worth of man. The well-nigh innumerable references to sufferings, complaints and misery give us a score in minor that is relieved by the theme in major, " Mankind is to be pitied ! " It is an ancestor to the plea in later expressionism for the worth of man. At the end of the drama the Daughter of Indra promises to carry the cause of mankind " to the throne " of Indra himself.

The selection of a Daughter of the Gods instead of a Son is in accordance with Strindberg's hope of being reconciled to life through the agency of woman. Strindberg, of course, could not

[79] Strindberg, XXXVI, 225, 250, 252, 259, 265, 269, 275, 284, 286, 288, 290, 291, 292, 294, 296, 305–306, 307–308, 312–315, 316, 317, 319, 324, 325, 326, 329.

resist giving Indra's Daughter some touches which betray his disgust with women; for instance, the Daughter is a most abominable housekeeper. Yet Strindberg could well defend himself with the argument that it was necessary to give Indra's Daughter the guise as well as the experiences of mankind so that she could later report to the Almighty Father on the lot of men.

CONCLUSION

" A DREAM PLAY," like *To Damascus,* is an exquisite expressionistic drama. It is well rounded out with all the characteristics of expressionism; and these are, furthermore, well moulded into the art-product. Typification, autobiographical data, dream character, distortion, contrapuntal method and other factors leave not the echo of suspicion that *A Dream Play* can be anything but an expressionistic drama.

CHAPTER VI

CHAMBER PLAYS AND DRAMATIC FRAGMENTS

CHAMBER PLAYS

Opus 1. The Thunderstorm

L ANDAU comments on the musical construction of *The Thunderstorm:* [1] " Musikalisch ist der ganze Aufbau von Stücken, wie *Das Gewitter*, wo dieselben Motive wiederkehren, dieselben Themen stets von neuem angeschlagen werden." [2] It is true that the outstanding characteristic of this play is its similarity to music in construction, as analysis soon proves. The memories of the Master bob up constantly,[3] the new occupants of the house remain as shadows early in the drama,[4] the storm adds to the mood,[5] man is murdered when his honor is slain,[6] hate is in the atmosphere,[7] and the Master is proud that in spite of his fifty years he was not too old for the young wife, inasmuch as they soon had a child.[8]

There is also the autobiographical element behind the play. The Master is an image of Strindberg, and the Brother is modelled after Strindberg's own brother Axel, who used to visit the dramatist frequently.[9] Apart from this autobiographical factor and that of music, however, the play is almost lost in an impressionistic haze of memories. It is certainly not an outstand-

[1] Written 1907.

[2] Landau, " Strindberg als Dramatiker des Expressionismus," *Die deutsche Bühne,* May 24, 1920, p. 374.

[3] Strindberg, XLV, 11, 17, 20, 26, 29, 33, 34, 39, 40, 41, 42, 64, 74.

[4] *Ibid.,* pp. 9, 13, 20, 21, 22, 24, 25, 37, 48.

[5] *Ibid.,* pp. 21, 41, 47, 58, 68.

[6] *Ibid.,* pp. 15, 16, 28, 30, 52, 68.

[7] *Ibid.,* pp. 26, 43, 52, 53, 68.

[8] *Ibid.,* pp. 15, 16, 27, 51.

[9] Lamm, II, 375.

ingly expressionistic play, in spite of some factors. It might yield more readily to analysis according to norms of impressionism.

Opus 2. After the Fire

THE second of the chamber plays, *After the Fire*,[10] compares rather favorably with *The Thunderstorm*. It also has the autobiographical background, and the whole play is built up on the resurgence of the past, first in memories and then in fact, through the gutting of the burned dwelling. The memories, all built up on misinformation or fabrications, are blasted when the fire brings facts to light.

One item in the play [11] expresses the point of view that all things are woven together, but so woven that each individual seems to have the whole scene before him separately. The Stranger, who has discussed the product of the " world-weaver," also declares that he feels like a sleepwalker on the edge of a roof. He knows that he is asleep and yet he is awake. He also refers to the distortion of objective reality: ". . . when one is born without a film on the eyes, then one can see life and men as they are . . . and one would be a swine if he could thrive in this sludge. — But when one has had his fill of the blue mists he turns his eyes inside out and looks within his own soul. There one finds something really worth looking at — Himself! But when one has seen himself, he dies! " [12] This is obviously very close to expressionism, but the evidence is by no means convincing. *After the Fire* does not respond very well to expressionistic analysis.

Opus 3. The Ghost Sonata

IN *The Ghost Sonata* [13] we encounter once more a full-fledged expressionistic drama. The mere reading of the play carries

---

[10] Written 1907.
[11] Strindberg, XLV, 96–97.   [12] *Ibid.,* pp. 138–139.
[13] Written 1907 (see note in item 64, list of Strindberg's plays, p. 219).

conviction of the soundness of the judgment, and analysis furnishes the evidence. The play is filled with autobiographical data, antitheses, distortion, contrapuntal dialogue, pantomime, pause and continuous wide-awake dreaming. Strindberg's letter of March 27, 1907, to Emil Schering gives further strength to the evidence of expressionism: *The Ghost Sonata* " ist furchtbar wie das Leben, wenn einem die Schuppen von den Augen fallen und man ' Das Ding an sich ' sieht." [14]

The autobiographical content of the play is found especially in the discussions of the Student and the Young Lady concerning the annoying duties of a household. In a letter of April 7, 1907, Strindberg indicates the importance of some of these details: " Vergessen Sie nicht die Sojaflasche, das Kolorit, unter der ich jetzt dreissig Tage gelitten; habe gefärbtes Wasser gegessen! " [15] Lamm shows rather clearly that the drama gathered much material from Strindberg's troubles in March, 1907; he had difficulties with servants, with his quarters, with food, and with all that goes to make up a household.[16] The recurrence of the same ideas in *The Pelican* shows how much Strindberg was affected by forty days of household disorder.

For an immediate representative of Strindberg in the play there is no question but that the Student, a child of extraordinary vision, owing to his birth on a Sunday, is the dramatist himself. In any attempt at identification, however, we must bear in mind the caution that Strindberg administered to Schering: " Nun bitte ich Sie, lesen Sie meine neuen Dramen nur als solche; es ist Mosaik wie gewöhnlich, aus fremden und eigenem Leben; aber bitte, nehmen Sie es nicht als Selbstbiographie oder als Bekenntnisse. Was nicht mit der Tatsache stimmt, ist gedichtet, nicht gelogen." [17] One cannot take the characters out of an expres-

---

[14] Strindberg, *Werke*, Abt. 8, Bd. III, 202.
[15] *Ibid.*, p. 207.
[16] Lamm, II, 399.
[17] Strindberg, *Werke*, Abt. 8, Bd. III, 204 (letter of April 2, 1907).

sionistic play and fit them exactly to individuals any more than one can take an expressionistic painting and make the details of line and color agree with the original object. A psychoanalyst would do the well-nigh impossible and make identifications, but the critic of expressionistic drama is responsible only for pointing out likenesses and distortions.

The characters of *The Ghost Sonata* are certainly a queer lot. The Old Man, Director Hummel, and the cook are vampires who seem like devastating dragons out of fairy lore. The Old Man is eighty years of age,[18] but he has an infinitely long life behind him;[19] and, from his interest in the destinies of all people,[20] it would seem that time has had no place in his life. He is also a " troll "-man [21] and " has been everything." [22] If this drama is " Mosaik wie gewöhnlich, aus fremden und eigenem Leben," then surely this character of the Old Man must be a distortion of Strindberg's experiences with a certain individual or else a group of individuals.

The Student, too, is an unusual figure. He is a " Sunday child " and is gifted with vision that children born on week-days never have.[23] He sees the Milkmaid when she is invisible to the Old Man; [24] likewise, he sees the Dead One, when the Old Man sees nothing; [25] and, later, only the Student and the Old Man see the Milkmaid.[26] The Student also considers the Young Lady beautiful, and the Old Man remarks that the Young Man sees what others cannot.[27]

The Milkmaid and the Dead One are naturally enough silent

---

[18] Strindberg, XLV, 158.
[19] *Ibid.,* p. 163.
[20] *Ibid.,* p. 158 (also has knowledge of everyone, *Ibid.,* p. 157).
[21] *Ibid.,* p. 178.   [24] *Ibid.,* p. 150.
[22] *Ibid.,* p. 168.   [25] *Ibid.,* p. 166.
[23] *Ibid.,* p. 159.   [26] *Ibid.,* p. 173.
[27] *Ibid.,* p. 163 (this statement is obviously and perhaps intentionally ambiguous; a young man *always* sees in a certain young lady what others fail to observe).

figures, and many of the other characters have little or nothing to say. The Mummy, however, is another clear distortion of observed reality. In the early part of the play,[28] the Old Man says that the Colonel's wife sits inside the house like a mummy and worships her own statue, and Johansson later develops the concept with the aid of the Mummy's voice.[29] When the Colonel's wife is first shown to the spectators she appears like the distortion that the Old Man and Johansson have presented,[30] and she prattles meaningless stuff. Yet she talks seriously soon after meeting the Old Man and toward the end of the play gives him the rôle of Mummy.[31]

This element of distortion also extends to the afternoon tea which is first described to us as a " ghost supper." [32] When the guests are finally assembled for this tea, the atmosphere is such that the social function becomes quite spectral.[33] The whole play is, in fact, an excellent illustration of the principle of distortion. Things are distorted in order that we may get a closer view of truth subjectively.

The speech of the Student toward the end of the play is especially significant in showing the pattern of distortion in this play. He implies that his conversation with the Young Lady should be interpreted in the same manner that he presents an experience of his father's. The Student's father had invited a large number of guests. Weary with the day's work and with the struggle " att dels tiga, dels prata skit med gästerna " the father finally told all his guests to " go to hell! " The Student, too, is weary and strikes through everything.

> By keeping silent too long one collects the still waters that rot, and so it is in this house too. There is something rotten here. And I thought that it was paradise when I saw you enter here for the first time. . . . Then it was on a Sunday morning I stood and looked inside. I saw a Colonel

---

[28] Strindberg, XLV, p. 159 (see Lamm, II, 394).   [31] *Ibid.*, p. 194.
[29] *Ibid.*, p. 175.   [32] *Ibid.*, p. 174.
[30] *Ibid.*, p. 179.   [33] *Ibid.*, pp. 190–193.

who was no colonel. I had a noble benefactor who was a bandit and had to hang himself. I saw a Mummy who was none and a maid — by the way, where do you find virginity? where beauty? In nature and in my mind when it is dressed in Sunday clothes. Where is honor and faith? In the sagas and the fancies of children. Where can I find anything that maintains what it promises? — In my imagination! * * * There are poisons that blind you and poisons that open the eyes — I must have been born with the latter, for I cannot regard the ugly as beautiful, nor call evil good — I cannot! Jesus Christ descended into hell; that was his wandering on earth, — this madhouse, this prison, this morgue of an earth. And the madmen killed him when he wished to deliver them, but the thief was let loose. The robber always gets sympathy! Woe! Woe unto us all! Saviour of the World, save us — we perish." [34]

The Student shows clearly that all objective reality is after all not what it seems. One has to turn within himself in order to find something that " maintains what it promises." Essential reality is within the ego and not in the empirical world.

This turning to one's own ego almost brought Strindberg to the point of creating a new dramatic form which he called the monodrama, a play in which only one character would be on the stage and the dialogue would be maintained between this one character and voices off stage.[35] There is a hint of this type of play in *The Stronger* [36] in which there are two characters on the stage, but only one speaks throughout the entire play. The one clear example of the monodrama is the Prologue to *A Dream Play*. In this Prologue Indra's Daughter alone appears on the stage and the dialogue is maintained by the voice of Indra off stage. But, had Strindberg proceeded with the monodrama, he might have sunk so wholly within the ego that his drama would have been in serious danger of turning into monomania drama. As it is, Strindberg has well developed the expressionistic monologist in *To Damascus* and *The Great Highway*.

Music as sound occurs rather infrequently in *The Ghost Sonata*,[37] but the drama well illustrates the contrapuntal form of

---

[34] *Ibid.*, pp. 208–210.
[35] Lamm, II, 365.
[36] Written 1888–89.
[37] Strindberg, XLV, 150, 195, 210, 211.

dialogue. Antitheses, for example, meet us throughout the drama in different guise. Fame and blame go together.[38] The Student's father and the Old Man are both described as scoundrels and as benefactors in their relations with each other.[39] The Old Man and his fiancée had plighted everlasting troth, but at the time of the play they do not even recognize each other.[40] The Old Man says that during his entire life he has always taken but now he has the irresistible desire to give.[41] The Old Man refers to the Dead One as " a well-doing scoundrel." [42] Johansson says: " This is a horrible house . . . and the Student desired to come here as though to a paradise." [43] The Student declares that his father was well but crazy.[44] And, finally, the Student speaks of the ugly and the beautiful, of good and of evil.[45] These antitheses may appeal to one as more or less accidental, but from our knowledge of *A Dream Play* with its mass of antitheses it is safe to assume that Strindberg was still consciously emphasizing " this curious world of contradictions " when he was writing *The Ghost Sonata*.

The dialogue and staging furnish other examples of the contrapuntal method: the collapse of the house,[46] the Japanese screen,[47] the statue of the Colonel's wife,[48] the vision of the Milkmaid,[49] hyacinths and the hyacinth room,[50] the opera [51] and the vampires.[52]

Pantomime is not employed very much,[53] but pause occurs

[38] Strindberg, XLV, 152.
[39] *Ibid.,* p. 154.
[40] *Ibid.,* p. 161.
[41] *Ibid.,* p. 164.
[42] *Ibid.,* p. 167.
[43] *Ibid.,* p. 177.
[44] *Ibid.,* p. 207.
[45] *Ibid.,* p. 209.
[46] *Ibid.,* pp. 151, 160, 165, 169, 170, 188.
[47] *Ibid.,* pp. 177, 182, 194, 196, 210.
[48] *Ibid.,* pp. 149, 158, 159, 163, 174, 176, 177, 179.
[49] *Ibid.,* pp. 150–151, 152, 160, 170, 172, 173, 193.
[50] *Ibid.,* pp. 149, 159, 165, 174, 181, 188, 189, 196–198, 209.
[51] *Ibid.,* pp. 156, 164, 165, 171, 173, 178.
[52] *Ibid.,* pp. 163, 169, 184, 192, 193 (Old Man); 199–201, 205, 209 (Cook).
[53] *Ibid.,* pp. 150, 157, 172.

with astonishing frequency.[54] These elements, however, must not be considered too seriously in judging a drama. When, as in *The Ghost Sonata*, they accompany other expressionistic factors, they help to complete the evidence, but when they stand alone they are almost useless as evidence.

The Ghost Sonata is a clear example of the dream form of play, unless one is thinking of gentle fairy-tale dreams. Lamm does not think that this play has dream form, but at the same time he says that Strindberg has substituted caricature for reality.[55] Lamm calls it " deformed reality." From our knowledge of expressionism we readily see that this " deformed reality " is dream distortion, or distortion that arises through inner experiences. *A Dream Play* gave us distortion of the arrangement of elements, and *The Ghost Sonata* gives us in addition a distortion of the elements themselves. In fact, through this factor of distortion, *The Ghost Sonata* must be placed with the expressionistic dramas. The other evidence does much to determine the character of this play, but the element of distortion is the most powerful of all.

Opus 4. The Pelican

THE fourth chamber play takes us back to the one-act plays of the 'nineties, as Lamm observes.[56] *The Pelican* [57] seems like a continuation of *Facing Death*,[58] except that in the former play the Mother is still very much alive. She has murdered her husband both physically and spiritually, according to a letter received by the Son. The letter further reveals that the Mother has been the vampire in the family, that she is murdering the children as surely as she did the Father.

[54] *Ibid.*, pp. 152, 154, 166, 181, 183(2), 184(2), 186, 190 (whole page slowly and with pauses), 191(6), 192, 195, 199, 201, 203, 204, 205, 206(2), 207(2), 208.

[55] Lamm, II, 393–395.

[56] *Ibid.*, p. 405.

[57] Written 1907.

[58] Written 1893.

This play has expressionistic elements. The figure of the Mother is certainly a distortion of reality by magnification, for no such human vampire could long escape the prison or the insane asylum. She is a good reproduction of the cook in *The Ghost Sonata;* and, like the cook, owes her existence partly to Strindberg's unhappy experiences in his bachelor quarters during March, 1907. *The Pelican* is really a distorted view of Strindberg's difficulties with food, warmth and household sanitation.

In *The Ghost Sonata* there were visionary creatures and dead ones that walked about. In *The Pelican,* however, the supernatural is manifested especially by inanimate objects. The rocking-chair symbolizes the spirit of the dead father, so much so that whenever the chair rocks the Mother is convinced that some invisible creature is seated there.

Strindberg once thought of calling this play *The Sleepwalker.*[59] In many respects the people in the drama are " sleepwalkers in the broad daylight." The Son-in-law warns the Mother that the Daughter is beginning to awaken from her sleepwalking.[60] And the Daughter, in a conversation with the Son, cries out, " Hush! I am walking in my sleep, I know, but I don't want to be awakened! For then I should not be able to live! " The Son replies: " Well, but don't you think we are all sleepwalkers? "[61] A little later in the same conversation the Daughter remarks: " I can hear your thoughts in the silence. . . . When people meet, they talk, talk everlastingly simply that they may conceal their thoughts . . . to forget, to stupefy themselves . . . they wish to hear the news of others, but they hide their own! " Gerda knows that she is a sleepwalker but she doesn't want the rude awakening, so she talks endlessly to stupefy herself. The Son, who has awakened,[62] is so distressed by what he sees that he immediately proceeds to get drunk and stay drunk that he may preserve the

[59] Lamm, II, 406.
[60] Strindberg, XLV, 238.
[61] *Ibid.,* p. 246.
[62] *Ibid.,* p. 251.

condition of former days; otherwise, he fears that he will commit suicide.[63] The Mother cries out that at last she is awakening " as though out of a long, long sleep." [64] But Gerda assures her a little later that she is still a sleepwalker.[65]

Music, as sound, is employed in *The Pelican*. As the play opens, Chopin's *Fantaisie Impromptu, Oeuvre Posthume,* opus 66, is played off stage. The stage direction before the second scene states that Godard's *Berceuse* from *Jocelyn* is being played off stage, but there is no indication how long the music continues. The last part of the drama is accompanied by Ferrari's waltz, *Il me disait,* which is likewise played off stage. The contrapuntal method also has some place in this drama; the spooky rocking-chair gains attention frequently,[66] the Son has always been cold and hungry,[67] and the figure of speech comparing the Mother with the pelican is employed several times.[68]

In *The Dance of Death*, II, the vampire was very active during the progress of the drama and thus added materially to the sense of the struggle. In *The Pelican,* on the other hand, the larger part of the vampire's work has preceded the drama and we are given only the last few spasms of this stage nightmare. As Lamm also observes,[69] *The Pelican* is grotesque while *The Dance of Death* is tragic.

The Pelican has a number of expressionistic factors, but is not a strong play of the expressionistic type. We must admit that the judgment of *The Pelican* may suffer through too close association with the more artistically moulded *The Ghost Sonata,* and also suffers from too much attention to food and household matters in general. The play should at least be put on the frontiers of expressionism, if not entirely within the domain.

[63] *Ibid.,* p. 267.
[64] *Ibid.,* p. 269.
[65] *Ibid.,* p. 274.

[66] *Ibid.,* pp. 236, 256, 263, 264–266, 268, 271.
[67] *Ibid.,* pp. 216, 218, 223, 227, 247, 250.
[68] *Ibid.,* pp. 229, 264, 266, 275, 279.
[69] Lamm, II, 412.

Opus 5. The Black Glove

THE fifth [70] of the chamber plays has for its subtitle " A Lyrical Fantasy," which should augur well for expressionistic material. The play is indeed lyrical and is a fantasy, but on reading it we find altogether too much scampering about of the Brownie to permit expressionistic interpretation. The elements of monologue, pantomime, pause, music as sound, and contra-puntal·technique are all present; but in spite of these elements the play is staged and toned in the mists of the impressionist's moments of beauty. Even the Brownie comments somewhat unfavorably on an expressionist's attempt to get at the heart of reality.

> *The Old Man.* Who is there? Are you a living thing . . .
>
> *The Brownie.* To be is to be apprehended . . .
> You have apprehended me!
> Therefore I am!
>
> *The Old Man.* But I wish to feel, I want to take hold of you!
> For otherwise you don't exist for me!
>
> *The Brownie.* You cannot grasp the rainbow but it *is* nevertheless!
> The mirage of the desert, of the sea, exists —
> I am a mirage; don't come too close to me,
> For then you will no longer see me,
> Though I continue to be.[71]

The Brownie further informs the Old Man that the latter's attempt to find unity in the world of multiplicity has not been very fruitful, for it is so easy to prove multiplicity. Once more essential happiness comes from memories as the Brownie opens the casket which contains relics of the past. The Old Man goes into ecstasy, and Sinding's *Frühlingsrauschen* adds to the mood.

The Black Glove with its musical background tempts one to put it in the expressionistic classification. Evidence once more holds up a forbidding hand.

[70] Written 1908-9.   [71] Strindberg, XLV, 316.

DRAMATIC FRAGMENTS

The Hollander

THE fragment *The Hollander* [72] has type figures in the dramatis personae. The Hollander is really the Flying Dutchman who is being punished because he had unfaithful wives. [73] In *A Dream Play* the Flying Dutchman had already been through seven marriages, but in *The Hollander* he has a background of only six. The seventh wife is Lilith, Adam's first wife and the mother of all demons, according to rabbinical documents. [74] Lilith is also of the flesh, fully as much as Wedekind's *Lulu*. Quite fittingly she first appears to the Hollander in a window, surrounded by men. The Mother in the drama is a rather shadowy figure; and Ukko, servant to the Hollander, and himself an unsuccessful artist, is apparently a grotesque. Ukko may also be a distortion of Geijerstam, for Ukko saves the colors which the Hollander prepares and the latter is suspicious that his assistant intends to use them for his own glory. In the same way, Geijerstam rendered much assistance to Strindberg, but the latter felt that the assistant was building his literary works almost entirely on the Strindbergian material. [75]

The first part of the play is certainly of dream fabric. The Hollander is seated on a bench in a small park of a seaport. He speaks in a long monologue until interrupted by the appearance of Lilith in the window. Then, another monologue is later broken by the entrance of the Mother. The dialogue considers the six wives of the Hollander; and, according to the husband, each of the wives was at fault! The Mother, who is clearly not of earth

[72] Written 1902 (see Lamm, II, 336).
[73] See above, pp. 186–187.
[74] Strindberg, *Samlade otryckta skrifter*, I, 217.
[75] See Erdmann, *Strindberg*, p. 773. Note also that in the novels *Götiska rummen* and *Svarta fanor*, Strindberg, XL and XLI, Geijerstam is portrayed in the character of " *Little* Zachris " (see Erdmann, p. 769).

stuff alone (perhaps she is the All Mother, the Eternal Feminine), promises to give the Hollander illusions once more; she will put him in society in the guise of a great painter. Hardly has she gone before the Hollander wishes that the apothecary were open that he might buy sleeping powders. His wish is no sooner expressed than the apothecary himself appears and delivers the powders. Another rubbing of the Aladdin lamp of desire, and the Hollander receives a spoon. But he discovers that he cannot differentiate between reality of consciousness and of dream, so he cries out: " This is just like a dream; what need have I then of sleeping powders! " [76]   So he throws away the powders and the spoon. Ukko appears and attaches himself as servant to the " great master," and a maid comes out of the apartment house to ask if her " Master " desires anything. The Mother evidently has fulfilled her promise. The Hollander is, in the very first scene, already a great painter, and his quarters are a luxurious apartment in the building opposite the park. This first scene is clearly dream stuff all the way through; indeed, radiation from the dream desire of the Hollander.

In the second tableau the Hollander is installed in his apartment and Ukko is his assistant artist. Lilith calls, and, despite all the warnings and protests on the part of Ukko, she is admitted. The Hollander seems to have known her before. He remembers as though in a dream, an ugly dream, that he has seen Lilith in a window surrounded by men. Lilith explains that she actually was the person in the window, but it was an innocent affair, her relative's birthday party. The Hollander also dimly recalls that he knew her, or someone like her, in Amsterdam; but " must have dreamt it! You see that when a man has lived as long as I have, dreams and experiences are blended." [77]   Clearly enough, Lilith is just what her name explains, Adam's first wife, and the mother of at least six demons: the Hollander's former wives! She is,

---

[76] Strindberg, *Samlade otryckta skrifter*, I, 216.   [77] *Ibid.*, p. 235.

however, also portrayed as typical woman,[78] for as such she gives the Hollander dream remembrances of his former wives and of other women he has known.

In a very short time the Hollander and Lilith agree to live together. The former claps his hands, the scenes open and the Hollander points to their home: "Step in, my Wife, in your home! — May God watch over our union!"[79] An Unseen Choir also sings:

> Eros Basileus!
> Ruler of all!
> Bow down hearts and minds!
> Extinguish hate and selfishness!
> Thou who guidest worlds
> With love almighty!
> Eros Basileus!

Ukko enters, observes the pair, and makes his comments on "love-hate, the sweet poison, the gentle scourge! the mild Fury born of night and hate!" Ukko ends his speech with the exhortation, "O Love, come, complete the work."

Love has evidently completed the work by the time of the third tableau, for already the sex struggle has begun. Lilith soon departs and the Hollander breathes more easily again. The fragment ends in this tableau with a comment by Ukko that the whole town knows Lilith, even if the Hollander does not. This statement carries a dual implication: Lilith as an individual woman in the play is a harlot; and she is a typical woman. This does not mean that all women are harlots, but implies that woman is essentially unmoral. She is lacking in the intellect that pronounces ethical distinctions, and consequently must yield either to the urge of her instincts or else be controlled by a stronger

---

[78] "Madonna worshipers" may deny that Lilith is typical woman; or, indeed, Laura in *The Father*, or Alice in *The Dance of Death.* They should not forget, however, that even Strindberg worshiped woman as "Madonna" at the same time that he appraised her as woman.

[79] Strindberg, *Samlade otryckta skrifter,* I, 246.

being, a man. Lilith remains typical even though she is qualified as a harlot.

This fragment has autobiographical elements, with the Hollander as mouthpiece for the dramatist. The drama is also a fair example of *Ausstrahlungen des Ichs*, for everything develops through the one character, the Hollander. All the figures are products of his own mind, and the scenes are visions flowing from his imagination. The unwritten fourth tableau is the same in setting as the first, a possible indication that the last tableau would return to the original dream fabric.

The drama also makes use of music as sound [80] and of the contrapuntal method. Antitheses,[81] the element of hate,[82] the idea of reconciliation through woman,[83] all build up the contrapuntally styled dialogue. Monologue [84] and pause [85] add a trifle to the technical evidence. The determining factor, however, is *Ausstrahlungen des Ichs*, which is so strongly in evidence. The fragment, in view of this analysis, should be classed with the expressionistic dramas.

" TOTEN-INSEL "

" Toten-Insel " [86] also has characteristics of expressionism, and might have developed into an expressionistic drama had it been carried beyond the second scene. The dramatis personae answer the qualifications for type figures: the Watchman, the Instructor, a Shadow Figure, an Invisible Choir, the Dead One, Assir (who was the Dead One in the first division of the play), the Wife, First Daughter, Second Daughter, the Son, the Colleague.

---

[80] Strindberg, *Samlade otryckta skrifter*, I, 204, 242, 246.
[81] *Ibid.*, pp. 205, 228, 244, 247, 250, 251, 253
[82] *Ibid.*, pp. 208, 209, 211, 247, 249.
[83] *Ibid.*, pp. 208, 211, 245.
[84] *Ibid.*, pp. 203–204, 205, 215, 216–219, 223.
[85] *Ibid.*, pp. 234, 235, 236, 238, 239, 251, 254.
[86] Written 1906.

The scene is laid in Hades with Böcklin's painting of *Toten-Insel* on a curtain for the background. A coffin is brought in, the Invisible Choir sings and the Dead One awakens. His mind, however, is still earth-bound, so he continues to think of earthly things. The Dead One is obviously a professor who has been pained almost to death by the frantic effort to get to school on time, read his themes, get enough sleep, pay his bills, borrow money and manage his wife. The wife, like many Strindbergian females, seemed to radiate more unkindness and meanness than love. Above all, the Dead One wants repose! The first scene closes with a speech from the Instructor: " Peace, Dead Man, have out your sleep for once. No school bell shall awaken you. The ringing now is over! The term has ended, examinations are set aside and summer leave begins! " [87]

In the second scene the Dead One is renamed " Assir," meaning " Earthman." According to the Swedenborgian principle that one continues after death what one has done in life,[88] Assir also proceeds with his earthly task of correcting themes. The Instructor interrupts him with a question:

> *Instructor (sitting down).* What are you correcting?
>
> *Assir.* Themes! Here is one who has written on " Life is a dream."
>
> *Instructor.* Well? What do you think of it?
>
> *Assir.* Why, life can't be a dream. Then it would be just nonsense!
>
> *Instructor.* But why? Can't a dream be instructive? Have you never had a dream of that kind? [89]

They talk of dream for a time without coming to any definite conclusion, except that Assir cannot determine what is dream and what is reality. The Instructor then cautions him: the professor should be a bit more careful in the correcting of themes. The dream motif runs through the entire scene until the Instructor

[87] Strindberg, *Samlade otryckta skrifter,* I, 299.
[88] Lamm, II, 403.
[89] Strindberg, *Samlade otryckta skrifter,* I, 300.

touches upon drama and says: " If life is a dream, then a drama
is a dream of a dream, even though you have employed it as
reality." [90]   The scene and the fragment both come to an end as
Assir longs for closer contacts " with Nature."

> *Assir.* But I want good company and beautiful landscapes.
>
> *The Instructor.* You will receive everything you wish . . . as long as
> your desire is reasonable! . . . Well, then, have a good trip!
>
> *Assir.* But light! light! After all this darkness!
>
> *The Instructor.* After the night comes the day; only in the darkness
> can a light shine; the moon gives no light in the daytime, but the
> midnight sun gives sunshine in the deep of the night! [91]

What there is of this drama is assuredly of an expressionistic
nature. That the dream fabric is consciously employed is well
illustrated by the Instructor's comments on life and drama. The
fragment *Toten-Insel* should also be included in our list of
Strindberg's expressionistic dramas.

[90] Strindberg, *Samlade otryckta skrifter*, I, 308.   [91] *Ibid.*, pp. 309–310

CHAPTER VII
CONCLUSION

THERE is need for a restatement of the problem discussed in this work. The first part of our book presented a systematic arrangement of the critical literature on expressionism in order to set down norms for the study of Strindberg's dramas. We put aside the problem of the aesthetics of expressionism as not pertinent to our particular field of inquiry, for we hold that the present work of systematization is a necessary basis for all other problems in this subject. Not until we know what the expressionists themselves have set forth in theory and practice is it possible for us to examine dramas for expressionistic content and form; nor, indeed, would it be possible even to discuss the aesthetic worth of expressionism. First of all, the word welter of expressionistic criticism must be ordered; and this has been done in our first part. We have established norms through a synthetic study of a large number of critics.

Likewise, in the part devoted to the study of Strindberg's dramas we have made each analysis in the light of the earlier study. We have pointed out the nature and the extent of Strindberg's dramatic expressionism [1] in relation to the elements set forth in Part I. All other problems were dismissed as irrelevant to this work.

To be more precise, we have dismissed some problems that are relevant to the subject but are not pertinent to the immediate discussion. Expressionism in Strindberg's historical dramas and in his non-dramatic works has been dismissed for practical

---

[1] The historical dramas were excluded; see pp. 86–87 above.

211

measures. Moreover, we have been rather silent regarding one
important issue, the relation of Strindberg's dramas to the religious aspect of expressionism.[2] It will be obvious to the readers
of Strindberg, or of this book, that the religious element plays a
strong part in the dramas, especially the post-Inferno plays.[3]
There is, however, a tangle in this religious material that cannot
be solved by a gesture accompanying another study. In the first
place, one would be obliged to consider Strindberg as a Lutheran,
a Unitarian, an atheist, a Swedenborgian, a Buddhist, a Roman
Catholic and a non-confessional mystic;[4] and one should be more
than indifferently learned in each. Secondly, Oswald Spengler's
statement concerning " the second religiousness "[5] of a Culture
World invites speculation that would necessarily throw the
study into an entirely different light. If Spengler is right,[6] we
may be close to a significant historical phenomenon in expressionism, despite Spengler's petulant dismissal of the movement:
that is, " the second religiousness " in Western Culture. Certainly
a study of Nietzsche,[7] Strindberg, G. B. Shaw [8] and expressionism
must challenge any fond prejudice that Christianity is surviving
in Western Civilization, especially if one also has observed the
events of the last fifty years. Likewise, our eyes should be opened
by the growing scepticism in science and the consequent disintegration of positivistic foundations. The Western World has
practically discarded its religion and is becoming weary of its

[2] See above, pp. 57–58.
[3] See *To Damascus, Easter, Advent, There are Crimes and Crimes,
The Bridal Crown, A Dream Play, Moses, Socrates, Christ, The Black
Glove* and *The Great Highway*. And there are more!
[4] See Karl Möhlig's *Strindberg und der Katholizismus,* and Liebert's
Strindberg — Seine Weltanschauung und Seine Kunst.
[5] See note 8, Part I, Chapter V.
[6] Right in assuming that we too shall have a " second religiousness "
in the Western World.
[7] Spiero refers us to Friedrich Rittelmeyer, *Friedrich Nietzsche und die
Religion,* München, 1920.
[8] See especially Shaw's *Back to Methuselah.*

science.[9] George Bernard Shaw coolly invites us to formulate a new religion if we would save ourselves,[10] and expressionism claims to have in itself the essence of religion, a new spirituality that in no wise depends on religious institutions. We have obviously a problem of great significance in the religious aspect of expressionism, but its partially speculative nature and its great dimensions naturally forbade inclusion in this study.[11]

In the second half of this book we have analyzed Strindberg's dramas individually, so our responsibility rests in the honesty and the accuracy of our work. There is little possibility that anyone versed in expressionistic criticism will object to our discussions of the post-Inferno dramas. Indeed, even a cursory reading of dramas like *To Damascus, A Dream Play* and *The Ghost Sonata* leaves no room for doubt. They are clearly what the German critics call expressionistic dramas.

Some critics may feel a slight shock in learning that *The Father* must be grouped with the expressionistic dramas, for this play has long been fondled as a naturalistic drama, especially as an example of early naturalism. Yet it is evidence that has forced us to make a reclassification. There are no ulterior motives behind this work; no feverish desire to force expressionism into Strindberg's dramas; and, further, no frantic endeavor to unearth something new. It is not the play of a critic's fancy, but the compulsion of evidence that determines the expressionistic character of *The Father.*

There can no longer be any reasonable doubt regarding the expressionistic nature of a number of Strindberg's dramas. We have studied these dramas according to the norms established from the German movement in expressionism, and the results are

[9] Note, for instance, Fosdick, " What is Religion? " and Bridgman, " The New Vision of Science." *Harper's Magazine,* March, 1929.

[10] Shaw is not alone in making such a plea.

[11] The study would be, " The Relation of Literature of the Last Fifty Years to ' the Second Religiousness.' "

at hand.   The so-called naturalistic dramas, *The Father* and *The Dance of Death,* must be recognized as expressionistic dramas. The *To Damascus* trilogy, *The Great Highway, A Dream Play* and *The Ghost Sonata* are obviously expressionistic.   To this list we must add *Advent, There are Crimes and Crimes, Easter, The Hollander, Toten-Insel* and possibly also *The Pelican* and even *The Bridal Crown.*

Later criticism may rebuild this mosaic, but at present we can scarcely come to other conclusions.   This is the result of applying expressionistic norms to Strindberg's dramas.

BIBLIOGRAPHY

A LIST OF STRINDBERG'S DRAMAS

THE following is a list of items of Strindberg's dramas with titles in Swedish, German and English; also with dates of writing, publication and production, when these can be ascertained. The Roman numerals refer to the volume numbers in the *Samlade skrifter*.

This list has been compiled from the Landquist edition of Strindberg's *Collected Works*, the Carlheim-Gyllensköld edition of *Posthumous Works*, Strindberg's letters to Emil Schering, and Lamm's monumental work on Strindberg's dramas. The work last mentioned is the most authoritative of all for dates of writing and has been followed closely. Landquist's edition is most convenient for dates of first publication and production; the letters to Schering, for the verification of some dates. The dates of publication and production refer to the first appearance in Sweden unless otherwise stated. Hedvall's *Strindberg på Stockholms scenen (1870–1922)*, which is not at present available to me, may help to complete the data offered.

1. En namnsdagsgåva, eller, Gnat (Ein Namenstagsgeschenk; A Name's-day Gift). Written 1869. Sent to the theater; lost.

2. Fritänkaren, I (Der Freidenker; The Freethinker). Written 1869. Published 1870. Produced — .

3. Hermione, I. Written 1869. Published 1871. Produced — .

4. Jesus av Nazareth. Begun 1870; not completed.

5. Erik XIV. Written 1870; burned by Strindberg.

6. I Rom, I (In Rom; In Rome). Written 1870. Published 1870. Produced 1870.

7. Blotsven. Written 1870; burned by Strindberg.

8. Den fredlöse, I (Der Friedlosen; The Outlaw). A drama based on the earlier drama Blotsven. Written 1871. Produced 1871. Published 1876.

9. Mäster Olof, II (Meister Olof; Master [Magister] Olof). Written in prose, 1871–72. Published 1881. Produced 1881. The drama was rewritten at least five times, for five manuscripts are extant in Sweden.

215

10. Anno fyrtioåtta, I (Anno 48). Written 1875. Published 1881. Produced — .

11. Mäster Olof, II (Meister Olof; Master Olof). Written in verse 1876. Published 1878. Produced 1890.

12. Efterspel, Fragment, Mäster Olof, II (Nachspiel, Meister Olof; Post-ludium, Master Olof). Written 1877. Published 1878. Produced — . This Postludium contains within its frame the miracle play, De Creatione et Sententia vera Mundi.

13. Gillets hemlighet, IX (Das Geheimnis der Gilde; The Secret of the Guild). Written 1879–80. Published 1880. Produced 1880? Note the statement by Landquist: "Gillets hemlighet uppfördes första gången på K. Dramatiska teatern där det gick 6 gånger. Dramat upptogs på Svenska teatern i Stockholm 7 maj 1906."

14. Lyckopers resa, IX (Glückspeters Fahrt; Lucky Per's Journey). Written 1881–82. Published 1882. Produced 1883.

15. Herr Bengts hustru, IX (Ritter Bengts Gattin, oder, Frau Margit — Sir Bengt's Wife). Written 1882. Published 1882. Produced 1882.

16. Höstslask, eller, den samhällsvådlige reformatorn. Toalettpjäs, av Rococo. Fri översättning, XVI, 198–208 (Herbstschlacker, oder, der staatsgefährliche Reformator, dramatische Parodie; Autumn-Splash, or, the Reformer Dangerous to Society). Written 1884. Published 1884. Produced — .

17. Marodörer, XXIII, 449–486 (Marodeure; Marauders). Printed as manuscript in ten copies, 1886. Later rewritten as Comrades in collaboration with Axel Lundegård.

18. Fadren, XXIII (Der Vater; The Father). Written 1887. Published 1887. Produced, Danish translation by Axel Lundegård, 1887, in Copenhagen; 1888 in Stockholm; 1890 by the Freie Bühne.

19. Kamraterna, XXIII (Die Kameraden; Comrades). Written 1887–88, in collaboration with Axel Lundegård; see item 17. Published 1888. Produced 1910.

20. Fröken Julie, XXIII (Fräulein Julie; Miss Julia). Written 1888. Published 1888. Produced 1892, Freie Bühne; 1906, Stockholm.

21. Fordringsägare, XXIII (Gläubiger; Creditors). Written 1888. Published 1890. Produced 1890.

22. Hemsöborna, XXV (Die Leute auf Hemsö; Hemsö Folk). Written 1888. Produced 1889. Published 1905, German; 1914, Swedish.

23. Paria, XXIII (Pariah). Written 1888. Published 1890. Produced 1908.

24. Den starkare, XXV (Die Stärkere; The Stronger). Written 1888–89. Produced 1889, Copenhagen. Published 1890.

25. Samum, XXIII (Simoom). Written 1889. Published 1890. Produced 1892.

26. Himmelrikets nycklar, XXV (Die Schlüssel des Himmelreichs; The Keys of the Kingdom of Heaven). Written 1891–92. Published 1892. Produced —.

27. Debet och kredit, XXV (Debet und Credit; Debit and Credit). Written 1892. Published 1893. Produced —.

28. Första varningen, XXV (Die erste Warnung; The First Warning). Written 1892. Published 1893. Produced 1910.

29. Inför döden, XXV (Vor dem Tode; Facing Death). Written 1892. Published 1893. Produced 1910.

30. Moderskärlek, XXV (Mutterliebe; Motherlove). Written 1892. Published 1893. Produced —.

31. Leka med elden, XXV (Spiel mit dem Feuer; Playing with Fire). Written 1892–93. Published 1893, Germany; 1897, Sweden. Produced 1908.

32. Bandet, XXV (Das Band; The Link). Written 1892–93. Published 1893, Germany; 1897, Sweden. Produced 1908.

33. Till Damaskus, första delen, XXIX (Nach Damaskus, erster Teil; To Damascus, Part I). Written 1897–98. Published 1898. Produced 1900.

34. Till Damaskus, andra delen, XXIX (Nach Damaskus, zweiter Teil; To Damascus, Part II). Written 1898. Published 1898. Produced —.

35. Advent, ett mysterium, XXX (Advent, oder Das Mausoleum, ein Mysterium; Advent, a " Mysterium "). Written 1898. Published 1899 with the drama in item 36 under the inclusive title Vid högre rätt, eller, Rus (Vor höherer Instanz, oder, Rausch; Before a Higher Court, or, Ecstasy). Produced —.

36. Brott och brott, XXX (Verbrechen und Verbrechen; There are Crimes and Crimes); see drama in item 35. Written 1898–99. Published 1899. Produced 1900.

37. Folkungasagan, XXXI (Die Folkungersage; The Folkung Saga). Written 1899. Published 1899. Produced 1901.

38. Gustav Vasa, XXXI. Written 1899. Published 1899. Produced 1899.

39. Erik XIV, XXXI. Written 1899. Published 1899. Produced 1899.

40. Gustav Adolf, XXXII. Written 1899–1900. Published 1900. Produced 1912.

41. Kaspers Fet-Tisdag, XXXIII (Kaspers Fastnacht; Casper's Shrove-Tuesday). Written 1900. Produced 1901. Published. 1915.

42. Midsommar, XXXIII (Mittsommer; Midsummer). Written 1900. Published 1901. Produced 1901.

43. Påsk, XXXIII (Ostern; Easter). Written 1900. Published 1901. Produced 1901.

44. Dödsdansen, första delen, XXXIV (Der Todestanz, oder, Totentanz, erster Teil; The Dance of Death, Part I). Written 1901. Published 1901. Produced 1909.

45. Dödsdansen, andra delen, XXXIV (Der Todestanz, oder, Totentanz, zweiter Teil; The Dance of Death, Part II). Written 1901. Published 1901. Produced 1909.

46. Kronbruden, XXXVI (Die Kronenbraut, oder, Kronbraut; The Bridal Crown; literally, The Crown-Bride). Written 1901. Published 1902. Produced 1907.

47. Svanevit, XXXVI (Schwanenweiss; Swanwhite). Written 1901. Published 1902. Produced 1908.

48. Carl XII, XXXV. Written 1901. Published 1901. Produced 1902.

49. Engelbrekt, XXXIX. Written 1901. Published 1901. Produced 1901.

50. Kristina, XXXIX (Königin Christine; Christina). Written 1901. Published 1903. Produced 1908.

51. Ett drömspel, XXXVI (Ein Traumspiel; A Dream Play). Written 1901-2. Published 1902. Produced 1907.

52. Holländarn, Samlade otryckta skrifter, I (Der Holländer; The Hollander); a fragment. Written 1902; see Lamm, II, 336. Published 1918.

53. Homunculus, en saga, Samlade otryckta skrifter, I (Homunculus, a Saga-Play); a fragment. Written 1902; see Lamm, II, 336. Published 1918.

54. Gustav III, XXXIX. Written 1902. Published 1903. Produced 1916.

55. Näktergalen i Wittenberg, XXXIX (Die Nachtigall in Wittenberg, oder, Luther; The Nightingale in Wittenberg). Written 1903. Published 1904. Produced —.

56. Genom öknar till arfland, eller, Moses, Samlade otryckta skrifter, I (Durch die Wüste zum gelobten Land; Through the Wilderness to the Promised Land, or, Moses). Written 1903? See Lamm, II, 354. Published 1918. Produced —.

57. Hellas, eller, Sokrates, Samlade otryckta skrifter, I (Hellas, or Socrates). Written 1903? See Lamm, II, 354. Published 1918. Produced —.

58. Lammet och vilddjuret, eller, Kristus, Samlade otryckta skrifter, I (Das Lamm und das wilde Tier; The Lamb and the Wild Beast, or, Christ). Written 1903? See Lamm, II, 354. Published 1918. Produced —.

59. Till Damaskus, tredje delen, XXIX (Nach Damaskus, dritter Teil; To Damascus, Part III). Written 1900–4. Published 1904. Produced — . (There had been no production by 1915, but the author saw one in the 1926–27 season, which was not the first appearance on the stage.)

60. Starkodder skald, ett forn-nordiskt sagodrama, Samlade otryckta skrifter, I (Der Skalde Starkodder, alt-nordisches Märchen-drama; The Skald Starkodder, an Old-Norse Saga-Drama); a fragment. Written 1903–6. Published 1918.

61. Förspel till ett drömspel, XXXVI (Vorspiel, Ein Traumspiel; Prologue to A Dream Play). Written September, 1906 (there are five extant manucripts of this Prologue and each differs somewhat from the others). Produced 1907. Published 1920. (It is not clear whether the Prologue was published before 1920, the date of Volume XXXVI of the Samlade skrifter.)

62. Oväder, XLV (Gewitter, oder, Wetterleuchten; The Thunderstorm). Written 1907. Published 1907. Produced 1907.

63. Brände tomten, XLV (Die Brandstätte; After the Fire). Written 1907. Published 1907. Produced 1907.

64. Spöksonaten, XLV (Die Gespenstersonate; The Ghost Sonata). Note Strindberg's letter to Schering of April 1, 1907, apropos of the title of this drama: " Es war mir eine grosse und neue Freude in meinem Osterschmerz dass Sie sofort mit der ' Gespenstersonate ' vertraut waren. (So müssen wir sie nennen nach Beethovens Gespenstersonate D-moll und Gespenstertrio; also nicht Spuk-sonate.)" Published 1907. Produced 1908.

65. Den blödande handen (Die blutende Hand; The Bleeding Hand). A chamber play. Written 1907. Burned by Strindberg.

66. Toten-Insel, eller, Hades, Samlade otryckta skrifter, I (German title used by Strindberg). Written 1907. Published 1918. A fragment.

67. Pelikanen, XLV (Der Pelikan, oder, Scheiterhaufen; The Pelican). Written 1907. Published 1907. Produced 1907.

68. Siste riddaren, XLIX (Der letzte Ritter; The Last Knight). Written 1908. Published 1909. Produced 1909.

69. Riksföreståndaren, XLIX (Der Reichsvorsteher; The Regent). Written 1908. Published 1909. Produced 1911.

70. Abu Casems tofflor, LI (Abu Casems Pantoffeln; Abu Casem's Slippers). Written 1908. Published 1908. Produced 1908.

71. Bjälbo-Jarlen, XLIX (Der Bjälbo-Jarl; The Earl of Bjälbo). Written 1908. Published 1909. Produced 1909.

72. Svarta handsken, XLV (Der schwarze Handschuh, oder, Fröhliche Weihnacht; The Black Glove). Written 1908–9. Published 1909. Produced 1911.

73. Stora landsvägen, LI (Die grosse Landstrasse; The Great Highway). Written 1909; see Lamm, II, 429. Published 1909. Produced 1910.

BIBLIOGRAPHY TO PART I

ALLESCH, G. JOHANNES VON, Die Grundkräfte des Expressionismus. Zeitschrift für Ästhetik und allgemeine Kunstwissenschaft, Bd. 19, 1925, 112–120.

AULHORN, EDITH, Zur Gestaltung seelischer Vorgänge in neurer Erzählung, Vom Geiste neuer Literaturforschung, Festschrift für Oskar Walzel, herausgegeben von Julius Wahle und Victor Klemperer, 70–79. Potsdam, 1924.

BAB, JULIUS, Die Expressionisten und das Drama. Die Schaubühne, September 19, 1916, 266–270.

BAB, JULIUS, Expressionistisches Drama. Die Schaubühne, September 26, 1916, 286–289.

BAB, JULIUS, Der dramatische Jugendstil. Die Weltbühne, August 22, 1918, 173–176.

BAB, JULIUS, Die Chronik des deutschen Dramas (1900–18). Four Volumes. Oesterheld & Co., Berlin, 1922.

BAB, JULIUS, Expressionismus, Das deutsche Drama, herausgegeben von R. F. Arnold, 783–811. Beck, München, 1925.

BACHMANN, FRIEDA, Die Theorie, die historische Beziehungen und die Eigenart des Expressionismus. The Germanic Review, July, 1927, 229–244.

BAHR, HERMANN, Expressionismus. Delphin, München, 1916. English translation by R. F. Gribble, Expressionism. Boni & Liveright, New York. 1926.

BARTELS, ADOLF, Die deutsche Dichtung der Gegenwart. Haessel, Leipzig, 1921.

BENZMANN, HANS, Expressionismus in der neuesten Dichtung. Gegenwart, February 1, 1919, 27–29; March 24, 1919, 81–89.

BINDING, R. G., Allgemeiner und dichterischer Expressionismus. Faust, November, 1921, 1–9 (Bound in Vol. I, 1922–23).

BLESSINGER, KARL, Das Problem des Expressionismus, III, Musik und Expressionismus. Der schwäbische Bund, February, 1920, 497–506.

BOYD, ERNEST, Expressionism without Tears, Studies from Ten Literatures, 231–251. Charles Scribner's Sons, New York, 1925.

BRANDENBURG, HANS, Das neue Theater. Haessel, Leipzig, 1926.

BRANDT, PAUL, Sehen und Erkennen, Eine Anleitung zu vergleichender Kunstbetrachtung. Kröner, Leipzig, 1925.

BRAUN, OTTO, Studien zum Expressionismus. Zeitschrift für Ästhetik und allgemeine Kunstwissenschaft, Bd. 13, December 3, 1918, 283–302.

BRUCK, MARTIN VAN DEN, Theodor Däubler und die Idee des Nordlichtes. Deutsche Rundschau, Bd. 47, 4, 1921.

BÜHLER, CHARLOTTE, Der Erlebnisbegriff in der modernen Kunstwissenschaft, Vom Geiste neuer Literaturforschung, 195–209. *See* Aulhorn, Edith.

CHENEY, SHELDON, A Primer of Modern Art. Boni & Liveright, New York, 1924.

DESSOIR, MAX, Vom Jenseits der Seele. Dritte Auflage, Ferdinand Enke, Stuttgart, 1919.

DICKINSON, T. H., An Outline of Contemporary Drama. Houghton Mifflin, Chicago, 1927.

DIEBOLD, BERNHARD, Expressionismus und Bühnen Kunst. Die Scene, September, 1916, 159–164.

DIEBOLD, BERNHARD, Unruh — Platz. Das literarische Echo, July 15, 1920, 1239–1240.

DIEBOLD, BERNHARD, Der Denkspieler Georg Kaiser. Frankfurter Verlags-Anstalt A.-G., Frankfurt am Main, 1924.

DIEBOLD, BERNHARD, Anarchie im Drama, Kritik und Darstellung der modernen Dramatik, 3. erweiterte Auflage. Frankfurter Verlags-Anstalt A.-G., Frankfurt am Main, 1925.

DREWS, ARTHUR, review of Max Dessoir's Vom Jenseits der Seele (dritte Auflage, Ferdinand Enke, Stuttgart, 1919). Preussische Jahrbücher, Bd. 178, October 1919, 136–140.

EDSCHMID, KASIMIR, Über den Expressionismus in der Literatur und die neue Dichtung. 3. Auflage. Reiss, Berlin, 1919.

EMMEL, FELIX, Das ekstatische Theater. Kampmann & Schnabel, Prien, 1924.

FREYHAN, MAX, Das Drama der Gegenwart. Mittler, Berlin, 1922.

FREYHAN, MAX, Georg Kaisers Werke. Schmiede, Berlin, 1926.

GOLDBERG, ISAAC, The Drama of Transition. Stewart Kidd, Cincinnati, 1922.

H., R., Impressionismus und Expressionismus. Deutsche Kunst und Dekoration, November, 1926, 131–133.

HASENCLEVER, WALTER, Das Theater von Morgen: I, Vom Geist des Theaters und seinem Verfall; II, Die Forderung einer geistigen Bühne; III, Entstehung. Die Schaubühne, May 11, 18, 25, 1916, 453–456, 474–477, 499–501.

HEINEMANN, KARL, Die deutsche Dichtung, Grundriss der deutschen Literaturgeschichte, siebente von Erick Ebermayer bis zur neuesten Zeit ergänzte Auflage. Kröner, Leipzig, 1927.

HERKE, KARL HEINZ, Vom Expressionismus zur Schönheit, Versuche über Entwicklung und Wesen der modernen Kunst. Matthias Grünewald, Mainz, 1923.

HESELE, HERMANN, Das Problem des Expressionismus, I, Ausdruck und Symbol. Der schwäbische Bund, December, 1919, 306–312.

HEYNICKE, KURT, Deutsche Volk und deutsche Kunst. Hellweg (Essen), January 23, 1924, 55–56.

HUEBNER, FRIEDRICH MARKUS, Expressionismus und Nichts Andres. Die Schaubühne, February 8, 1917, 123–127.

HUEBNER, FRIEDRICH MARKUS, Der Expressionismus in Deutschland. Nord und Sud, Bd. 44, 548, May, 1920, 176–186.

JOHST, HANNS, Die Tragödie und die Gestalt. Zeitwende, February, 1929, 5. Jg., H. 2, 147–158.

KAUFMANN, F. W., Franz Werfel. The Modern Language Journal, April, 1927, Vol. 11, 427–434.

KAULFUSS-DIESCH, KARL, Deutsche Dichtung in Strome deutschen Lebens. Voigtländers, Leipzig, 1921.

KAYSER, RUDOLF, Subjektivismus. Die Erhebung, herausgegeben von Alfred Wolfenstein, 347–353. Fischer, Berlin, 1919.

KAYSER, RUDOLF, Das Ende des Expressionismus. Der neue Merkur, July, 1920, 248–258.

KEIM, H. W., Expressionismus als Weltanschauung. Das literarische Echo, October 1, 1919, 40–41 (abstracted from Das junge Deutschland, II, 7).

KENTER, HEINZ, Franz Werfels Gerichtstag. Das literarische Echo, August 1, 1921, 1292–1297.

KERR, ALFRED, Dramen-Expressionismus. Die neue Rundschau, August, 1919, 1005–1014.

KNAPP, FRITZ, Impressionismus und Expressionismus. Neue Jahrbücher für Wissenschaft und Jugendbildung, Bd. 1, 4, 1925, 517–526.

KNEVELS, WILHELM, Expressionismus und Religion, gezeigt an der neuesten deutschen expressionistischen Lyrik. J. C. Mohr (Paul Siebeck), Tübingen, 1927.

KNUDSEN, HANS, Die Entwicklung des schauspielerischen Stils. Faust, December, 1921, 1–8 (Bound in Vol. I, 1922–23).

KÖRNER, JOSEF, Erlebnis — Motiv — Stoff, Vom Geiste neuer Literaturforschung, 80–90. See Aulhorn, Edith.

KOSCH, WILHELM, Das deutsche Theater und Drama seit Schillers Tod, Zweite völlig umgearbeitet Auflage. Vier Quellen, Leipzig, 1922, 55–69.

KRELL, MAX, Das Drama von heute. Das deutsche Theater der Gegenwart, Aufsätze herausgegeben von Max Krell, 1923.

KÜHN, HERBERT, Das Wesen des Dramatischen. Die neue Schaubühne, January, 1919, 3–6.

KÜHN, HERBERT, Das Gegenständliche des expressionistischen Dramas. Die neue Schaubühne, July 1, 1919, 204–206.

KÜHN, HERBERT, Das Wesen der neuen Lyrik. Die neue Schaubühne, December 1, 1919, 365–375.

KUMMER, FRIEDRICH, Deutsche Literaturgeschichte des 19. und 20. Jahrhunderts. Reissner, Dresden, 1922.

KÜPPERS, PAUL ERICH, Der Kubismus, Ein künstlerisches Formproblem unserer Zeit. Klinkhardt & Biermann, Leipzig, 1920.

LANDAU, PAUL, Strindberg als Dramatiker des Expressionismus. Die deutsche Bühne, May 24, 1920, 371–374.

LANDSBERGER, FRANZ, Impressionismus und Expressionismus. Klinkhardt & Biermann, Leipzig, 1922.

LEHMAN, KARL, Junge deutsche Dramatiker. Dieterich, Leipzig, 1923.

LEIS, HEINRICH, Kunst und Gemeinschaft. Hellweg (Essen), May 28, 1924, 391.

LEMKE, ERNST, Die Hauptrichtungen im deutschen Geistesleben. Quelle & Meyer, Leipzig, 1914.

LEYEN, FRIEDRICH VON DER, Deutsche Dichtung in neuer Zeit. Diederichs, Jena, 1922.

MARTENS, KURT, Die deutsche Literatur unsrer Zeit. Rösl & Cie., München, 1921.

MARZYNSKI, GEORG, Die Methode des Expressionismus, Studien zur seiner Psychologie. Klinkhardt & Biermann, Leipzig, 1921.

MATTHIAS, LEON, Der Stierkampf: Ein Gespräch über das Drama, Die Erhebung. Fischer, Berlin, 1919, 353–360.

MIELKE, HELLMUTH, UND HOMANN, HANS J., Der deutsche Roman des 19. und 20. Jahrhunderts, sechste Auflage. Reissner, Dresden, 1920.

NAUMANN, HANS, Die deutsche Dichtung der Gegenwart (1885–1923). J. B. Metzlersche Verlagsbuchhandlung, Stuttgart, 1923.

OESTERHELD, ERICH, Vom Traum und Traumspiel. Die deutsche Bühne, September 29, 1919, 458–459.

ORLOWIUS, HANS, Über den Expressionismus und seine Verirrungen. Preussische Jahrbücher, October, 1919, 143–148.

PFISTER, OSKAR, Der psychologische und biologische Untergrund expressionistischer Bilder. Ernst Bircher, Bern, 1920. Translated into English by Barbara Low and M. A. Mügge, Expressionism in Art, Its Psychological and Biological Basis. Dutton, New York, 1923.

PICARD, MAX, Expressionismus. Die Erhebung. Fischer, Berlin, 1919, 329–338.

PIRK, ROBERT, Georg Kaiser als Regieproblem. Die deutsche Schaubühne, June 16, 1919, 307–309.

RHEINER, WALTER, Expressionismus und Schauspiel. Die neue Schaubühne, January, 1919, Bd. 1, 14–17.

RIEMANN, ROBERT, Von Goethe zum Expressionismus. Dieterich, Leipzig, 1922.

ROH, FRANZ, Nach-Expressionismus. Klinkhardt & Biermann, Leipzig, 1925.

RÖHL, HANS, Geschichte der deutschen Dichtung, sechste, durchgesehene Auflage. B. G. Teubner, Leipzig, 1927.

SCHEFFAUER, HERMAN GEORGE, The New Vision in the German Arts. Ernest Benn, London, 1924.

SCHLEMMER, HANS, Der Expressionismus in der modernen Dichtung und die Religion. Protestantenblatt, January 20, 1924, 10–12.

SCHMID, PAUL, Das Problem des Expressionismus, II, Das literarische Chaos. Ein kritischer Versuch. Der schwäbische Bund, January 1920, 462–469.

SCHNEIDER, MANFRED, Der Expressionismus im Drama. Hoffmann, Stuttgart, 1920.

SCHNEIDER, MANFRED, Einführung in die neueste deutsche Dichtung. Meyer, Stuttgart, 1921.

SCHREYER, LOTHAR, Die jüngste Dichtkunst und die Bühne. Die Scene, 1915, 171 f.; 1916, 37 ff. and 101 ff.

SCHULENBERG, WERNER VON DER, Das Reich ohne Raum. Das literarische Echo, July 15, 1920, 1230–1233.

SIEBURG, ERICH, Das Ethos im gegenwärtigen Drama. Hellweg (Essen), June 18, 1924, 459–462.

SOERGEL, ALBERT, Dichtung und Dichter der Zeit, Neue Folge, im Banne des Expressionismus. Voigtländer, Leipzig, 1926. (*A 1928 edition has also been published.*)

SPECHT, RICHARD, Franz Werfel, Versuch einer Zeitspiegelung. Zsolnay, Berlin, 1926.

SPENGLER, OSWALD, Der Untergang des Abendlandes, Umrisse einer Morphologie der Weltgeschichte: Erster Band, Gestalt und Wirklichkeit,

60. bis 63. Auflage; Zweiter Band, Welthistorische Perspektiven, 50. bis 53. Auflage. Beck, München, 1927. English translation by Charles F. Atkinson, The Decline of the West: Vol. I, Form and Actuality; Vol. II, Perspectives of World History. Knopf, New York, 1926, 1928.

Spiero, Heinrich, Die Heilandsgestalt in der neueren deutschen Dichtung. Eckart, Berlin, 1926.

Stammler, Wolfgang, Deutsche Literatur vom Naturalismus bis zur Gegenwart. Jedermanns, Breslau, 1927.

Steiner, Fritz, Das Theater und der Expressionismus. Die deutsche Bühne, April 19, 1920, 309–312.

Storck, Karl, Deutsche Literaturgeschichte, neunte vermehrte Auflage. Metzler, Stuttgart, 1920.

Strindberg und die deutschen Bühnen, Aufsätze. Drei-Masken, Berlin, 1915.

Stuart, Donald Clive, The Development of Dramatic Art. Appleton, New York & London, 1928.

Tischendorf, Käte, Geist und Seele. Die Schaubühne, October 24, Bd. 178, 1916, 381–384.

Tränckner, Chr., Der Expressionismus in der Dichtung. Preussische Jahrbücher, November, 1919, 246–261.

Utitz, Emil, Die Überwindung des Expressionismus. Ferdinand Enke, Stuttgart, 1927.

Walzel, Oskar, Franz Werfels Spiegelmensch. Berliner Tageblatt, 175, 1921.

Walzel, Oskar, Expressionistische Drama. Internationale Monatsschrift für Wissenschaft Kunst und Technik, August, 1919, 789–810.

Weininger, Otto, Geschlecht und Charakter. Braumüller, Wien und Leipzig, 26. Auflage, 1925. English translation published by W. Heinemann, London, 1906 (?).

Witkowski, Georg, Ernst Barlach's " Der tote Tag." Das literarische Echo, January 15, 1920, 471–475.

Wittner, Victor, Der Standpunkt des neuen Erzählers. Das literarische Echo, November 1, 1920, 141–144 (abstracted from Frankf. Zeitung, 72 — 1 M).

Wolff, Rudolf, Die neue Lyrik. Dieterich, Leipzig, 1922.

Zeydel, Edwin H., The Trend of Literature in Germany since the War. The Modern Language Journal, December, 1925, Vol. 10, 165–171.

Zickel, Reinhold, Dichter, Zeit und Gott. Das literarische Echo, March 15, 1920, 736–737.

Ziesche, K., Vom Expressionismus. Vier Quellen, Leipzig, 1920.

BIBLIOGRAPHY TO PART II

STRINDBERG'S WORKS

Samlade skrifter, John Landquist, Editor. 55 Volumes, Bonnier, Stockholm, 1913–24.

Samlade otryckta skrifter, Professor Carlheim-Gyllensköld, Editor. 2 Volumes. Bonnier, Stockholm, 1918.

Werke, Emil Schering, Translator. 8 Abteilungen, 49 Bände. Georg Müller, München, 1908–28.

Bibliothèque Cosmopolite, Collection scandinave, Delamain et Boutelleau, Paris: contains a number of dramas, some of which are translated into French by Strindberg himself. See *Le Songe* and *Deux Féeries*.

PLAYS IN ENGLISH TRANSLATION

Collections

1. Plays, first series, The Dream Play, The Link, The Dance of Death, translated by Edwin Björkman. Charles Scribner's Sons, New York, 1912.

2. Plays, second series, There Are Crimes and Crimes, Miss Julia, The Stronger, Creditors, Pariah, translated by Edwin Björkman. Charles Scribner's Sons, New York, 1913.

3. Plays, third series, Swanwhite, Simoom, Debit and Credit, Advent, The Thunderstorm, After the Fire, translated by Edwin Björkman. Charles Scribner's Sons, New York, 1913.

4. Plays, fourth series, The Bridal Crown, The Spook Sonata, The First Warning, Gustavus Vasa, translated by Edwin Björkman. Charles Scribner's Sons, New York, 1916.

5. Plays, Creditors, Pariah, translated by Edwin Björkman. Charles Scribner's Sons, New York, 1912.

6. Plays, The Father, Countess Julie, The Outlaw, The Stronger, translated by Edith and Wärner Oland. J. W. Luce, Boston, 1912.

7. Plays, Comrades, Facing Death, Pariah, Easter, translated by Edith and Wärner Oland. J. W. Luce, Boston, 1912.

227

8. Plays, Swanwhite, Advent, The Storm, translated by Edith and Wärner Oland. J. W. Luce, Boston, 1914.

9. Miss Julie and Other Plays (The Creditor, The Stronger Woman, Motherly Love, Paria, Simoom). Modern Library Series, Boni and Liveright, New York, 1918.

10. Pariah, Simoom, translated by Horace B. Samuel. Hendersons, London, 1914.

11. Three One-Act Plays (The Outcast, Simoom, Debit and Credit), translated from the German of Emil Schering by Mary Harned. Poet Lore, Boston, 1906, Vol. 17, No. 3, pp. 8–44.

12. Simoom, Debit and Credit, The Outcast. R. G. Badger, Boston, 1911.

13. Simoom, Debit and Credit, The Outcast. Poet Lore Plays, R. G. Badger, Boston, 1912.

14. Easter and Other Plays (The Dance of Death, The Ghost Sonata, A Dream Play), translated by E. Classen, C. D. Locock, Erik Palmstierna and James Bernard Fagan. Anglo-Swedish Literary Foundation, Jonathan Cape, London, 1929.

Individual Plays

The numbers after see *in this section refer to items given in the Collections.*

Advent, translated by Claud Field, R. G. Badger, Boston, 1914; Four Seas Publishing Co., 1914. See 3, 8.

After the Fire. See 3.

Bridal Crown, The. See 4.

Comrades. See 7.

Creditor, The, translated by Francis J. Ziegler, Brown Bros., Philadelphia, 1910; by Francis J. Ziegler, R. D. Badger, Boston, 1911; by Mary Harned, Poet Lore, Boston, 1911; Vol. 22, No. 11, pp. 81–116; by (?), N. L. Brown, Philadelphia, 1915; in Fifty Contemporary One-Act Plays, selected and edited by Frank Shay and Pierre Loving, D. Appleton and Co., New York and London, 1924, pp. 261–288. See 2, 5, 9.

Dance of Death, The. See 1, 14.

Debit and Credit. See 3, 11, 12, 13.

Dream Play, A. See 1, 14.

Easter (and stories from the Swedish of August Strindberg) translated by Velma Swanston Howard, Stewart and Kidd, Cincinnati, 1912. See 7, 14.

Facing Death, translated by Olive M. Johnson, privately printed, Easton, Pa., 1911; also in the Dramatist, 1911, Vol. 2, No. 4, pp. 173–184. See 7.

Father, The, translated by N. Erichsen, J. W. Luce and Co., Boston, 1907; also in Chief Contemporary Dramatists, first series, selected and edited by Thomas H. Dickinson, Houghton Mifflin, Boston, 1915, pp. 599–626; in Types of Domestic Tragedy, World Drama Series, edited by R. M. Smith, Prentice-Hall, Inc., New York, 1928. See 6.

First Warning, The. See 4.

Ghost Sonata, The. See 4 (The Spook Sonata), 14.

Gustavus Vasa. See 4.

Link, The. See 1.

Lucky Pehr, translated by Velma Swanston Howard, Stewart and Kidd, Cincinnati, 1912; D. Appleton, New York and London, 1923.

Master Olof, translated by Edwin Björkman, from the prose version of 1872, American Scandinavian Foundation, New York, 1915.

Miss Julia: Julie, translated by Arthur Swan, Poet Lore, Boston, 1911, Vol. 22, No. 3, pp. 161–194; Miss Julia, by Edwin Björkman, Charles Scribner's Sons, New York, 1912; Countess Julia, by C. Recht, N. L. Brown, Philadelphia, 1912; in Poet Lore Plays, R. G. Badger, Boston, 1912; Fröken Julie, Brown Bros., Philadelphia, 1912. See 2, 6, 9.

Motherlove, translated by Francis J. Ziegler, Brown Bros., Philadelphia, 1910; 2d edition, N. L. Brown, Philadelphia, 1916. See 9.

Outlaw, The (The Outcast). See 6, 11, 12, 13.

Pariah. See 2, 5, 7, 9, 10.

Simoom. See 3, 9, 10, 11, 12, 13.

Stronger, The, translated by Francis J. Ziegler, Poet Lore, Boston, 1906. Vol. 17, No. 1. pp. 47–50. R. G. Badger, Boston, 1911. See 2, 6, 9 (The Stronger Woman).

Swanwhite, translated by Francis J. Ziegler, Brown Bros., Philadelphia, 1909; also a 2d edition. See 3, 8.

There Are Crimes and Crimes, translated by Edwin Björkman, Charles Scribner's Sons, New York, 1912. See 2.

Thunderstorm, The. See 3, 8 (The Storm).

Prose Works in English Translation

By the Open Sea, translated by Ellie Schleussner, F. Palmer, London, 1913; Huebsch, New York, 1913; under title On the Seaboard, by Elizabeth

230 *Strindberg's Dramatic Expressionism*

Clarke Westergren, Stewart and Kidd, Cincinnati, 1913; Grosset, New York, 1915.

Confession of a Fool, The, translated by Ellie Schleussner, S. Swift and Co., London, 1912; Small, Maynard and Co., Boston, 1913; with an introduction by Ernest Boyd, Viking Press, New York, 1925.

Fair Haven and Foul Strand, McBride, Nast and Co., New York, 1914.

German Lieutenant and Other Stories, The, A. C. McClurg and Co., Chicago, 1915.

Growth of a Soul, The, translated by Claud Field, W. Rider and Son, London, 1913; McBride, Nast and Co., New York, 1914.

Have Plants Nerves? Tucker Publishing Company, New York, 1900.

Historical Miniatures, translated by Claud Field, George Allen and Co., London, 1913.

Inferno, The, translated by Claud Field, G. P. Putnam's Sons, New York and London, 1913.

In Midsummer Days and Other Tales, translated by Ellie Schleussner, H. Latimer, London, 1913; McBride, Nast and Co., New York, 1913.

Legends, Autobiographical Sketches, A. Melrose, London, 1912.

Married, translated by Ellie Schleussner, J. W. Luce, Boston, 1913; in Modern Library Series, Boni and Liveright, New York, 1917.

Red Room, The, translated by Ellie Schleussner, H. Latimer, London, 1913; G. P. Putnam's Sons, New York and London, 1913.

Son of a Servant, The, translated by Claud Field, with an introduction by Henry Vacher-Burch, W. Rider and Son, London, 1913; G. P. Putnam's Sons, New York and London, 1913. See above, The Growth of a Soul.

(Easter and) Stories from the Swedish of August Strindberg, translated by Velma Swanston Howard, Stewart and Kidd, Cincinnati, 1912.

Zones of the Spirit (taken from Strindberg's four volumes of Bluebooks), translated by Claud Field, with an introduction by Arthur Babillotte, G. Allen and Co., London, 1913; G. P. Putnam's Sons, New York and London, 1913.

CRITICAL LITERATURE

ANWAND, OSKAR, Strindberg. Ullstein, Berlin, 1924.

BAB, JULIUS, Expressionismus, Das deutsche Drama, herausgegeben von R. F. Arnold, 783–811. Beck, München, 1925.

BABILLOTTE, ARTHUR, August Strindberg. Das hohe Lied seines Lebens. Xenien, Leipzig, 1910.

BERG, R. G., Litteraturbilder, andra samlingen. Stockholm, 1919.

BIGEON, MAURICE, Les Revoltes Scandinaves, 2d ed. Paris, 1894.

BÖÖK, FREDRIK, Sveriges moderna litteratur. Norstedt, Stockholm, 1921.

BOOR, H. DE, Schwedische Literatur. Jedermanns, Breslau, 1924.

BRUNIUS, A., Kätterier, Essayer. Svenska Handelsförlaget, Stockholm, 1923.

CASTRÉN, G., Studier och kritiker. Stockholm, 1918.

CLARK, BARRETT H., A Study of the Modern Drama. Appleton, New York and London, 1925, 1928.

CLAUSSEN, CHR., En digterskjaebne, August Strindberg. En biografisk-psykologisk Skitse. Kristiania & København, 1913.

DAHLSTROM, CARL, August Strindberg, the Father of Dramatic Expressionism. Papers of the Michigan Academy of Science, Arts and Letters, 10 (1928), 261–272. Published 1929.

DIEBOLD, BERNHARD, Anarchie im Drama, 3. erweiterte Auflage. Frankfurter Verlags-Anstalt A.-G., Frankfurt am Main, 1925.

EKLUND, J., En obeaktad uppsats av Strindberg: Du hasard dans la production artistique. Samlaren, Uppsala, 1924.

ELDH, CARL, Arthur Sjögren, Valfrid Spångberg, Valter Bratt, Gösta Westman, Elsa Dalström, Anna Branting, Bo Bergman, Gideon Forssel, Vad jag mins om Strindberg, Vecko-Journalen, årg. 6, 1915, 662, 704, 722, 734, 774, 814, 833, 894, 914.

ENGSTRÖM, ALBERT, August Strindberg och jag. Bonnier, Stockholm, 1923.

ERDMANN, NILS, August Strindberg. En kämpande och lidande själs historia, 2 volumes. Wahlström & Widstrand, Stockholm, 1920. German translation, August Strindberg, Die Geschichte einer kämpfenden und leidenden Seele, by Heinrich Goebel. Haessel, Leipzig, 1924.

ESSWEIN, HERMANN, August Strindberg, ein psycholg. Versuch. Piper, München, 1907.

ESSWEIN, HERMANN, August Strindberg im Lichte seines Lebens und seine Werke. Müller, München, 1909.

FALKNER, FANNY, Strindberg i blå tornet. Stockholm, 1921. German translation, Strindberg im blauen Turm. Müller, München, 1923.

FISCHER, MAX, August Strindberg, Beiträge zur Kenntnis der religiösen Psyche unserer Zeit. Grünewald, Mainz, 1921.

FRITZE, R., Strindbergs "Vater." Xenien, Leipzig, 1918.

GEIJERSTAM, GUSTAF AF, Hvad vill Lektor Personne? Gernandt, Stockholm, 1887.

GOEBEL, HEINRICH, Einleitung, Strindbergs Ein Traumspiel. Philipp, Leipzig, 1918, 3–18.

GOLDMAN, EMMA, Social Significance of Modern Drama. Badger, Boston, 1914.

HÄGG, JONAS (B. Meijer), Några ord om Herr Strindberg och hans nya skådespel (Mäster Olof). Gleerup, Stockholm, 1878.

HANNSON, OLA, Das junge Skandinavien, Vier Essays, Pierson, Dresden & Leipzig, 1891. Swedish translation, Det unga Skandinavien, 11 delen. saml. skr. Tidens, Stockholm, 1921.

HANSSON, OLA, Errinerungen an Strindberg. Neue Rundschau (Berlin). November, December, 1912.

HARDEN, MAX, Editor, Strindbergs Dramen, Deutsche Aufsätze. Müller, München, 1911.

HEDBERG, OSCAR, Strindberg. En urolig Tids urolige Aand. Olson, Hellerup, 1924.

HEDBERG, TOR, Ett Decennium, Del. I, Literatur; Del. III, Teater. Bonnier, Stockholm, 1912–13.

HEDÉN, ERIK, August Strindberg. En ledtråd vid studiet av hans verk. Nutiden, Stockholm, 1921; German translation, Strindberg, Leben und Dichtung. Beck, München, 1926.

HEDVALL, Y., Strindberg på Stockholms scenen (1870–1922). N. S. Lundström, Stockholm, 1923.

HELLER, OTTO, Prophets of Dissent. Knopf, New York, 1918.

HELLSTRÖM, VICTOR, Strindberg och musiken. Norstedt, Stockholm, 1917.

HELMECKE, CARL A., Buckle's Influence on Strindberg. Philadelphia, 1924 (Dissertation, University of Pennsylvania).

HENDERSON, ARCHIBALD, Modern European Dramatists, revised edition. Appleton, New York, 1926.

JAMESON, STORM, Modern Drama in Europe. Collins, London, 1920.

JASPERS, KARL, Strindberg und van Gogh. Versuch eine pathographischen Analyse unter vergleichender Herausziehung von Swedenborg und Hölderlin, 2. ergänzte Auflage. Springer, Berlin, 1926.

KAUS, OTTO, Strindberg. Eine Kritik. Piper, München, 1918.

KOTAS, W. H., Die skandinavische Literatur der Gegenwart, seit 1870. Dioskuren, Wiesbaden, 1926.

KROGVIG, ANDERS, Bøker og mennesker, 150–175. Aschehoug, Kristiania, 1919.

LAMM, MARTIN, Strindbergs dramer. 2 Volumes. Bonnier, Stockholm, 1924–26.

LANDAU, PAUL, Strindberg als Dramatiker des Expressionismus. Die deutsche Bühne, May 24, 1920, 371–374.

LAURIN, CARL G., Ros och ris. Från Stockholms teatrar 1903–13. Norstedt, Stockholm, 1914.

LEVERTIN, OSCAR, Diktare och drömare. Stockholm, 1898; or, Vol. 8 saml. arb. Bonnier, Stockholm, 1908.

LEVERTIN, OSCAR, Svensk litteratur, Vol. 13. saml. arb. Bonnier, Stockholm, 1908.

LIDFORSS, BENGT, August Strindberg och den litterära nittiotals reklamen. Framtiden, Malmö, 1910.

LIDFORSS, BENGT, Levertinskultens apologet. En vidräkning med doc. F. Böök. Framtiden, Malmö, 1910.

LIEBERT, ARTHUR, August Strindberg — Seine Weltanschauung und seine Kunst, 3. Auflage. Pan Verl., Berlin, 1925.

LIND-AF-HAGEBY, LIZZIE, August Strindberg, the Spirit of Revolt. Appleton, New York, 1913.

LINDBERG, PER, Tillkomsten af Mäster Olof. Bonnier, Stockholm, 1915.

LINDBLAD, GÖRAN, August Strindberg som berättare. Studier i hans tidigare prosa. Norstedt, Stockholm, 1924.

LINDEBERG, G., Svenska diktarsilhuetter. Stockholm, 1923.

LINDGREN, HELLEN, August Strindberg. Ett utkast med 10 bilder, Ord och Bild, årg. 8, 1899, 433–455.

LINDSTRÖM, E., Strindbergs " Mäster Olof " dramer. Lund, 1921.

LOISEAU, GEORGES, Auguste Strindberg et son œuvre, 5–104 (Preface to the second edition of " Mademoiselle Julie "). Paris.

LUNDEGÅRD, A., Några Strindbergsminnen knutna till en handfull brev. Tidens, Stockholm, 1920.

LYND, ROBERT, Old and New Masters, 123–130. T. Fischer Unwin, London, 1919.

MAG, OLAF, Erläuterungen zu Strindbergs phantast. Drama, Ein Traumspiel. Dietrich, München, 1917.

MARCUS, C. D., Strindbergs Dramatik. Müller, München, 1918.

MARCUSE, LUDWIG, Strindberg. Das Leben der tragischen Seele. F. Schneider, Berlin, Leipzig, 1922.

MARHOLM, LAURA (FRAU OLA HANSSON), Wir Frauen und unsere Dichter, 165–198. Wiener-Mode, Wien und Leipzig, 1895.

MAURY, L., Les confessions de Strindberg (Introduction to " Le fils de la servante," Bibliothèque Scandinave, IV. Paris, 1921).

MÖRNER, BIRGER, Den Strindberg jag känt. Bonnier, Stockholm, 1924.

Möhlig, Karl, Strindberg und der Katholizismus. Bergland, Elberfeld, 1923.

Molander, Olof, Harriet Bosse. Norstedt, Stockholm, 1920. German translation by H. Goebel. Haessel, Leipzig, 1922.

Neuhaus, Johannes, August Strindberg im Leben und Streben. Hendricks, Halle, 1916.

Nielsen, R. Jahn, August Strindberg og hans Digtning. Jespersens, Kjøbenhavn, 1909.

Oczeret, Herbert, Strindberg ein Zeitproblem. Leipzig, 1920.

Palmblad, Harry V. E., Strindberg's Conception of History. Columbia University Press, New York, 1927.

Palmblad, Harry V. E., review of Martin Lamm's " Strindbergs dramer," Scandinavian Studies and Notes, Vol. X, No. 4, November, 1928, 115–117.

Paul, Adolf, Strindberg-Erinnerungen und -Briefe. Langen, München, 1914. Swedish translation, Strindbergminnen och brev. Stockholm, 1915.

Personne, J., Strindbergs litteraturen och osedligheten bland skolungdomen. Carl Deleen, Uppsala, 1887.

Proost, K. F., August Strindberg. Zijn leven en werken, Een inleiding. J. Ploegsma, Zeist, 1922.

Rahmer, Sigismund, August Strindberg, eine pathologische Studie. E. Reinhardt, München, 1907.

Réja, Marcel, Avant-propos, L'Inferno d'Auguste Strindberg. Société du Mercure de France. Paris, 1898.

Rydh, Hanna, De historiska källorna till Strindbergs Mäster Olof. Bonnier, Stockholm, 1915.

Schleich, Carl Ludwig, Erinnerungen an Strindberg nebst Nachrufen von Ehrlich und von Bergmann. Müller, München, 1917. Swedish translation, Hågkomster om Strindberg. Stockholm, 1917.

Schleich, Carl Ludwig, Besonnte Vergangenheit. Lebenserinnerungen, 1859–1919. E. Rowolt, Berlin, 1921.

Schönebeck, E., Strindberg als Erzieher. Oldenburg & Co., Berlin, 1923.

Smirnoff, Karin (daughter of Strindberg and Siri von Essen), Strindbergs första hustru — Siri von Essen. Bonnier, Stockholm, 1925.

Soergel, Albert, Dichtung und Dichter der Zeit. Neue Folge. Im Banne des Expressionismus. Voigtländer, Leipzig, 1926.

Sprengel, David, De nya poeterna. Gernandts, Stockholm, 1902.

STORCH, ALFRED, August Strindberg im Lichte seiner Selbstbiographie. Eine psychopathologische Persönlichkeitsanalyse. Bergmann, München & Wiesbaden, 1921.

STRECKER, KARL, Nietzsche und Strindberg. Mit ihrem Briefwechsel. Müller, München, 1921.

Strindberg und die deutschen Bühnen, Aufsätze, Drei-Masken. Berlin, 1915.

Svenska pressen om August Strindberg och religionen, samlade af H. S., Söderhamn, 1885.

TAUB, H., Strindbergs Traumspiel. Eine metaphysische Studie. Müller, München, 1917.

THOMPSON, VANCE, Strindberg and his Plays. McDevitt-Wilson, New York, 1921.

UDDGREN, GUSTAF, August Strindberg, Början till en biografi, Åhlén & Åkerlund, Göteborg, 1909.

UDDGREN, GUSTAF, Andra boken om Strindberg, Åhlén & Åkerlund, Göteborg, 1912.

UDDGREN, GUSTAF, Strindberg the Man, translated by A. J. Uppvall, Four Seas, Boston, 1920.

UPPVALL, A. J., Strindberg, a Psychoanalytic Study with Special Reference to the Oedipus Complex. Badger, Boston, 1920.

WEININGER, OTTO, Taschenbuch und Briefe. Tal, Leipzig, 1919, 2 Strindberg letters, 99–102.

WIEN, ALFRED, August Strindberg. Borngräber, Berlin, 1913.

WIESE, LEOPOLD VON, Strindberg — Ein Beitrag zur Soziologie der Geschlechter. Duncker & Humblot, München, 1918.

WIESE, LEOPOLD VON, Strindberg und die junge Generation. Rheinland, Köln, 1921.

WIESELGREN, O., Strindbergs " Inferno " och dess verklige bakgrund, Svensk Tidskrift, årg. 3, 1913.

ZETTERLUND, RUNE, Bibliografiska anteckningar om August Strindberg. Bonnier, Stockholm, 1913.

STRINDBERG LETTERS

BJØRNSON: Ein Brief A. S. an Bjørnson, 1884, Weserzeitung, erstes Morgenblatt, September 30, 1916.

BRANDES: Tilskueren, July, 1916, 97–122; Die neue Rundschau, November, 1916, 1491–1509.

GAUGUIN: Brief Strindbergs an Gauguin, Neueste Züricher Zeitung, April 13, 1922. See also Cassirer, Else, Künstler-Briefe aus dem 19. Jahrh. Bruno Cassirer, Berlin, 1919.

GEIJERSTAM: Strindbergs "Scheidebrief" an Geijerstam, Frankfurter Zeitung. Morgenblatt, April 10, 1917.

GRANDINSON: Ett Strindbergsbref, Svenska scenen, March 15, 1915, 101–102.

HANSSON, OLA: A. Strindbergs Breve til mig fra Holte, Tilskueren, 29, Halvbd. 2, 1912, 31–49.

KIELLANDS BREV TIL A. S., edited by J. Landquist, Samtiden, 33 aargang, 1922, Kristiania, 419–434.

KJELLBERG: Några Strindbergs bref till Isidor Kjellberg, edited by N. P. Svensson, Ukens Revy, årg. 9, 1922, 368–375, 396–403, 426–430.

LIE, JONAS: Unbekannte Strindberg Briefe, edited by E. Lie, Berliner Tageblatt, February 12, 1922.

NIETZSCHE-STRINDBERG LETTERS: Frankfurter Zeitung, February 9, 1913; La Revue (Revue des revues), Vol. 101, pp. 301 ff., 1913; Mercure de France, Vol. 102, 1913; North American Review, Vol. 198, 1913; Tagliche Rundschau (Berlin), February 8, 1913 ff.; Der Türmer, May, 1913.

SCHERING: Briefe an Emil Schering. Müller, München, 1924.

STRINDBERG'S SISTER, Vår Lösen, 9–10 årg., 1918–19, 181.

STRINDBERG, J. O.: Bref från A. S. till J. O. S. under åren 1870–1900, utg. af S. J. Erdtman. Björk & Börjesson, Stockholm, 1915.

WRANGEL: Ett och annat om mina förbindelser med A. S. och om hans brevsamling, Ord och Bild, 30 årg., 1921, 459–478.

See also Engström, Krogvig, Lamm, Lundegård, Molander, Paul, Smirnoff, Strecker, Weininger, and appendixes to the Landquist edition of Strindberg's Collected Works (Samlade skrifter).

INDEX

Italicized figures refer to items given in footnotes